Measuring Happiness

Measuring Happiness
The Economics of Well-Being

Joachim Weimann, Andreas Knabe, and Ronnie Schöb

The MIT Press
Cambridge, Massachusetts
London, England

© 2015 Massachusetts Institute of Technology

Original German-language edition—*Geld macht doch glücklich: Wo die ökonomische Glücksforschung irrt* (ISBN 978-3-7910-31941)—published by Schäffer-Poeschel Verlag für Wirtschaft, Steuern und Recht GmbH, Stuttgart (© 2011).

All rights reserved. No part of this book may be reproduced in any form by any electronic or mechanical means (including photocopying, recording, or information storage and retrieval) without permission in writing from the publisher.

MIT Press books may be purchased at special quantity discounts for business or sales promotional use. For information, email special_sales@mitpress.mit.edu

Set in Sabon by the MIT Press. Printed and bound in the United States of America.

Library of Congress Cataloging-in-Publication Data

Weimann, Joachim, 1956–
[Geld macht doch glücklich. English]
Measuring happiness : the economics of well-being / Joachim Weimann, Andreas Knabe, and Ronnie Schöb.
  pages cm
Includes bibliographical references and index.
ISBN 978-0-262-02844-8 (hardcover : alk. paper)
1. Quality of life—Economic aspects. 2. Well-being—Economic aspects. 3. Happiness—Economic aspects. 4. Money—Psychological aspects. 5. Wealth—Psychological aspects. 6. Economics—Psychological aspects. I. Knabe, Andreas. II. Schöb, Ronnie III. Title.
HN25.W4313 2015
306—dc23
2014019585

10 9 8 7 6 5 4 3 2 1

to our families

Contents

Preface ix

I The Economics of Happiness and Its Most Important Results

1 The End of Materialism? 3
2 Economists' Way of Thinking: "More Is Better Than Less" 9
3 The Easterlin Attack 17
4 If Money Doesn't Make Us Happy, What Then? 35
5 The Economic Determinants of Happiness 57
6 What Is to Be Done If Money Doesn't Make Us Happy? 75

II What Is Happiness Research Telling Us?

7 Are We Measuring Correctly? 89
8 How Much Truth Is There in the Easterlin Paradox? 113
9 Unemployed and Happy?! 131
10 The Importance of Relative Position 141
11 Conclusion 151

Appendix 155
Notes 191
References 193
Index 209

Preface

We noticed during our research on life satisfaction that we were dealing with a theme that touches many people. Around this theme there are many myths, open questions, and small mysteries. A theme with such characteristics is perfect for a thrilling work of nonfiction. And so our book came to be. It should be a thrilling book, entertaining to read but still reporting on the latest scientific developments. This book was preceded by much preliminary work. The beginning was marked by an extensive study that we conducted on the issue of the life satisfaction of unemployed and employed people. We would like to express particular thanks to the Fritz Thyssen Stiftung, which funded that study. Substantial preliminary work took place within the framework of a report we prepared for Germany's Bundesministerium der Finanzen (Federal Ministry of Finance).

We originally published this book in German under the title *Geld macht doch glücklich: Wo die ökonomische Glücksforschung irrt*. The book received positive feedback from colleagues in academia and appreciative reviews in the German-speaking popular media. This encouraged us to bring it to the attention of an international audience. We would not have been able to do so without the help of our translator, Brian Browne, who did a wonderful job of not only thoroughly translating the content of the book but also carrying over its somewhat colloquial style. We are grateful for the effort he put into the project. We also want to thank the Börsenverein des deutschen Buchhandels (Association of the German Publishing Trade) for supporting the translation financially.

We would especially like to thank all those whose assistance helped bring this book to fruition. Christine Bayer-Schöb and Sarah Schöb read and commented as meticulously as Barbara Weimann, and Christine Lücke, Alexander Plum, and Florian Timme carried out valuable work researching the literature and the data. Our thanks go to them and to Paul Bethge and John Covell of the MIT Press, who worked on the project with energy and dedication.

Joachim Weimann, Andreas Knabe, and Ronnie Schöb
Berlin and Magdeburg, June 2014

I
The Economics of Happiness and Its Most Important Results

1
The End of Materialism?

The question of what makes people happy is very old, and it hasn't been answered yet. Or perhaps, to be more precise, we can say that there are many answers to the question. The influence of the spirit of the age on how the question is answered shouldn't be underrated. After the Second World War, it was quite clear what people in the Western world wanted and what could be done to make them happy: Make them forget the horrors of war and help them to overcome the hardships that arose from it. Above all, people wanted economic prosperity and a future they could believe in. In postwar Western societies, striving for happiness meant, first and foremost, striving for prosperity and security.

The European student revolts of 1968 and the peace movement in the United States marked the dawn of a new age in which other values began to gain ground against the predominance of these earlier goals. Political participation, emancipation, and the desire in general to "dare more democracy" (as Willy Brandt put it) appeared alongside the strictly material goals. But the desire for higher income and better living conditions held its ground against the emerging environmental and civil rights movements of the 1970s and the 1980s. In Europe, the environmental movement succeeded in promoting ecological awareness and firmly establishing an understanding of environmental interrelationships in society. However, even these successes didn't prevent people from striving for material things. And that has changed little to this day.

But is money really everything? Of course not, but that has never been the point. What has always mattered is having the money to buy goods and being able to afford the things that we assume make us happy. This includes paying for the necessities of life just as much as taking vacation trips, attending cultural events, and generally taking the time to enjoy the fruits of our labor. That is attested by the simple fact that over the last hundred years incomes have increased and working hours have decreased considerably (Lee et al. 2007). Our economic prosperity is continually rising—a fact we lose sight of in the midst of daily reports of crises, problems, maladministration, and grievances. It nevertheless remains a fact. With our hard work and ambition we ensure that material progress doesn't come to a standstill. Slow growth is perceived as problematic, an economy that isn't growing is thought to be in crisis, and a decline in economic performance is considered a catastrophe. And yet we are currently experiencing an ever-increasing readiness in society to enter into a debate on whether we have taken things much too far.

The fundamental themes of this discussion are whether there are not more important values than economic prosperity and whether striving for economic prosperity is likely to violate those values. Today this theme comes in many shapes and sizes and is generally orchestrated against consumerism, neoliberalism, and the other usual suspects. But this isn't completely new. The green movement, the peace movement, and especially the student movement were linked to widespread criticism of capitalism, which was sparked by, among other things, an excessively strong orientation toward materialistic values. But in the past only relatively small segments of society backed such criticism—small groups that, although they attracted a great deal of attention, never really got beyond the status of a minority.

Nowadays, however, this discussion is taking place in mainstream society and in parliaments and has managed to penetrate the inner circles of economic debate. Economists on a broad front are dealing with the question of what makes people happy—and this is rather an unusual task for economists. Why it is unusual is a long story. We will tell a small part of the story in the next chapter, and the whole story in the appendix.

At the political level there is a debate on the question of whether it still makes sense to continue to use gross domestic product (GDP) to assess the situation of a country. (In the past, a related measure—gross national product, abbreviated GNP—was more commonly used.) To put it simply, GDP measures economic performance by adding up the value of all the goods and services produced within a country. Thus, GDP is confined to the strictly material. But aren't we making a mistake if we rely entirely on this one measure? Shouldn't other measures be taken into account? Economic prosperity is, of course, not an end in itself, but it serves as an indicator of people's happiness. At the same time, we are assuming tacitly that people are better off when they are better provided for and when they are able to consume more. Is this assumption admissible? Aren't we in danger of overlooking happiness if we only use material things in the form of GDP as our yardstick?

Economic research pertaining to happiness played no small part in setting the debate surrounding this question in motion. Indeed, it was economists who discovered, in the mid 1970s, that people's average life satisfaction didn't seem to depend on their incomes. This finding became known in the literature as the Easterlin Paradox, after the economist Richard Easterlin. As a consequence of it, simply equating economic growth and an increase in economic prosperity with an increase in well-being was no longer generally accepted. Since that time it has become fashionable to consider whether there aren't better measures of changes in well-being than GDP.

Since 1990, the United Nations has been using the Human Development Index (HDI), a set of indicators (among them indicators of life expectancy and educational attainment) that is claimed to indicate a country's stage of development better than GDP can. The top three countries in the rankings published in 2012 are Norway, Australia, and the United States. At the bottom of the ladder is Niger.

But the HDI no longer stands alone. The number of indicator systems has increased steadily, and all of them are problematic. Let's take as an example a relatively new indicator with the promising name Happy Planet Index. Three quantities are drawn together in this index: life expectancy, average life satisfaction (measured on a scale from 0 to 10), and the so-called ecological footprint (representing the extent to which a country exploits its natural resources). The Happy Planet Index is relatively simple to calculate: The indicators of life satisfaction and life satisfaction are multiplied, and the result is divided by the index for the ecological footprint. The results are astonishing. The United States is in 105th place in the world rankings, and Germany is in 54th—both easily surpassed by some developing countries, including Morocco and Egypt. And the reason for this is simple. Although Americans have a high life expectancy and, on average, grow rather old, they are also very active economically and leave a correspondingly large ecological footprint. This footprint is small, however, in Cuba and Vietnam (which are in twelfth and second places) and in Costa Rica (which is at the top of the list).

How should we judge the Happy Planet Index? It is certainly a well-intended attempt to summarize the various measures of well-being. But memories of the Arab Spring are still fresh in our minds. Egyptians took to the streets, risking their lives and shouting into the microphones of Western journalists that they were doing it all because they wanted to live like people in the West. Should they have been told to go home because their Happy Planet Index was much better than that of Germany or the United States?

Indicators are used to try to condense information. This works, but it has two decisive disadvantages. The first is that a good deal of information is lost in the process of consolidation. The second is that using indicators makes it necessary to decide which components should be included in the indicator and how they are to be weighted. Both decisions can be shown to be highly arbitrary. Who would presume to decide how life expectancy is to be weighted relative to carbon dioxide emissions in an index?

GDP has a significant advantage over other indicators: It is largely safe from manipulation, since it consists largely of data generated by market processes. The data cannot, therefore, be influenced by value judgments made by members of an elite who presume to know what indicators should be used to measure the welfare of a country (which is, essentially, nothing other than the welfare of the people who live in that country).

Research into the economics of happiness has certainly contributed to the proliferation of other indicators. It also provides a set of tools that, similar to GDP, solves the aggregation problem without any element of arbitrariness. Economic happiness research obtains information on people's life satisfaction by asking them about it directly. Such research is carried out in many countries by means of extensive social surveys. Some of the most widely used surveys are the General Social Survey (GSS) in the United States, the British Household Panel Survey (BHPS) in the United Kingdom, and the Sozio-oekonomisches Panel (SOEP) in Germany. These surveys are conducted on a large number of households—for example, more than 55,000 people are interviewed for the GSS. In the BHPS and the SOEP, the same people are questioned every year in order to be able to recognize trends and isolate effects that are not a result of their personalities (which remain constant with time) but instead can be ascribed to changes in external factors. Members of surveyed households are required to undergo a very comprehensive interview and are asked about various aspects of their lives. The question that particularly interests the happiness researcher typically comes at the end of the interview. Here is a translation of the wording used in the Sozio-oekonomisches Panel:

> Finally we would like to ask you about your satisfaction with your life in general. Once again, please answer using the following scale, in which "0" means completely dissatisfied and "10" means completely satisfied. How satisfied are you with your life, all things considered?

It is immediately clear that this question asks a respondent to aggregate everything that influences his or her life satisfaction into a single number. Adding up all the figures provided by the respondents in the SOEP and dividing the sum by the number of respondents yields a single number that summarizes the average life satisfaction of the respondents. Happiness research aggregates life satisfaction just as GDP sums up total economic performance in one number. And life satisfaction depends just as little on what "experts" think as GDP depends on arbitrary weightings. It depends solely on the subjective aggregation of the individuals concerned.

It may well be this characteristic, above all else, that allows happiness research to make use of the latest efforts to improve the measurement of prosperity and happiness in life. These endeavors take place primarily in newly created commissions that have been assigned the task of thinking about the alternatives to GDP. One of the best-known of these commissions, France's Commission sur la Mesure da la Performance Économique et du Progrès Social, was appointed by President Nicolas Sarkozy. Several Nobel laureates and a number of leading happiness researchers served on that commission, which began its work in 2008 and presented its result in a report published in 2009 (Stiglitz et al. 2009).

We will discuss the work of the Commission sur la Mesure da la Performance Économique et du Progrès Social and other similar initiatives in chapter 6. For present purposes, it should be noted that the governments of many countries appear to share the feeling that GDP has had its day and that something better is now needed. Although experience with indicators has not been very good, indicators are still fashionable. But, most of all, happiness research seems to provide the promise of a better measurement for evaluating people's satisfaction. In any case, this research and its results have played a significant role in all the commissions and initiatives, and its advocates are working to ensure that the new indicators play a greater role in politics.

Happiness research is expected to continue to grow more important, since we are only at the beginning of its development and since it is a comparatively young discipline. But what are we to make of happiness research, and what can we expect from it? Where do its strengths lie? Does it have any weaknesses? These are the questions we will pursue in this book. The economic determinants of life satisfaction (in particular, income and employment) will be one focus, but we will also consider the more personal aspects and what happiness research has to say about them. We will present the results of our own research, show that happiness research does indeed have strengths and weaknesses, and note that some of its strongest results have to be put into perspective.

Our aim is to present the most comprehensive possible picture of the possibilities and limitations of happiness research. In order to do this, we will proceed as follows.

In part I, we will describe what happiness researchers have accomplished to date. We will begin by explaining why economists find what happiness research does new and unusual. When one compares the happiness approach against the approach of classical economics, it becomes clear what happiness research can, and cannot, achieve. Once we have gained insight into economists' way of thinking "so far," we will confront this point of view with the most powerful and exciting proposition that happiness research has produced: the Easterlin Paradox. After that, it is likely to be clear how varied the positions adopted in the debate centered on happiness research are. Within this spectrum of views there are many very interesting and helpful findings of happiness research that are less radical (and less contentious) than the Easterlin Paradox. We will devote chapters 4 and 5 to those results. We will return to the Easterlin Paradox in chapter 6, describing the consequences that arise from Easterlin's finding if the formulation used by Easterlin and others is accepted.

In part II, we will subject the main finding of happiness research to a critical analysis. We will begin, in chapter 7, by dealing with the question of whether the method employed by empirical happiness research really allows us to measure what we want to measure. In chapter 8, we will turn our attention to the heart of the debate and question whether the Easterlin Paradox exists at all, using more recent data and providing a new interpretation of the data. Together these two elements will show that the Easterlin Paradox, in the strict form in which it has commonly been formulated, does not exist. The analysis will be completed in two chapters in which we will take a closer look at two specific issues that play important parts in the debate on the Easterlin Paradox. In chapter 9, we will present our own empirical research, which clearly demonstrates that previous happiness research has had too narrow a view of "happiness" and that there is an urgent need to broaden its perspective. The discussion centered on the Easterlin Paradox has shown, above all, that too little attention has been paid to relative position. But what are the consequences when greater attention is given to relative position? We will address that question in chapter 10.

2
Economists' Way of Thinking: "More Is Better Than Less"

The public has only a rather vague idea of what economists actually do and what they research. Some people believe that economists are constantly busy with stock exchange prices or that they are always thinking about what policy the European Central Bank or the Federal Reserve should adopt. Economists do, in fact, do those things. However, if we want a fundamental description of what is at the heart of the economic way of thinking, central banks and the stock exchange have no role to play. The basic problem that economists have to grapple with is, quite simply, that the resources that are available fall well short of meeting people's needs. We have a fundamental and permanent scarcity problem, and economists deal with solutions to that problem. To tackle it, we need economic systems. This is where the stock exchange and the central bank have significant roles to play. That is why we eventually end up at these highly developed and complex institutions, even though we are still essentially dealing with scarcity.

A scarcity problem can be very simply pictured as an allocation problem. Suppose there is a cake of a certain size, and a number of hungry people would like some cake. If every individual states how much cake he or she would like to have, and if all the claims to the cake are totaled up, it will be clear that the cake isn't big enough to meet all the demands. And therein lies the problem. How is the cake to be shared? How are we to decide who gets how much? Of course, this problem has been simplified enormously. In actual fact, the size of the cake is naturally not fixed. If the skillful use of resources results in the baking of a bigger cake, the scarcity problem is relieved. We will, however, remain with the extreme simplification.

Imagine that, besides the cake, there is also some healthy whole-grain bread with a vegetarian spread. One possible solution would be that each person receives the same amounts of cake and whole-grain bread. That probably would please few of them—those who like only cake would be just as dissatisfied as those who prefer whole-grain bread.

Another solution might be to put prices on the cake and the bread, and make the act of eating a piece of cake conditional: Only a person who is prepared to pay a certain price is allowed to eat cake. If we assume that all those involved have the same income, this eliminates any issues of fairness, which are not of concern at this point. Putting price tags on the cake and the bread would require each individual to decide how much the cake is worth to him relative to the bread, and only the individuals whose valuation is at least as high as the price being asked will get to eat some cake. If we then also succeed in setting the price in such a way that there is a demand for exactly the number of pieces of cake that are on the platter and all the bread is also eaten, we have achieved a great deal: None of the cake is wasted, since it has been completely eaten up, and only those who had the highest valuation for the cake received a piece. Precisely such a solution to the scarcity problem is achieved in markets, and it is certainly not the worst solution. To be more exact, one can think of no better solution. The scarce resources are completely distributed to those who gain the most benefit from them. That is why economists have such a particular liking for markets. They are wonderful instruments for easing scarcity problems.

Our very simple example allows us to clarify some important fundamentals of economic theory. First, economists assume that only individuals themselves can know what is most useful to them and what is not. Therefore, the decision as to whether an individual does or doesn't get a piece of cake is made by that individual. No one else is entitled to make a statement about what utility someone derives from eating a piece of cake. This holds in general. The utility someone experiences is just as much a deeply subjective matter as his life satisfaction. Every individual can judge for himself how satisfied he is, what generates utility, and what feelings he has. Therefore, it is inappropriate for the state, a central planning body, or any other authority to stipulate what is useful for people and what isn't useful.

History is full of examples in which despots or well-meaning political parties nevertheless claim to have the right to determine what is good for people and what is not. History also teaches us that this hasn't often gone well. It has never turned out well for people who have had to suffer under outside influence. In the vast majority of cases it has also not gone well for those in power, for in the long run the desire for self-determination has, as a rule, proved strong enough to prepare the ground for uprisings and revolutions.

What thought processes are involved when people choose to spend their money on cake or on something else? This is a fundamental question for economics. How we view the most important actors in economic life depends on the answer to this question. The goal of economic research is to derive general theories of how economic systems function. In order to do that, it is necessary to have a model of how the individual actors make decisions in such systems. Do they do so spontaneously? Do they sometimes decide one way and sometimes another? Is a piece of cake worth two dollars to them at one moment and four dollars a moment later? Or can we assume that people decide systematically on the basis of rational calculation? The latter is what economists assume, and they can cite good reasons for doing so.

The rational-choice model assumes that people act rationally in the sense that they do only what serves their own true goals, motives, and desires. This model forms the basis of modern economic theory. It is, therefore, worthwhile to take a look at how economists arrive at this model.

Making decisions means choosing among a number of alternatives. If you go shopping in a supermarket, you can choose from millions of possible combinations of the goods on offer. By the time you reach the checkout, you will have selected a particular basket of goods. The question is "How do people actually do that?" In order to be able to say something about it, economists use an ingenious trick which they owe to Paul Samuelson, in our opinion the greatest economist of the twentieth century. We have him to thank for the theory of revealed preference. In the appendix, we will describe in detail how this theory came about and what significance it has for economics. For the purposes of this chapter, explaining the principle should suffice.

The theory of revealed preference provides a justification that allows us to assume that the basket of goods you take to the checkout was put together on the basis of rational calculation. Here is how it goes: Let us assume that you want to buy tea and you have a choice among twenty different types of tea. You choose vanilla tea. Now let us assume that you choose once again, but this time there are only ten types of tea to choose among. Vanilla is one of them, and we observe that you select it again. These two observations provide sufficient information. The theory of revealed preference proves that when the observed behavior of people contains certain regularities (such as the one observed in our tea example) it may be assumed that the people whose decisions have been observed have employed rational calculation in making these decisions. In the present case, this means that whenever you choose vanilla tea from a larger selection of teas you will also be expected to choose vanilla tea from a smaller selection. To come to this conclusion it isn't necessary to make any assumption at all about what motivates people deep inside.

The theory of revealed preference is based exclusively on observations. It requires absolutely no psychology. If someone displays some behavior that satisfies the postulates of the theory of revealed preference (which isn't difficult), researchers can assume that his or her decisions are the results of rational calculation. Beyond that, scientists are also justified in using a very concrete model of this rational calculation, the basic features of which are as follows: Given a choice between two alternatives, people are always able to state whether they prefer one of them or whether they have no preference for one over the other. Such comparisons can be drawn for all the options available, and that results in an ordering of all the alternatives. Economists speak of a preference ordering in which all the alternatives are listed. The list is complete (it contains all the alternatives), and the ordering is transitive (if a consumer prefers lemonade to iced tea, and prefers iced tea to mineral water, it follows that he prefers lemonade to mineral water). With such a preference ordering, rational behavior on the part of the consumer is to choose the alternative that is at the top of his list over all the alternatives available to him when making any decision. That is precisely what we do when we shop at a supermarket. Of all the goods on offer, we select those that we can afford and that we think are best for us. Just as in the case of the vanilla tea, if less of the goods that we have placed lower down on the list are available, we will not change our choices concerning items that are higher on the list.

What is ingenious about the theory of revealed preference is that, as we have already noted, it is based solely on observations. We can assert that people choose rationally on the basis of a preference ordering without having to rely on psychological tests or otherwise having to find out what is going on inside their heads, what they like, and what they don't like. It is enough to observe what they reveal through their behavior. There is a catch, though. The theory of revealed preference allows us to assert that people are consistent in their behavior with regard to a preference ordering that represents their tastes, preferences, and motives. The theory does not, however, say anything about what generates utility for people. How could it? After all, economists believe very strongly that only an individual can say and judge what is useful to him and what is not. Thus, the theory can predict absolutely nothing about human behavior. The statement that people maximize their utility is meaningless if nothing can be said about what generates utility. This would then mean that any behavior is consistent with the theory. A theory that doesn't rule out anything is nothing but a tautology. Consider this weather report: "If the cockerel crows from his favorite spot, the weather may change. Then again, it may not." Neoclassical theory would be just as useless if it didn't say something about what generates utility.

Thus, neoclassical economics is in a dilemma: the clearer the need for a statement on what generates utility, the less consistent such a statement would be with the postulate that utility is purely subjective. A trick helps us find a way out of this dilemma. Instead of saying what creates utility in concrete terms, it is helpful to recognize that people prefer to have a wider range of choice. When you shop at a supermarket, it is not only your preferences that dictate what you put in the basket; your income also plays a significant role. Only things that you can afford are worth considering. For this reason, champagne generally goes by the board, and filet mignon ends up on your table only once in a blue moon. Many products are out of your reach because your budget is simply too small. A higher income, however, leads to a wider range of choice, and neoclassical economics resorts to the assumption that this is precisely what we prefer. If you can decide between a narrower and a wider range of choice, you decide in favor of the latter. It is in this sense that the neoclassical motto "more is better than less" is to be understood. It doesn't say that people always want to have more of everything; it says that a higher income increases people's opportunities to do or consume things they consider useful or worth consuming. It is for this reason that people prefer a higher income to a lower one. A higher income enables them to get things high on their list that they couldn't previously get because they couldn't pay for them.

How serious is the neoclassicists' assumption that more income is better than less? Who would seriously contradict it? Don't we observe people doing their best to increase their income? Trade unions call strikes, pensioners take to the streets, managers at all levels of the hierarchy work till they drop, workers stand beside an assembly line for hours, and cooks at McDonald's flip hamburgers eight hours a day for the minimum wage. In these ways, all these people reveal that they lean toward the neoclassical view. They find it better to have more money rather than less. Reports of lottery winners refusing to accept their winnings or donating them to charity are quite rare. Isn't it, then, possible to state that neoclassical economics is quite right in assuming that people strive for the highest possible income?

It would indeed be rather hard to justify not making this assumption. However, we really should also interpret it in the sense of neoclassicism.

This is not about money as such; it is about people having the income to be able to do the things that increase their own utility. It then follows that maximizing their income without any conditions can't be their goal. For instance, neoclassical labor market theory assumes people don't like working. Work is seen as a burden that tends to reduce individual well-being. That assumption is probably quite realistic if we ignore people (such as, arguably, professional football players and university lecturers) who are privileged enough to have a job that provides them with fulfillment and in which they have unlimited fun. It follows, then, that working people are faced with a conflict. On the one hand, they don't want to work; on the other hand, they want to consume. Owing to this conflict, there are also situations in which people decide *against* higher income—for example, when they can have more free time in exchange. A person who receives an unexpectedly large inheritance may "buy" more free time with the additional money by working less.

There are certainly other situations in which it can be observed that people freely choose to forgo income. This often happens if moral considerations come into play. We know from experience that people are willing to help others even if that results in a reduction in their income. People give gifts, and people sometimes display reciprocal behavior (that is, reward others who have treated them kindly). Experimental research in economics has observed and described many such cases under laboratory conditions. Although it isn't completely clear whether behavior in the real world can be inferred from laboratory observations, it is hard to imagine that things observed in the laboratory don't play any role at all in real life. What appears to be clear, however, is that it is easier to be "kind" with a high income than with a tight budget.

So there are a few limitations to the general principle of "more is better than less," but these don't really alter the fact that the notion that people fare better if they have more income clearly dominates the economic way of thinking. Even indications of the undoubted existence of altruistic behavior change nothing in this regard. An altruist is also happy to have more income, because he can then donate more to UNICEF or the Red Cross.

The focus on gross domestic product as a measure of the prosperity of a country and its citizens is therefore logical. GDP provides a figure that brings together the quantity of all goods and services produced or consumed by the inhabitants of a country. This value is nothing other than a monetary valuation of people's preferences revealed in their consumption. It isn't necessary to undertake an exogenous evaluation in order to distinguish between "good" and "bad" consumption or to make other value judgments. People consume what is useful to them. If it weren't useful, why would they spend their money on it? At the same time, the sum of all acts of consumption shows how large the consumption opportunities of society as a whole are. If people prefer to have more opportunities, a rising GDP shows that a society is becoming more able to provide these opportunities, and the economic prejudice lies in the fact that this is advantageous.

It should be pointed out that "more consumption" doesn't mean simply that people in a country drive more often, eat more, or buy bigger televisions. How this income is used is a matter of preferences, and preferences aren't restricted to private consumption. Ultimately, everything that surrounds us depends on the resources available to us and on our decisions on the use of these resources. The salaries of those who care for the elderly, investments in kindergartens, schools, and hospitals, transfer payments to needy people, development aid, and the social security system all have to be financed out of the incomes generated in other parts of the economy. A rising GDP is also a sign, therefore, that a society has achieved greater scope for better schools, for more generous systems of social support, and for the maintenance of its cultural assets.

All this is often overlooked when growth is discussed. Growth has fallen into disrepute, as has GDP as a measure of prosperity. The reason for this is the fear that we may be too careless in our treatment of the planet's limited resources. Growth is often seen as a purely quantitative phenomenon. As a rule, however, growth actually means, first and foremost, qualitative change. The quantitative growth of GDP changes our quality of life, not only by qualitatively improving private goods and services, but also by way of better cultural assets and social services. Is it surprising, then, that economists are, by and large, highly satisfied with GDP as a measure of prosperity?

3

The Easterlin Attack

Happiness and Income

Recent research into the economics of happiness differs radically in its methodology from all the methodological standards of neoclassical economics. From the point of view of neoclassical theoreticians, it is completely unnecessary to ask people how "happy" they are. They reveal their preferences through their behavior. It would not, for the most part, occur to economists to measure and compare utility quantitatively. But this is precisely what happiness researchers do when they ask people to rank their life satisfaction on a scale.

This method was first systematically applied to economic matters by Richard Easterlin (1974). It is noteworthy that his contribution was published not in a prominent scientific journal but in a collection of essays. Articles tend to land in collections of essays in economics when the authors aren't able to get them published in important journals. Indeed, Easterlin's seminal article was rejected by economics journals, presumably because his method was entering territory that was more forbidden than familiar for the profession. But not only that; Easterlin came to the conclusion that money didn't make people happy. This stood in such sharp contradiction to everything that neoclassical economists were accustomed to believing that only one reaction was possible: "That can't be true."

How valid the results of happiness research are is indeed an interesting question. There are two crucial points here. The first has to do with the quality of the data collected: Was the survey conducted properly? Were the same questions always asked? Were they asked everywhere? The second has to do with the validity of the information on life satisfaction: What are we actually measuring on this scale? Can we really compare the data. Do people always use the same scale? We will take a much closer look at these questions and similar ones later. Here, however, we will ignore them.

What picture does happiness research present when we assume that the data have been collected properly and that they possess all the characteristics that happiness researchers attribute to them? Instead of reporting on Easterlin's historical results (1974) or his later works (e.g., Easterlin 1995), we will take a look at more recent data from the United States, Great Britain, and Germany. We will look at these three countries not only because the data available for them are more recent, but also because they provide some of the best sets of data that happiness researchers can use: the General Social Survey (GSS) in the United States, the British Household Panel Survey (BHPS) in the United Kingdom, and the Sozio-oekonomisches Panel (SOEP) in Germany. We will begin with an overview of how well people were doing in these countries in the past.

Figure 3.1 shows, for the respective levels of the life-satisfaction scale (eleven points in Germany, seven points in the UK, three different categories in the US), what percentage of the population classified itself on each rung of the happiness ladder. As can be seen from the figure, things are going well, rather than badly, for people in all three countries. After all, 88.5 percent of all Americans reported being "pretty happy" or "very happy." If only 11.5 percent of the population classify themselves as "not too happy," one can certainly say that Americans seem to be quite successful in the "pursuit of happiness," one of the inalienable rights mentioned in the Declaration of Independence. Even without such historical backing, people in the United Kingdom and in Germany also seem to be pretty happy, on average. In the UK, 76.4 percent of the population report life-satisfaction scores strictly above the midpoint of the scale (5 to 7) and thus tend to be more satisfied with their lives; only 9.4 percent tend to be dissatisfied (1 to 3). In Germany, 77.6 percent of people are more satisfied with their lives, as indicated by the scores (6 to 10) above the midpoint of the scale, and (again) only 9.4 percent report satisfaction scores in the bottom half of the scale (1 to 4).

Of course, this distribution of subjective life satisfaction says nothing about what the reported life satisfaction depends on. Neoclassical economists would have a strong suspicion as to what is responsible for people's life satisfaction. The higher the income, the greater the quantity of resources available to people. In accordance with the standard neoclassical assumption that more is better than less, it immediately follows that there should be a positive correlation between income and life satisfaction. Since the examined surveys also naturally provide detailed

United States

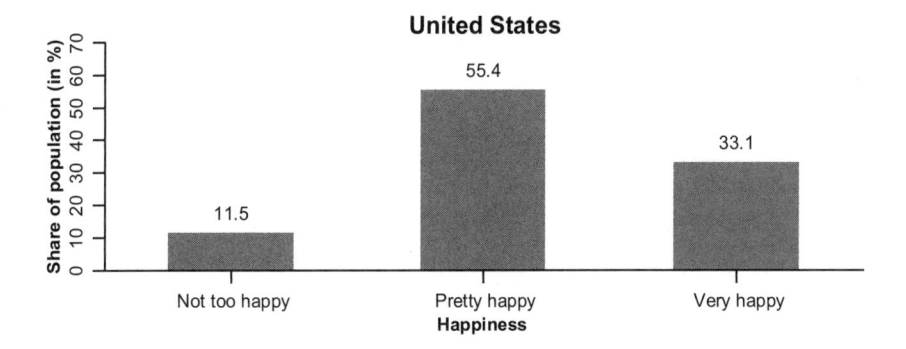

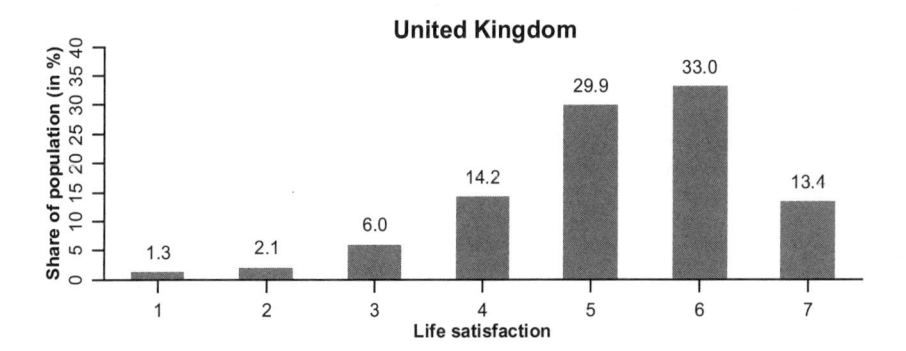

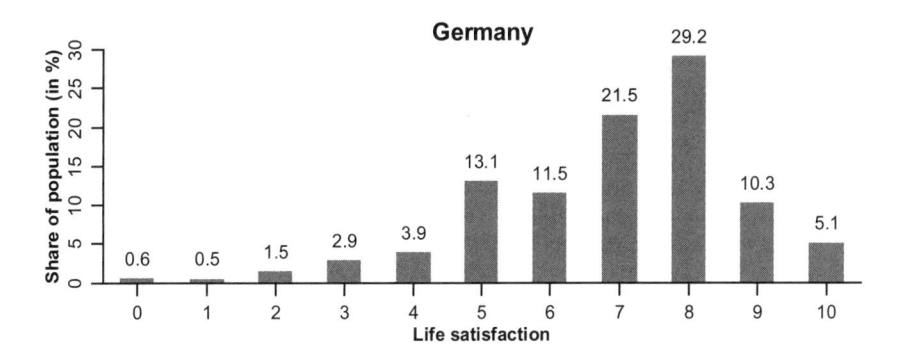

Happiness	Share (%)
Not too happy	11.5
Pretty happy	55.4
Very happy	33.1

United Kingdom

Life satisfaction	Share (%)
1	1.3
2	2.1
3	6.0
4	14.2
5	29.9
6	33.0
7	13.4

Germany

Life satisfaction	Share (%)
0	0.6
1	0.5
2	1.5
3	2.9
4	3.9
5	13.1
6	11.5
7	21.5
8	29.2
9	10.3
10	5.1

Figure 3.1

Relative distribution of subjective well-being (average distribution of life satisfaction or happiness).
Sources: GSS (1972–2012), BHPS (1996–2008), SOEP (1992–2010), authors' calculations.

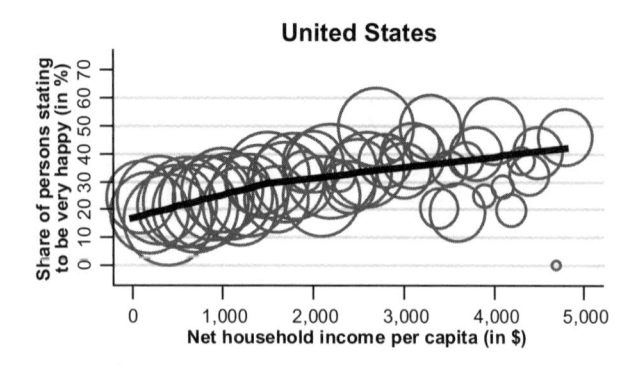

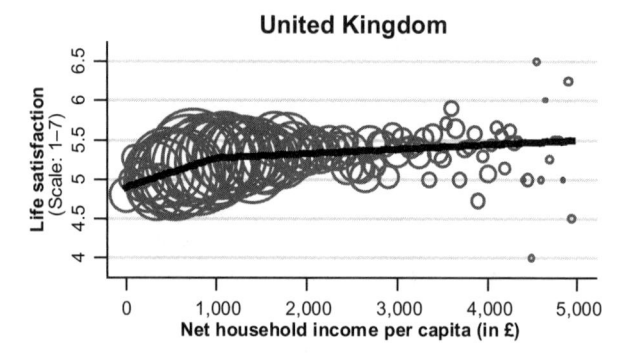

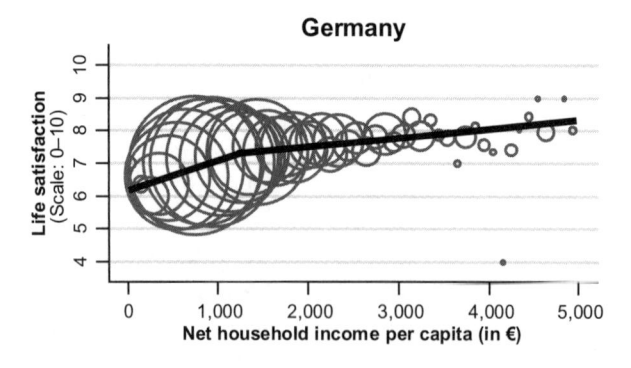

Figure 3.2

Relationship between income and subjective well-being. The size of a circle is proportional to the number of people with a certain income level.
Sources: GSS (2006–2012), BHPS (2008), SOEP (2012), authors' calculations.

information about respective net household income and size of household, it is straightforward to examine the relationship between life satisfaction and net income. Figure 3.2 shows the results.

The findings are clear and provide little cause for concern for neoclassical economists. In all three countries, there is indeed a positive correlation between life satisfaction and disposable income. This isn't altered by the fact that this correlation is weaker for higher incomes than for lower incomes. For example, in Germany the effect of a 100-euro increase in disposable income is about three times as great on a per capita monthly net income below approximately 1,200 euros than on one above 1,200 euros. (The threshold corresponds to the mean per capita household income.) We should keep in mind here that a large proportion of the observations in the low-income segment concern families with three or more members; thus, although their household income exceeds 3,000 euros, their per capita income falls markedly short of the 1,200-euro mark. In the United Kingdom, the effect of a given absolute increase in income on life satisfaction is about seven times as large for net household incomes below £1,000 as for those above this threshold. In the United States, the effect of income on happiness is about twice as large for households with a net household income below $1,500 as for those with higher incomes.

So far the findings haven't been particularly exciting, and if things were to remain that way one could confidently continue working with economic models that are based solely on the assumption that people prefer a higher income to a lower income because they will then be happier (or, rather, will display a higher level of life satisfaction). But things don't remain that way. One initial observation that begins to raise suspicion is the way life satisfaction changes if individual income changes from one year to the next. This is easy to show with the aid of panel studies (observing one and the same individual from year to year), and it leads to a surprising result. If income remains constant over time (in real terms—that is, adjusted for inflation), life satisfaction decreases. (See figure 3.3.) In the United States, among households whose incomes didn't change much from one year to the next (they stayed in the same income bracket, where the GSS divides the interval between 0 and $160,000 into 25 brackets), about 15.55 percent reported moving to a higher happiness category, whereas 19.6 percent stepped down at least one happiness category. Hence, among those people whose incomes didn't change much, the share of those whose happiness decreased exceeds the share of those whose happiness increased by 4.05 percentage points (the value depicted in figure 3.3). As one would expect, among people whose incomes decreased the share of people whose happiness decreased too is substantially larger than the share of happier people, whereas the opposite holds true for people whose incomes increased. When examining British and German data, we obtain similar results. When people's incomes remain constant from one year to the next, there are more people becoming less happy than there are people whose happiness increases.

More detailed analyses of the data suggest that life satisfaction declines even if there is a slight growth in income. It increases only if there is a comparatively strong increase in income. This is surprising, since for constant or slightly rising income the quantity of resources available also remains constant or rises slightly. Why should the people concerned then feel less satisfied?

Once we establish that (as figure 3.2 shows) people with higher incomes are happier than those with lower incomes, it should then follow that if *everyone's* income rises then everyone feels better. However, that is not the case! Easterlin showed in his 1974 article (and in later works) that there is no positive correlation between GDP growth and average life satisfaction of the population. This finding can also be reproduced using the data introduced earlier. Figure 3.4 shows the development of GDP per capita and average subjective well-being over the time interval for which happiness data are available. In all three countries, inflation-adjusted per capita GDP has risen substantially. With cyclical influences put aside, the positive growth trend characterizing industrial nations since the end of the Second World War has also appeared in the period for which happiness data are available. Inhabitants of industrialized countries have been enjoying a constantly rising standard of living for a very long time. In most countries, this has manifested itself not only as an increase in average income but also in better provision of cultural and social goods. It is by no means an exaggeration to claim that since the Second World War every generation has been considerably better off materially than the preceding generation and worse off than the next generation. This has not, however, led to increases in people's satisfaction. As figure 3.4 shows, average happiness didn't change at all in any of the three countries.

The relationships represented in figure 3.4 show exactly what Easterlin showed as early as 1974. And there we have it, the Easterlin Paradox: Although people with higher incomes are happier than those with lower incomes, raising the incomes of all does not lead to an increase in average life satisfaction. (See Easterlin 1995, p. 44.)

It can be shown that the Easterlin Paradox doesn't hold true only for the United States, the United Kingdom, and Germany. A series of studies

United States

[Bar chart: Negative −5.48; Unaltered −4.05; Positive 2.40. Y-axis: Increased happiness − decreased happiness (in %). X-axis: Change in net income.]

United Kingdom

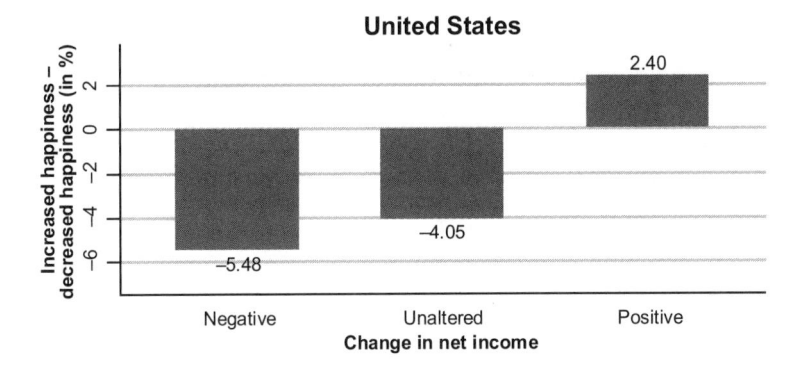

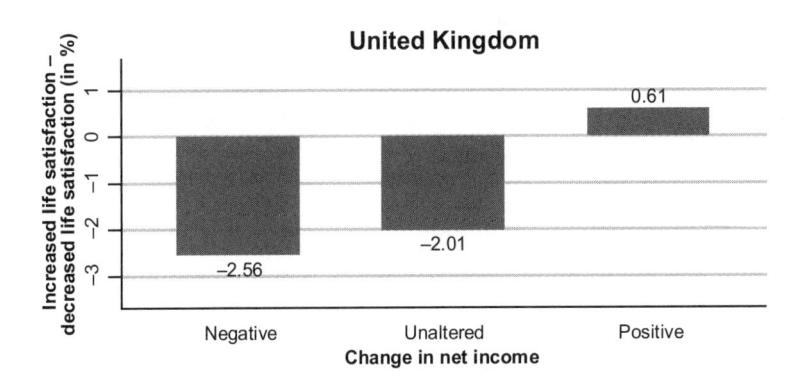

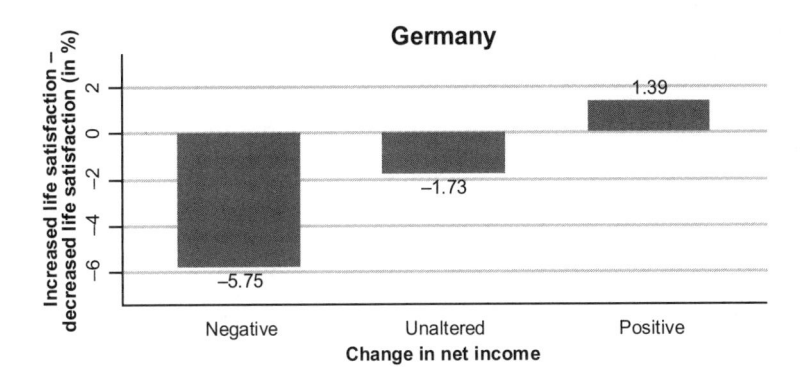

[Bar chart: Negative −2.56; Unaltered −2.01; Positive 0.61. Y-axis: Increased life satisfaction − decreased life satisfaction (in %). X-axis: Change in net income.]

Germany

[Bar chart: Negative −5.75; Unaltered −1.73; Positive 1.39. Y-axis: Increased life satisfaction − decreased life satisfaction (in %). X-axis: Change in net income.]

Figure 3.3

Changes in income and subjective well-being. This figure shows the percentage-point difference between the share of people who report being in a higher happiness category from one year to the next and the share of people who report being in a lower happiness category. "Unaltered" refers to persons with net income changes of less than 1 percent (United Kingdom and Germany; inflation-adjusted) or with a net income within the same income bracket (United States; there are 25 income brackets in the interval between 0 and $160,000 annual income).
Sources: GSS (2006–2010), BHPS (2003–2008), SOEP (2003–2010).

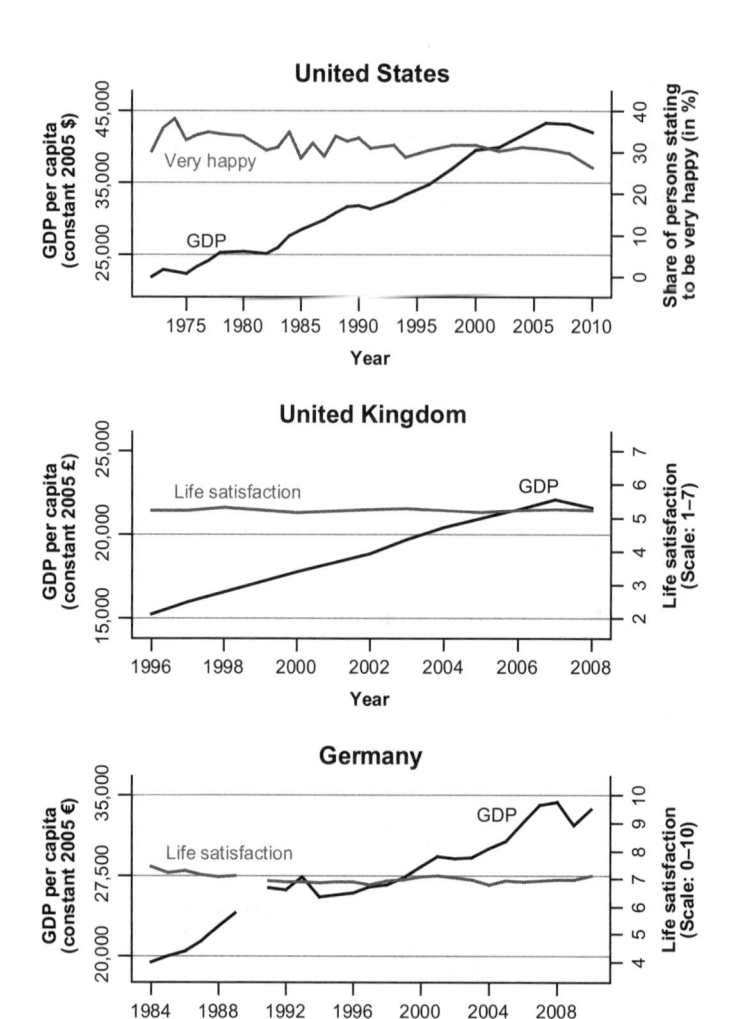

Figure 3.4

Income and life satisfaction. This figure presents GDP per capita (inflation-adjusted) and average life satisfaction (United Kingdom, Germany) or the share of people who report being "very happy" (as opposed to "pretty happy" or "not too happy," US data).
Sources: GSS, BHPS, SOEP, OECD.

reproduce Easterlin's findings for different countries and data sets.[1] Admittedly, it is very likely that the income-happiness paradox holds only for wealthy nations, although Easterlin (2010) claims that it also holds for poor countries. People in poor countries profit from an increase in average income in a completely different way than people in developed countries. As long as such basic needs as food, drink, and a roof over their heads are not yet fully satisfied, every additional increment of money in their pocket contributes to greater life satisfaction. The equivalent of about 4,000–10,000 US dollars per year is needed to cover these basic needs. People with less benefit from a rise in income considerably more than people whose incomes lie above the "10,000-dollar barrier." (See, for example, Veenhoven 2006.) There certainly are poor people in industrial nations, but poverty is typically defined in relative terms. Many relatively poor people in developed countries wouldn't be considered poor in absolute terms in international comparison. For example, recipients of unemployment assistance in Germany, which equals the minimum welfare level, are certainly not well off by German standards, but they still receive enough support for housing and living expenses to jump over the "10,000-dollars-per-year barrier." The proportion of absolutely poor people in developed countries is comparatively low, whereas the great majority of people in developing countries are very poor.

It makes sense that poor people will benefit more from a rise in income in absolute terms than richer people. But figure 3.4 tells us that, in the end, the level of the average income isn't relevant to the level of average life satisfaction in the rich industrialized countries. That's strong stuff, and it's contradictory to the usual convictions of the economics profession. We observe that people strive for material possessions, and that they do so with considerable effort. Some work till they drop, and others are prepared to commit crimes, just to have a higher income. This behavior, easily observable all over the world, leads economists to agree with the theory of revealed preference that people generally "prefer more to less." Moreover, this preference for "more" can't be denied. In light of the Easterlin Paradox, however, it proves to be a kind of collective misapprehension. People believe they would feel better if they earned more money, but in fact their life satisfaction remains constant even if they become as rich as they want. This is based on averages, but it still holds even though an individual will, of course, feel much happier if he can raise his income considerably within a year. We will provide an explanation for this paradoxical result in a moment, but first we should keep clearly in mind what the finding illustrated in figure 3.4 actually means.

If the data we have used to understand the development of life satisfaction really show how satisfied the German population (for instance) was with life between 1984 and 2010, figure 3.4 is truly astonishing. You can always argue that you knew all along that money alone doesn't make you happy, but that argument is a bit weak. Income, as measured by GDP, is only an indicator that many things have changed, including several things that don't contribute directly to GDP. For instance, the Easterlin Paradox says that all the efforts we make to get on in life are to no avail. Strictly speaking, it also says that our lives have not become more bearable just because we are able to earn more with much easier work than our forebears could earn with their work.

The working day of a present-day worker can't be compared to the normal day of an industrial worker of the 1950s or the 1960s. For instance, a typical worker in Germany has a 35-hour week and six weeks' leave entitlement secured by a bargaining agreement, enjoys protection against dismissal, and receives a handsome vacation bonus that a trade union has negotiated for him. On average, our generation works much less than the generation before us, and not as hard. The amount of physical work is steadily decreasing in industrialized societies, as is the difficulty of such work. We have more and more machines that relieve us of hard work, of tasks detrimental to health, and of dangerous jobs. But it's no use—we still don't feel any better.

The quality of health care and the generosity of welfare systems that citizens enjoy today surpass anything that has come before. Life expectancy is increasing continually, and medical advances are seen and felt by everyone. But that doesn't fill us with joy, either.

If one looks at it this way, and gives thought not only to vile money but also to everything that can be and has been done with money, it is understandable that most economists have only one comment to make concerning the Easterlin Paradox: "It can't be right." But if the data measure what they purport to measure, then we have to accept these findings, in spite of all the reservations of the guild of mainstream neoclassical-oriented economists. If Easterlin's finding were to be found correct, it would have enormous repercussions for everything that has been sacred for economists until now. That the theory of revealed preference would not be particularly useful in providing a basis for the development of economic theory would be the least of our problems. We will see how far reaching the consequences are when we look at the conclusions for economic policy that some economists draw from the Easterlin Paradox. However, before we do that we need to resolve the conflict between the findings from figures 3.2 and 3.4: How can it be that at a given time there is a positive correlation between income and life satisfaction (richer people are happier than poorer people), but that this correlation disappears over the long term (average life satisfaction remains constant despite rising average income)?

The two findings no longer contradict each other if we allow not only the absolute level of income to be important but also how much a person earns relative to others. In other words, a person's relative position in society also counts. How satisfied a person is therefore depends, first and foremost, on how he or she fares against some reference level. In the case of earnings, the reference income may be the income of other people—for example, a person's neighbors and colleagues. It may also be the person's own income in the preceding year, or his expected future earnings. Both figure 3.2 and figure 3.4 can be reconciled with the hypothesis that relative income comparisons are decisive for life satisfaction.

Comparison with the income of "another" is all the more gratifying the higher up the income scale a person is. That's why those near the top of the scale at a certain time feel better than those much further down. And that is exactly what we see in figure 3.2. On the other hand, there is no positive effect on average life satisfaction if everyone's income rises, since the average relative position is unchanged. Figure 3.4 illustrates this relationship. The overriding importance of relative positions plausibly explains the contradiction between the two findings, and the Easterlin Paradox disappears.

The notion of relative positions, or rather the competition for such positions, has a very bad reputation among economists. As productive and beneficial as competition may otherwise be, when it comes to relative positions it seems to be hopelessly inefficient. The reason for this is simple. Across all the members of a group, the relative positions remain constant, as there is always a first place, always a second place, and always a last place. The person in each respective position changes during the process of competition, but the rise of one person is always connected with the relegation of another to a lower position; thus, on balance, no gain can result. In other words, someone who increases his income, and thereby rises in the hierarchy, will do so at the expense of someone who is pushed down. One person's success is another person's loss. People who are satisfied with what they have achieved thus find themselves in competition, because they have to keep up if they don't want to get pushed down in the hierarchy and suffer relative losses.

Competing for relative position inevitably leads to attempts to "keep up with the Joneses," a phrase popularized by Arthur R. Momand in a comic strip that debuted in 1913. Figure 3.5 illustrates this relationship. It shows the relationship between income and life satisfaction at three points in time: t_1, t_2, and t_3. The circled clusters of points describe the relationship between income and life satisfaction at each time. With time, the clusters of points shift to the right—that is, the society becomes richer. The three paths drawn between two points in time indicate possible changes for individual members of the groups. Path 1 represents a person at the bottom of the income hierarchy at t_1 who is still there at t_2. This is why, although his income grew strongly, his life satisfaction increased very little, if at all. Path 2 represents a person who didn't succeed in keeping up with the Joneses. His income remained constant; however, because the income of everyone else increased, his relative position is significantly worse at t_2 than at t_1. Dropping down in the hierarchy has considerably reduced his satisfaction with life. The achiever, represented by path 3, fares quite differently. Not only is he able to raise his absolute income between t_2 and t_3; he can also climb upward in the hierarchy, with a considerable gain in life satisfaction as his reward. The bold line (which we would like to name the Easterlin line in honor of its discoverer) represents the average relationship. It shows that steadily increasing income doesn't lead to an increase in average life satisfaction.

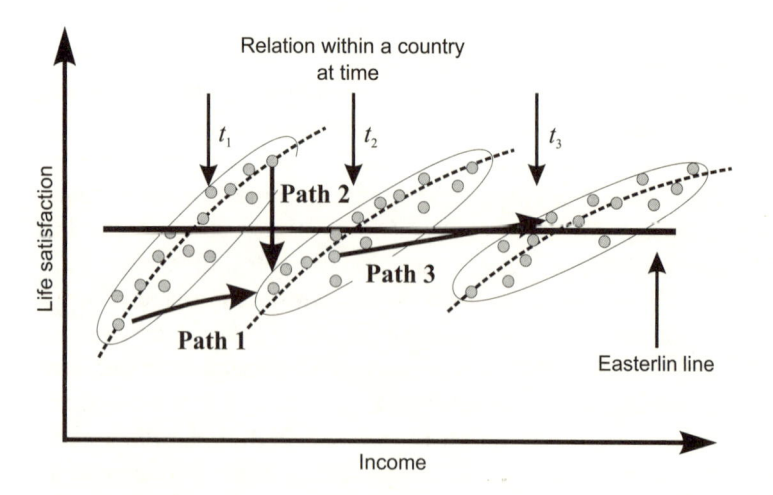

Figure 3.5

Relation between income and life satisfaction (freely adapted from Clark, Frijters, and Shields 2008).

We can be quite sure that relative position plays an important role in our lives. If you are not entirely convinced of this, imagine the following situation: One day your boss calls you into his office and, after offering you a cup of coffee, tells you that you will get a raise in pay of 5 percent for your good work. You are delighted, your satisfaction with life immediately goes up substantially, and you are happy as you leave your boss's office. In the hall you encounter a colleague, who sees where you are coming from and notices your beaming face. "So," he asks as he pats you on the shoulder, "did you get a 10 percent raise, too?" Now don't say that this wouldn't bother you. But why is it that your colleague's remark puts your life satisfaction into free fall?

Explanations

Relative income position is of practically no significance in neoclassical economics. Only a few authors have addressed this issue from a theoretical perspective, and it has not progressed any further than being an anecdote in the history of economic theory.[2] It was empirical life-satisfaction research, set in motion by Easterlin, that first put this issue at the top of its agenda. The main focus of such research was the question of with whom people compare themselves and how important these comparisons are. This was first pursued by Clark and Oswald (1996), who assumed that people compare themselves against a reference group made up of people similar to them—people of the same age and education who live nearby. Using British data on job satisfaction, Clark and Oswald showed that a person's position relative to the reference group had a strong influence on his or her satisfaction. Similar results were found for life satisfaction in Germany (Ferrer-i-Carbonell 2005) and for happiness in the United States (Luttmer 2005), and those results have been confirmed for Great Britain (Sloane and Williams 2000) and Canada (Lévy-Garboua and Montmarquette 2004).[3]

The empirical findings change little if we go beyond the world of work and examine reference groups consisting of people of the same age and gender in a neighborhood.[4] However, Clark, Kristensen, and Westergård-Nielsen (2009) show that life satisfaction rises with the income of the immediate reference group. They say that the reason for this is that living in a "better area" may well be accompanied by a higher life satisfaction than living in a poor district. Only within a reference group do the old relations hold sway once again: The higher a person is in the hierarchy, the happier the person is. The significance of relative position has also been established for Germany. Ferrer-i-Carbonell (2005) shows that people in the states of the former West Germany compare their income with the income of others more than the people in the states of the former East Germany do. Moreover, it makes a difference whether an individual compares himself with people who have more than he has or with people who have less. Poorer German citizens perceive having less income than their reference group as seriously limiting their happiness, whereas the rich experience no further gain in life satisfaction merely from being at the top of the ladder. Ferrer-i-Carbonell concludes that this is due mainly to comparisons from the bottom to the top.

It is not only the income of others that can serve as a reference. A person's own past income also sets a reference value, and expectations of future income may also play a role. When current income is compared with past income, the term *internal reference income* is used. What happens to this reference value if a person's own income rises? If the internal reference income then also increases, the rise in the person's income will have only a temporary effect, because people adjust to the gain by setting their benchmark higher. And this is exactly what seems to happen, at least according to a famous study by Brickmann, Coates, and Janoff-Bulmann (1978). They examined the life satisfaction of 22 lottery winners over a long period and found that life satisfaction had already begun to decline again one year after the win, even though it was still somewhat above the level that existed before the win. Gardner and Oswald (2007), however, found that winning a lottery also led to a noticeable increase in life satisfaction in the long run.

Adaptation nevertheless plays an important role. We become accustomed to earning more, and after a while we no longer experience the same boost in happiness we did the moment we first saw the larger number on our paycheck. This can lead to a feeling akin to being on a hamster wheel or a hedonic treadmill—a feeling that one has to earn more and more. Van Praag and Frijters (1999) estimate that an increase in income of one euro leads to a 60-euro-cent rise in a person's internal reference income. This means one needs the first 60 cents of the additional euro to satisfy his higher level of demands. The effect of an increase in income is always greatest at the beginning; it attenuates more and more with time.

Although the presence of adaptation to internal reference income is well documented, the reasons for its existence are not yet fully understood. Quoidbach et al. (2010) asked about 350 employees of the University of Liège about their ability to savor positive emotions. Specifically, respondents were asked to imagine various kinds of positive events, such as finishing an important task or spending a romantic weekend away, and then select their potential reactions from a list that included typical savoring behavior (displaying positive emotions, staying present, anticipating or reminiscing about the event, telling other people about the experience). Quoidbach et al. found that people with higher incomes displayed significantly less savoring behavior than people with lower incomes. Of course, this does not immediately imply that income causes less savoring. Instead, it might be the case that people who—for reasons not related to money— are less able to savor also are less easily satisfied and strive more for success, which might in turn be why their incomes are higher. To shed more light on causality, Quoidbach et al. randomly split the respondents into two groups. Member of one group received a questionnaire featuring a picture of a large stack of money; the questionnaire given to members of the other group did not have the picture. Members of the group that had been shown a simple reminder of money reported lower savoring scores, which suggests a true causal effect of money on people's ability to savor. Quoidbach et al. also conducted a related experiment with Canadian university students. After the subjects were randomly divided into two groups, members of one group were given a questionnaire with a picture of money on the front page; members of the other group received a neutral questionnaire. They were then asked to eat a piece of chocolate before completing the questionnaire. Without the students' noticing, observers rated how much they appeared to enjoy eating the chocolate (by observing their facial expressions and measuring the time they spent eating). When gender differences (female students took more time to enjoy the chocolate than male students) and individual differences in general tastes for chocolate were taken into account, it could be observed that students who initially saw the picture of money enjoyed the chocolate significantly less than students in the control group. Quoidbach et al. draw the conclusion that money impairs the ability to savor everyday pleasures. According to their interpretation, hedonic adaptation to income can thus be explained by the two-sided nature of money: Although it enables people to consume a larger set of more expensive goods and experiences, it also reduces their ability to enjoy the many smaller pleasures of everyday life. Even though this experimental design helps to overcome the causality problem, it can't fully clear up the reasons why showing people a picture of money causes them to enjoy a small pleasure less. What kinds of thoughts are triggered by a picture of money? Are people reminded of their own financial situation (which might be good or bad)? Do they think that they should have more money? Do they get the feeling that the experimenter wants them to act as if they wanted more money?

Adaptation to income has natural consequences for the behavior of employers. Grund and Sliwka (2007) found that employees who had received a greater pay increase than others were considerably more satisfied. If that is generally the case, a company that wants to keep its employees happy may want to grant frequent and substantial raises. Since (for obvious reasons) there are limits on this, it is no wonder that life satisfaction declines with increasing length of employment with a company. Increase in pay that are too regular and too predictable are also not advisable, though. For a long time, remuneration in the German civil service was based on length of service. Pay increased automatically every two years irrespective of how hard the civil servant had worked, and every employee was able to read the earnings he could expect directly from the pay tables. We think it is clear that guaranteed increases in income also affected the internal reference income and therefore had less of an effect on life satisfaction.

The German civil service also provides us with a fine example of an external reference point. Until a few years ago, professors in Germany were paid according to a relatively rigid salary scheme with three levels: C2 for professors at universities of applied sciences (i.e., teaching-oriented colleges), C3 for professors at universities of applied sciences and associate professors at research universities, and C4 for full professors at research universities. A story was circulating among economists: To increase the productivity of the C4 professors, a C5 professorship should be created that would differ from a C4 professorship only in the number of its designation—the salary, the equipment in the department, and the teaching duties should remain the same. Intense competition for the "higher status" would result in tremendous increases in productivity. Since then, empirical research on life satisfaction has found evidence that this conjecture concerning a pure status effect may well be correct. Whereas the effect of an increase in income diminishes with time, an increase in status has a positive long-term effect on life satisfaction. (See Di Tella, Haisken-DeNew, and McCulloch 2010.)

It is well known that people can't eat money and can't live in money. If income creates life satisfaction, presumably that is because it provides more scope for consumption. But higher income doesn't have to be accompanied by higher consumption. For example, a family that has borrowed money to build a house can use unexpected increases in income to increase their mortgage repayments. This will change the family's asset situation but not its consumption pattern. Instead, there will be an increase in the family's anticipated consumption at a later time, since with the higher repayments the mortgage will be paid off sooner and the family's interest burden will be lighter. In this context, economists say that consumption depends not on *periodic* income but rather on *permanent* income, which is calculated for the whole life cycle and which includes savings and future earnings.

Do we obtain other results if we use permanent income instead of periodic income? There is some evidence that the income-happiness relationship is stronger when one is comparing long-run averages of income and subjective well-being between individuals than when one is looking at short-run changes in these measures for one individual. This could be interpreted as illustrating the importance of stable personality traits and individual values (Luhmann et al. 2011) or as indicating that people's permanent income plays a larger role in well-being than temporary income changes. The problem is that permanent income is not easily observable. Although past income may, to some extent, be reflected in current wealth,[5] expected future income certainly is not reflected in current wealth. For this reason, the existing results should be viewed with caution. Important evidence, however, was provided by Knabe and Rätzel (2011). Using the average income earned during the ten years around the time under consideration as the approximate value for permanent income, they found that permanent income has an additional positive effect that goes beyond the effect of periodic income, and that its magnitude is similar. An increase in income a person receives only for a short time thus affects his satisfaction in several ways. For one thing, it raises his periodic income, which raises his satisfaction. For another, the additional income also leads to a slight rise in his permanent income, which increases his satisfaction. The person's permanent income, however, is calculated over all the years of his life, so not only does it increase in the period in which the additional income is earned; it also increases in the long term, and so it will also result in increased satisfaction in the other years of his life. Together these two effects determine how an increase in income affects subjective well-being. Life-satisfaction research generally considers only the first effect—the effect of income at the time it was earned. The positive effects of temporary income flows in other periods in life are ignored. This suggests that the effects arising from income increases are systematically underestimated in the literature.

Underestimation also arises from the fact that converting income into assets can have long-term effects if the possession of assets itself already leads to increased life satisfaction. So if homeowners or owners of old masters directly experience joie de vivre from the fact that they possess these assets (and not from actually using these assets), the income effect will be underestimated once more.

Such considerations suggest not only that it may be possible to eliminate the Easterlin Paradox by referring to the importance of relative position, but that the Easterlin Paradox may be attributable (at least partly) to a measuring problem in empirical life-satisfaction research. Are we measuring the right thing when we ask about life satisfaction? We will return to this point later. For now, we will continue on the path we have taken above, and will assume that everything is in order with the empirical results we have introduced thus far. If we are indeed trapped on a hedonic treadmill, what should we do? A number of economists have given some thought to this, and there is more to their answers than there would seem to be at first glance. But before we let those economists have their say, we must clarify one point. The Easterlin Paradox claims that an individual's satisfaction with life doesn't really depend on his or her income. But then what does make an individual more or less content?

4
If Money Doesn't Make Us Happy, What Then?

International life-satisfaction research is based on many data sets, not only on the American GSS, the British BHPS, or the German SOEP. For example, for Europe we have the European Social Survey (ESS) and the European Value Study (EVS), and comparable surveys exist for other countries and continents. In this chapter we will discuss some of the regularities that can be found in almost all of these data sets. On the basis of these surveys, we may be justified in assuming that the regularities involve relatively stable relationships. These surveys will then provide us with some clues as to what actually makes people happy and what does not. In this regard, there are some things we can influence and others that we cannot. We will begin with the latter.

The Happiness That Lies Within Us

The heritable things

Is happiness innate? When we feel happy or unhappy, is it because of our genes? If it is, then we can in fact stop thinking about what makes us happy, because life satisfaction is something we are born with and we have no way of changing it. However, it is hard to imagine that we have so little influence on our own life satisfaction. Doesn't a man forge his own destiny? What would there be to forge if our happiness were determined by our genes alone? On the other hand, it is also difficult to imagine that a person's genetic makeup has no influence at all on how contented he or she is wandering along life's path. It is probably more a matter of finding out to what extent our satisfaction is determined by our genes and how much it depends on our personal life circumstances and our own destiny. There are different ways of approaching this question. One is to examine how pronounced the variations in a person's life satisfaction are. Significant changes in subjective life satisfaction would suggest that it is largely determined by changing life circumstances. If, on the other hand, we were to find that life satisfaction scarcely changes no matter what happens, that would indicate a strong influence of the unalterable genetic makeup.

Our life satisfaction is likely to change particularly dramatically when significant events take place in our lives. These can be hard strokes of fate (such as a serious disease) or experiences of good fortune (such as winning a lottery). It shouldn't be surprising, then, that happiness researchers have been particularly interested in both lottery winners and seriously ill people. Some studies show that people have a very strong ability to adapt to changed circumstances in their lives. For example, lottery winners' feelings of happiness are of relatively short duration. After a while, a winner's life satisfaction declines again. According to new studies, however, lottery winners nevertheless remain happier than before the win, but not as dramatically as one might think. On the other hand, some respected studies have shown that people who were paralyzed in accidents regain their life satisfaction when given enough time to adapt to their new life circumstances. Schulz and Decker (1985), for instance, found that the life satisfaction of middle-aged and elderly paraplegics barely differed from that of their healthier contemporaries of similar age. Patterson et al. (1993) found a similar adaptation in people who had suffered serious burns. Wu (2003) observed that patients with heart disease became satisfied with their lives once again.

The aforementioned results should, however, be treated with some caution. Measuring a high level of adaptation to changed life circumstances on a scale with a limited range doesn't necessarily mean that the adaption has actually taken place. Perhaps the dramatic life event also changed the meanings of the endpoints of the satisfaction scale. For this reason, we cannot conclude from measured adaptation that a person's happiness in life is largely invariable.

A more promising approach is to use the results of research in which differences in the life satisfaction of identical twins and non-identical twins have been investigated. Lykken and Tellegen (1996) have done research of this kind. The basic idea is very simple: Compare identical and non-identical twins and, in each case, find out to what extent the life satisfaction of the siblings varies. If the differences between the twins who have exactly the same genes are less than the differences between the twins whose genes vary more significantly, genetic makeup may influence on life satisfaction. Lykken and Tellegen found the differences between identical twins to be significantly less than those between non-identical twins. Perhaps, then, our genes have a substantial say in matters concerning our satisfaction with life. Diener et al. (2009a), however, point out that this doesn't mean that our degree of happiness is set in concrete, so to speak. They draw an analogy with research on intelligence. It is known that a person's intelligence is also hereditary to a considerable extent. We nevertheless saw a dramatic increase in average intelligence during the twentieth century. Despite the mighty power of our genes, life circumstances still play an important role.

Personality and values
Aside from genetic predisposition, there are grounds for suspecting that an individual's personality is not unimportant in life satisfaction. After all, personality is also determined to a considerable degree by genes. Psychological research assumes that about half of our personality traits are inherited. These personality traits are measured by means of the Big Five personality traits. That method is based on a model whose foundations were laid in the 1930s—a model that has undergone intensively empirical testing since that time. It was found that people can essentially be categorized according to five characteristics of their personality, which in turn can easily be ascertained by means of a questionnaire.

It seems reasonable to pursue the question of whether there is a connection between the five personality traits and life satisfaction. Such a connection can in fact be demonstrated for at least two of these traits. (See Diener and Lucas 1999.) Psychologists categorize emotional stability and reactivity under the heading *neuroticism*. Someone who scores high on neuroticism is more prone to negative emotions than someone who scores low, and more often experiences anxiety, insecurity, sorrow, or embarrassment. A low score is associated with high ego strength, which imparts inner peace and security. It isn't surprising that people with the latter characteristics report higher levels of life satisfaction than those who score high on neuroticism. A similarly clear connection can be found with regard to extroversion. People with a high level of extroversion are sociable, open to others, and often cheerful and optimistic. Introverted people don't care about being sociable, like to be alone, and are not as open to positive feelings as the extroverted type is. In this case, life satisfaction is positively correlated with the value of this measure. There is a tendency for people with a higher score on extroversion to also report higher life satisfaction.

The other three personality traits are not significantly correlated with life satisfaction. *Openness to experience* measures a person's eagerness to try new things and says something about how imaginative he is, but it says nothing about whether he is satisfied with life. *Agreeableness* measures how we interact with other people. People scoring high on agreeableness tend to have a cooperative rather than a competitive attitude and tend to be altruists rather than egoists. But all this doesn't lead to a significantly higher life satisfaction. This is certainly a surprising finding—don't we always hear that it is better to give than to receive? That may well be true, but empirical research in psychology has found nothing to indicate that people who are prepared to give are systematically happier. *Conscientiousness*, the last personality trait of the Big Five, also says little about whether someone is content with his life. Apparently people who are inclined to be chaotic, careless, and inexact have the same chance of achieving high levels of life satisfaction as people who are organized, neat, and deliberate.

As in many other contexts, the question here is "How reliable are the results obtained by life-satisfaction researchers?" Diener and Lucas (1999) found that personality was a reliable indicator of life satisfaction and that it seemed to have more influence than life circumstances. On the other hand, Dolan, Peasgood, and White (2006) pointed out that some studies showed the correlation between personality and life satisfaction to be significantly weaker if, for example, religious convictions were taken into account. Despite these qualifications, it does seem to be the case that one's personality has a say in how happy one is.

People's personal values might also be relevant to their subjective well-being. Personal values reflect a person's life goals and represent what is important to him. Schwartz (1992) distinguished ten value types (universalism, benevolence, tradition, conformity, security, power, achievement, hedonism, stimulation, and self-direction) that can be grouped according to the degree to which they reflect self-enhancement relative to self-transcendence and openness to change relative to conservation. All these values are established over an individual's lifetime and have proved to be quite stable. They may influence subjective well-being in complex ways. A detailed discussion of these effects is beyond the scope of this section,[1] but it is worthwhile to take a closer look at the relationship between subjective well-being and one specific value that we mentioned at the very beginning of our book—a value that certainly comes to mind when one thinks about the relationship between money and well-being. That value is materialism. Materialism is typically understood as the valuation of the possession and continued acquisition of material goods, based on the belief that material objects are important and valuable (Larsen et al. 1999). In Schwartz's (1992) categories, materialists emphasize values in the self-enhancement dimension (power and achievement).

How is materialism related to subjective well-being? The common view is that materialism is detrimental to living a satisfied life. The pursuit of extrinsic (materialistic) values (such as being financially successful, good-looking, or famous) is generally thought to involve an excessive amount of interpersonal comparisons, to promote antisocial behavior (such as theft), and to crowd out intrinsically satisfying behavior (such as engaging with other people or doing something to their benefit).[2]

Recent empirical studies have produced evidence that necessitates a more differentiated view of the complex interplay between materialism and well-being. Burroughs and Rindfleisch (2002) conducted a survey in the United States in which they asked a large number of questions eliciting respondents' personal values (which they then divided into materialistic and collective-oriented values) and their life satisfaction. Whereas earlier studies had looked at the influence of each value separately, this study's novel approach was to take into account the entire value system, and thus also the interactions between the different value dimensions. The surprising result was that materialistic orientation isn't always bad for well-being. People suffer from their materialistic orientation only when they also hold strong collective-oriented values (family, community, religion). If people don't hold strong collective values, being more materialistic doesn't appear to harm their subjective well-being. This finding indicates that it isn't materialism as such that makes people unhappy, but the value conflict it causes when people also have competing values in their overall value system.

Another potential limitation of the idea that materialism is bad for well-being is provided by the environmental-match perspective. Sagiv and Schwartz (2000) argue that what matters for people's well-being in relation to their personal values is not so much what these values are as how they relate to the value orientation of people in their environment. If they are congruent, that is beneficial for well-being, because such environments typically support people in their pursuit of their goals and reinforce their importance. Sagiv and Schwartz empirically support their idea using a small sample of Israeli students with business administration or psychology majors. Under the arguable assumption that business administration is more oriented toward materialism than psychology, which emphasizes collective-oriented values, having more materialistic values should make business students feel better but should reduce the well-being of psychology students. That is exactly what Sagiv and Schwartz found, but their results didn't go undisputed. Using a different method to measure the extent to which a person's values reflect extrinsic and intrinsic goals, Kasser and Ahuvia (2002) surveyed business students in Singapore and found that students with a more extrinsic value orientation (valuing money, image, and popularity) reported lower happiness, more anxiety, and worse physical health. Thus, materialistic values may be so detrimental to well-being that even a supporting environment doesn't suffice to lessen their negative effects. Similar results were obtained by Vansteenkiste et al. (2006) in Belgium. In their study, business students were compared with students who wanted to become preschool teachers. Business students were found to have more extrinsic goals than education students, whereas education students reported higher life satisfaction and less alcohol and cigarette consumption. Statistical analyses show that there is indeed a robust positive relationship between intrinsic motivation and happiness. Interestingly, however, a student's choice of subject isn't relevant to this relationship, so even business students suffer when they have a more extrinsic value orientation.

As we have seen, many studies support the claim that materialism is bad for happiness. The question remains, however, why this is the case. Sirgy (1998) proposed that this could be explained by the way people form expectations. When people have to evaluate their lives, they need some benchmark with which to compare their actual achievements. This benchmark is set by people's expectations about what they could have hoped to achieve. In his 1998 paper, Sirgy argues that materialistic people more often have inflated expectations. They orient themselves to some ideal view of how high their standard of living could be and what they feel they deserve. Since these expectations are hard to satisfy, materialists are dissatisfied with their material standard of living, and thus also with their lives. Non-materialists, on the other hand, more often form ability-based expectations that are based on how their achievements relate to their own past and how well off they are materially given their educational background and socioeconomic status. Since such expectations are easier to meet, non-materialists are typically happier than materialists.

In a recent paper, Sirgy et al. (2013) build on the idea that materialists and non-materialists differ in how much importance they attach to comparisons of their standard of living with some benchmark. Contrary to Sirgy's 1998 paper, they don't claim that materialists and non-materialists set their benchmarks differently; instead they argue that materialists compare their actual standard of living partly with an ideal-based benchmark and partly with an ability-based benchmark, whereas non-materialists often don't compare their standard of living against any benchmark at all. Whereas evaluations using ideal-based benchmarks reduce life satisfaction, the opposite may be true for comparisons with an ability-based benchmark, because such comparisons may exert positive effects on economic motivation (one's motivation for economic success or need for achievement), which in turn positively affects life satisfaction. An empirical analysis of data on more than 1,000 people in seven countries supports this view. Materialists report higher frequencies of comparing their standard of living to both ideal-based and ability-based benchmarks than non-materialists. Although this decreases their satisfaction with their standard of living, it also strengthens their economic motivation, giving them more hope and optimism. This puts materialism in a very different perspective.

Health and disability

Albert Schweitzer once said "Happiness is nothing more than good health and a bad memory." Most people would probably agree with at least the first part of that remark. Empirical studies—for example, the survey by Dolan, Peasgood, and White (2008)—consistently show a high correlation between health and life satisfaction. Care should, however, be taken when interpreting such correlations, since by no means do the existence and the direction of a causal relationship follow from the fact that two quantities show a trend in the same direction. For example, a positive correlation between economic trends and the purchase of gold jewelry doesn't mean that economic activity depends on the demand for gold, but simply that more luxury goods are bought in times of a booming economy. There is a high correlation between the flowering seasons of many plants, but this doesn't mean there is a causal relationship between the blossoming of tulips and that of daffodils.

In order to obtain more detailed information about causal relationships, one can use a fixed-effects model in which the observed differences in life satisfaction are adjusted for the factors that could influence life satisfaction but don't manifest themselves in the data and don't vary with time—mainly the personality of the person being observed, which, as we have seen, has a strong influence on life satisfaction. If panel data are available, we have observations of one individual over a longer period of time. If it can be assumed that personality scarcely changes over time, we can use statistics to eliminate its influence by looking solely at the changes that occur as a consequence of particular events that the person has experienced. The results of such studies show that there is still a correlation between health and life satisfaction when the influence of personality can be eliminated.

This still doesn't settle the matter of causality conclusively. It is entirely possible that it is not health that determines life satisfaction, but rather the reverse. People who are content with themselves and with life are more well balanced, perhaps have much less stress and definitely have fewer worries. Doesn't it seem reasonable that they go through life in better health? Today it is generally recognized that many physical problems have psychological causes. Accordingly, life satisfaction must influence a person's health. It is nonetheless equally certain that health must influence life satisfaction. Major life events, such as a heart attack or a major operation, cause drastic reductions in life satisfaction. Thus, people are healthier if they are happy, and they are happier if they are healthy.

Layard (2005) draws attention to another interesting finding. It appears that it is chiefly a person's subjective assessment of his own health that is responsible for influencing happiness, not the objective results obtained by the doctor. Whether this is good or bad news is difficult to decide. For hypochondriacs around the world it is bad news, because it means that even an imagined illness can lower life satisfaction dramatically. On the other hand, it may be comforting to people who are really ill that it is possible to become happier simply by developing a positive attitude toward one's illness and, as a result, to feel healthier than a doctor says one actually is.

One would expect a health problem that leads to a permanent disability to be particularly dramatic. As we have already mentioned, early findings suggested that disabled people could adapt to their new situations rather well, with relatively minor reductions in the quality of life. Those findings—especially those reported by Brickman, Coates, and Janoff-Bulman (1978)—have been seriously questioned. More recent papers show a much more varied picture. And different researchers sometimes come to different conclusions even when analyzing the same data sets. Consider, for example, the studies conducted by the psychologist Richard Lucas (2007) and those conducted by the economists Andrew Oswald and Nattavudh Powdthavee (2008). Lucas finds that disability is associated with a large decline in life satisfaction. In the years after the onset of disability, almost no adaptation occurred, so life satisfaction didn't recover. Oswald and Powdthavee, on the other hand, use the same data but bring empirical methods to bear. They also find that becoming disabled has a large negative effect on life satisfaction. After three years of disability, however, between 30 percent and 50 percent of the negative effect has disappeared. One way to read these studies is to take them as evidence that there is no scientific consensus on the ability of people to adapt to unfortunate life circumstances. Another possible conclusion is, however, that a belief in the power of adaptation based on the study by Brickman et al. isn't supported by more recent studies. Even if we don't know exactly how well people are able to adapt, we can be pretty sure that adaption is only partial and that unfortunate life events can have permanent effects on an individual's happiness.

It has now become customary to compare the life satisfaction of physically disabled people with that of healthy people using a measure that takes into account not only average life satisfaction but also the scatter around this mean value. This is expressed in a result that says what percentage of healthy people are happier than an average disabled person.[3] A value of 57 percent is obtained for people with a mild disability—barely more than the 50 percent obtained in a comparison of two groups of healthy people. For people with serious disabilities (especially those accompanied by permanently reduced mobility), these values increase dramatically. In various studies, they range from 87 percent to 94 percent—that is, up to 94 percent of healthy people are happier than a person with a serious disability.

To what extent people are able to adapt to changed life circumstances is, of course, an important question, especially in connection with disabilities. Some studies that have shown that the life satisfaction of seriously disabled people improves with time, but it is very difficult to interpret those findings correctly. In order for reliable statements to be made, information on the life satisfaction of healthy people and that of disabled people would have to be comparable between healthy and disabled persons or between the points in time before and after the onset of disability. It seems highly unlikely that this is possible. Imagine a healthy person who becomes a quadriplegic because of an accident. Is he using the same scale for evaluating his life satisfaction after the accident that he used before the accident? Does he associate a 10 on the scale with the same things before and after the accident? That hardly seems likely. Paralysis usually is irreversible, and the best possible condition is, therefore, one in which the person can sit in a wheelchair. For this reason, he measures his subjective life satisfaction on a completely different "scale" after the accident than before. Thus, his post-accident responses can no longer be compared with his pre-accident responses.

On the other hand, an increase in life satisfaction after an initial decrease following the onset of disability shows that, to a certain extent, adaptation has indeed taken place. People come to terms with their situation and adjust to their changed circumstances. They need time for this, and there is little to indicate that they are able to gain the same degree of life satisfaction with the disability that they had without it. But adapt they do, and there is something special about this adaptation. As Dolan and Kahneman (2008) note, it turns out that the ability to adapt to changed life circumstances is greater than healthy people can imagine. People tend to underestimate the different ways it is possible to adapt to a disability. This has an implication that is of some significance for matters of health policy.

Imagine there are two illnesses. Illness A is initially accompanied by a severe reduction in life satisfaction, but sufferers can adapt exceedingly well and with time they regain a high proportion of their old life satisfaction. Illness B isn't as bad as illness A to begin with, but it is harder to adapt to it, and so the life satisfaction associated with this illness is lower than with illness A. (Sufferers of illness A have, in the meantime, adjusted well.) If we want to judge which of these illnesses is worse, our decision will hinge on whether we ask people who have just contracted their illness (they will rate A as worse) or people who have suffered for a longer time (they will describe B as worse). This isn't entirely unimportant, since in a world in which we have long been forced to ration health services it is rather important to decide which illness should have greater treatment priority. (In case of doubt this will, of course, be the one that is worse.)

Age

One finding that has the potential to change our entirely personal view of things radically concerns the relationship between happiness and age. The results reported by Stone et al. (2010) were so unexpected (at least to people not familiar with happiness research) that *The Economist*, in its issue of December 16, 2010, devoted a long article to them. Stone et al. contacted more than 330,000 households by telephone and asked them how they judged their life satisfaction and to what extent they felt certain emotions, such as anger, stress, happiness, or sadness. The most important result was that life satisfaction is U-shaped. Young people are happy, but the more they grow up, the more responsibility they must bear and the unhappier they become. The nadir is reached at about the middle of the fifth decade of life. After that, everything begins to improve. The life satisfaction one experienced at the age of 20 isn't lost for good; it is regained at 70.

As we said, the finding of a U-shaped relationship between age and life satisfaction was not so unexpected for happiness researchers. Many studies have found similar results in very different data sets. Blanchflower and Oswald (2008) analyzed data from the United States and Western Europe and then extended their analysis to Eastern Europe, Asia, and Latin

America. In all regions examined, they found the U-shaped relationship. They concluded that middle-aged people hit a happiness low almost everywhere in the world. Nevertheless, their results are not undisputed. For example, Frijters and Beatton (2012) argue that life satisfaction doesn't change much between the ages of 20 and 50 and that the U shape is a statistical artifact of a sudden upward jump of happiness around the age of 60. Kassenböhmer and Haisken-DeNew (2012) find that the U shape disappears if one takes the time people spent in a panel into account because their attitudes and answering behavior seem to change as a result of their being interviewed year after year. This last point is particularly interesting, because it hints at the difficulty in estimating the age-happiness relationship. When one compares people of different ages at a given time, one cannot distinguish age effects from cohort effects (i.e., the fact that people of different age will have been born in different years and were thus growing up under very different circumstances). When one observes the same person over time, however, one cannot separate the age effect from the "time spent in the panel" effect. Using more sophisticated empirical tools, however, van Landeghem (2012) was able to separate these effects and to show that the age effect is indeed likely to be U-shaped.

An interesting experiment conducted by Lacey, Smith, and Ubel (2006) shows just how much our own idea of age differs from these findings. A group of 30-year-olds and a group of 60-year-olds were each asked which of the two groups had the higher life satisfaction. A majority in both groups agreed that the younger ones were more satisfied with life. But when asked about their own subjective life satisfaction, it turned out that it was the older ones who reported higher scores.

When we see the obvious negative side effects of aging, we conclude that older people must be worse off than younger people. We overlook the fact, however, that aging is accompanied by changes that have a positive influence on our quality of life. For instance, Stone et al. show that stress levels decline markedly with age and that the elderly worry less and don't get so annoyed. In short, age relaxes a person. In this regard, *The Economist* quotes the American philosopher William James: "How pleasant is the day when we give up striving to be young—or slender."

What Happens to Us

Marriage

In most modern cultures, it is the norm for people to get married at some point and then often to start a family. The institution of marriage is considered the "nucleus of society" and has proved remarkably stable. There have been plenty of attacks on it, though. It has been vilified as an old-fashioned invention of the petit-bourgeois and dismissed as no longer keeping up with the times. At times one had the impression that the spouse would be permanently replaced by the cohabitant, the more or less freely interchangeable temporary companion. But marriage has held its ground. People may marry later and have fewer children, but there can be no question of the demise of the institution of marriage. This suggests there must be something to this institution. In the end, does it make people happier?

There are other indications that marriage has a positive effect on people's lives. Married people display better physical and mental health, for example. They also hit the bottle or smoke a joint less often. The results of Gardner and Oswald (2004) are particularly impressive. They were able to show that married people have a longer life expectancy than unmarried people. This effect is especially pronounced for men. Marriage lengthens men's lives to the same extent that smoking shortens them. Since we know how damaging smoking is, it is clear how good marriage is for men. This effect is also seen in women, but it is only about half as strong. This can also be expressed in numbers: The probability of dying in the next ten years is 6.3 percent lower for a married man than for an unmarried man of the same age and physical condition. This probability is only 3.4 percent lower for married women. In the final analysis, we can only speculate why this is so. Perhaps the fact that women have a longer life expectancy than men per se simply plays a role. Extending a life expectancy that is already long even further may be more difficult than lengthening a comparatively shorter average lifetime. It could, of course, also be the case that men profit more from marriage than women do.

Health, income, and life expectancy are objective data that can be observed directly. They seem to indicate that people are better off being married. But do they also feel subjectively happier? Frey and Stutzer (2006) evaluated data on about 2,000 people who were questioned annually for as long as seventeen years within the framework of the German Sozio-oekonomisches Panel. Their results show that people experience a kind of happiness peak at the time they get married. Strictly speaking, they are happiest shortly after getting married. Their life satisfaction then declines, eventually returning to the pre-marriage level. Lucas et al. (2003) also used SOEP data to analyze the relationship between marriage and happiness. Even though they found that people reacted to marriage in very different ways (for some people, happiness just keeps on increasing every year after marriage; others seem to begin suffering immediately after marriage and never recover), there is clear evidence that on average people's happiness tends to return to its initial level after some years of marriage. These findings can be interpreted in various ways.

The first interpretation follows the usual pattern: People experience something that makes them happy, and their life satisfaction rises. Eventually they get accustomed to the new (better) state, so at some point they no longer gain any further feelings of happiness from it. The result is that they revert to their baseline level. In this interpretation it is adaptation that explains the decline in happiness. This result, however, didn't remain unchallenged. Quari (2010), who also used SOEP data, argues that happiness adapts only partially after marriage and remains permanently higher than it was when the partners were single. He argues that it is important to compare well-being after getting married with well-being before the relationship that eventually led to marriage began. If researchers look only at marital status, they typically compare the time when two persons were married with the time when they were cohabiting, which would certainly underestimate the true effect of having a steady partner.

The second interpretation reverses the causality. People don't get happier by marrying; they get married precisely when they feel especially happy, perhaps because they think that by marrying they can hold on to their happiness. In fact, feelings of happiness fluctuate quite independently of marital status. In other words, the return to the old level would have happened anyway, even without marriage.

A third interpretation is tied to a fundamental methodological problem of happiness research. We pointed this out earlier, and it will play an important role later in this book. We will use an example to explain it. Suppose that a 23-year-old unmarried man is asked, in a survey, to state how happy he is, on a scale from 1 to 10, at the moment. He may consider what 10 would mean for him—that is, in what situation he would be completely happy. Let us now suppose that in doing this he comes up with a dream scenario for his future life: He has graduated from a university and has landed a good job. At his side is a stunning woman whom he wants to marry and start a family with. Measuring his current life against this ideal situation, he checks the number 6. Five years later he is asked the same question again. In the meantime he has graduated and gotten a job that makes him happy and offers him good future prospects, and he has recently married. He should now check 10, but he probably has already reconsidered his ideal situation and therefore his former 10 is now only an 8. His satisfaction has nevertheless risen. The crucial point, however, is that he is now measuring his happiness on a scale different from the one used five years earlier. Now let us look ahead five years. He has two children, and his job is exhausting and stressful. What does 10 now correspond to—perhaps a situation in which he earns more and doesn't have to work as much and in which the children are developing well and are doing well at school, and the parents have a little more time for themselves. Life's focus has shifted once again, thus shifting the scale, and perhaps our 33-year-old now rates his happiness as 7. One possible interpretation of the ups and downs of his measured life satisfaction is that matrimony first made him happy and that getting accustomed to matrimony then made him a little unhappier. But such an interpretation is permissible only if we assume that the scale used to measure his life satisfaction was the same the whole time. Is it so implausible that perhaps this was not the case?

The methodological problem described above arises when we compare a person's life-satisfaction scores at different times. It doesn't arise if we make a cross-sectional comparison of married couples with different characteristics, as Frey and Stutzer (2006) did. They showed that couples with differing incomes benefit more from marriage than couples with similar incomes, which corresponds to Becker's idea (1973, 1974) that marriage is beneficial because it allows the partners to specialize, one working in the labor market and one working at home (that is, doing housework). Frey and Stutzer also found that couples with a similar level of education experienced more long-term happiness than couples with widely different levels of education. Different levels of education don't yet have a negative influence before the wedding or shortly thereafter, but the longer the marriage lasts the more important it seems to be that the spouses have similar interests.

All in all, there is considerable evidence that it is hardly a coincidence that the institution of marriage has proved stable.

Children

Three men are discussing the question of when human life begins. "Life begins when the egg cell is fertilized," says the first man. "No," objects the second man, "life begins at birth." The third man shakes his head. "You have no idea. Life begins when the children leave home and the dog is dead."

At first glance, happiness research appears to agree with the third man. More specifically, some studies show that people who have children are by no means happier than people without children—so long as their children are still living at home, at least. Only people with children who have left home are happier than people who grow old alone. Alesina et al. (2004) and Breterton et al. (2008) found that this result held true on average. The chronological sequence of satisfaction with life is what one would expect. Parents are least happy when their children are in puberty, but satisfaction with life already begins to decline after the birth of the first child. The expectation that the feared empty-nest syndrome will ensue after the children leave home seems, on the other hand, unfounded. Rather, it is a time for relief—on average, anyway.

These findings reflect the fact that bringing up children is accompanied by great burdens. Parents experience all kinds of limitations in their lives. Financially things become tighter, and leisure activities are put on hold for a long time because it is just not possible to take small children to bars or on extended hiking vacations in the Alps. All this seems to come at the expense of life satisfaction. On the other hand, there are the positive feelings parents display to their children, and being able to have these is said to increase happiness. On average, however, these feelings apparently don't suffice to balance out the limitations. It seems reasonable to suppose, however, that the stronger the parents' desire to have children is, the stronger these feelings will be. Morillo (2005) found that university graduates who have children were significantly happier than those without children. Even single mothers report higher levels of life satisfaction than single female graduates who have no children. Bucher (2009, p.100) puts it aptly: "Parenthood, one of the many options people have, makes them all the happier, the more convinced they are they want it."

Divorce from or death of a partner
People who are unhappy in their marriages will file for divorce when they hope to become happier by doing so. This means, however, that the positive effect of divorce on happiness can't be verified by comparing divorcees with married people. On the contrary, people who remain married are happier than people who have divorced. The positive effect of divorce first appears in a longitudinal study of divorcees—a study of changes in life satisfaction before, during, and after a divorce. The worst time in the life of a divorcee is *before* the divorce. Announcing that one will soon be divorced is enough to lead to an immediate improvement in life satisfaction.

The reason why the benefits of divorcing don't appear in a cross-sectional comparison is that we can't observe something that runs counter to the facts. In order to know exactly what benefits a divorce provides, we would have to know how (un)happy the two people would have become had they not divorced. This is a fundamental problem of happiness research. For instance, a small increase in life satisfaction may be observed after a person has been told that he will receive a raise in pay. But what would have happened if the raise hadn't materialized? It might well be that this would have led to an enormous decline in life satisfaction and that we therefore underestimate the "value" of the increase in pay if we don't take into account counterfactuals—a methodological problem that is difficult to solve. However, in the case of divorce referring to counterfactuals is entirely appropriate. Otherwise we might get the idea that the Roman Catholic Church is right in forbidding divorce and that people would be happier if it weren't possible for them to divorce.

Apart from that, findings from studies of life satisfaction are compatible with the purported experience of divorce attorneys. Women feel the worst two years before a divorce, men only one year before a divorce. This is consistent with the observation that women file for divorce considerably more frequently than men. After a divorce, life satisfaction starts to go up above the level it had, on average, during the entire marriage. This finding doesn't come as a surprise, either. In summary, these results demonstrate once again that it is wise to think very carefully about the person you choose to marry. The consequences of a bad decision for one's happiness can't really be corrected by getting divorced, since, as we said, those who stay married are happier.

Losing a partner to death differs greatly from losing a partner through divorce. It is known from the psychological and socio-medical literatures that the death of a life partner is one of the worst events in a person's life. Kaprio et al. (1987) reported a 20-fold increase in the suicide rate of women within a week of the death of a partner; for men the increase was even higher, at 70-fold. Life-satisfaction research supports these results.

Clark et al. (2008a) used data from the Sozio-oekonomisches Panel to investigate the effects of the death of the partner and found a dramatic decline in life satisfaction—a decline twice the size of that caused by unemployment and 2.5 times the size of the positive effect of marrying. In the case of a long illness or a period of nursing care, the unhappiness may begin years before the partner's death. After the funeral it takes a long time for the survivor to recover from the loss to some degree. Men have considerably more difficulty with this than women. On average, men take four years to return to their previous median level of life satisfaction, women only two years. This finding completes the picture. Men file for divorce less often than women, suffer more from a separation, and suffer more from the death of a life partner. Members of the allegedly stronger sex are obviously much more dependent on their relationships with their life partners than women, or less able to cope emotionally with separation.

Things are completely different if a person loses a partner unexpectedly (say, in an accident). The consequences are then much more serious than those of a natural death that was expected. Lehman et al. (1987) studied people who had lost a spouse in an automobile accident. Any adaptation to the new situation was almost impossible to detect. The survivors didn't succeed in coming to terms with what had happened. They tried to make sense of it long after the event, but to no avail. It is easy to imagine them replaying the accident in their thoughts again and again and asking themselves whether it could have been avoided. In this way, their grief lingers, and their life satisfaction declines permanently.

The World Around Us

Social contacts
It is not so much the great political achievements that make people happy as it is the things that people manage to achieve themselves in their immediate surroundings. In the late 1980s and the early 1990s, a number of American sociologists and political scientists were able to show the importance of social capital to the functioning of society and the well-being of the individual (Coleman 1988; Putnam et al. 1993; Putnam 1995). The term *social capital* refers to the individual's interactions with his or her immediate environment—first and foremost the individual's own family, then his or her neighbors, friends, and community. Putnam (1995) and Helliwell and Putnam (2004) showed that in the United States social capital has a strong correlation with health and with life satisfaction. People who live in a close network of family, friends, and neighbors, who get involved in their communities, or who are affiliated with religious groups are healthier and happier than others.

Social contacts provide us with a sense of community, emotional well-being and security, recognition, and support. Using the data from the German Sozio-oekonomisches Panel, Becchetti et al. (2008) showed that people who spent more time on community activities had a higher average level of life satisfaction. The results obtained by Powdthavee (2008) for Great Britain are even clearer. He compared people who had contact with friends several times a month, or even daily, with people who had such contact less than once a month. If we were to condemn a person accustomed to seeing his friends every day to seeing them only once a month, we would have to compensate him with £60,000 a year to maintain his life satisfaction at a constant level. Friends—particularly close ones—are precious, especially if the friendship involves speaking about very personal matters rather than about football or the weather.

Marked differences between men and women emerge in this context. According to the psychologist Nolen-Hoeksema (1991), women maintain more friendships than men but rather seldom make productive use of them. Instead of talking to their friends about how to solve a particular problem, they complain more and spend time discussing matters. Men are less open but more purposeful. They are more likely to try to solve problems, and less likely to get lost in long discussions. Although more recent studies have disproved the prejudice that men talk distinctly less than women, when solving problems women still appear to have a greater willingness to speak. For both men and women, according to the results of a psychological study of American college students conducted by Wheeler et al. (1993), friendship with a woman has a more positive effect on life satisfaction than friendship with a man. One reason for this may be that more openness and more emotional support is provided in friendships with women than in those with men. According to Kahneman et al. (2004), both positive and negative emotions are experienced more intensively when people are in contact with others than when they are alone. Loneliness leads to emotional flattening.

If we wanted to make recommendations for government action on the basis of findings on the importance of social capital, the advice would be to support everything that promotes social contacts. Examples include encouragement of marriage and tax incentives for registered clubs and associations and for non-profit organizations.

The environment
Market systems rely on prices to send reasonable signals of scarcity that people can use as a guide to make decisions about the use of scarce resources. But what happens if a market price for a good doesn't emerge? This is the case, for example, with goods for which no market exists. The most important examples of this can be found in the environment. For instance, clean air is a good for which no market exists. Similarly, there is no market for unspoiled landscapes, the conservation of species, or our climate system, and therefore there are no market prices for these goods. This is problematic, since it is nevertheless often necessary to place

a value on some environmental good. If a decision is to be made as to, say, whether a recreational area should be converted into an industrial area, it is important to be aware of the value of the recreational area when carrying out a rational analysis of the costs and benefits of such a step. Environmental liability law provides another example. Polluters would take their liability seriously if the cost of the damage caused by their emissions could be measured.

How can we specify the values of goods if we can't fall back on market prices? Not least thanks to Welsch (2002), happiness research is seen as promising to help solve this problem. The basic idea is as follows. For the purposes of simplification, let us imagine that a person's life satisfaction depends only on his income and the quality of his environment. If we now observe many people, with differences in earnings, exposed to different environmental conditions, but with a similar quality of life, we can derive a tradeoff between income and environmental quality. This provides information on the value of the environment expressed in terms of income. All that is needed to do this is the usual data from life-satisfaction research and a quantitative measure of the respective environmental quality (e.g., pollutant concentration).

Most of the studies valuing environmental goods using the life-satisfaction approach produce astonishingly clear and unambiguous findings, although the thorough discussion of the capabilities and limitations by Ferreira and Moro (2010) shows that the application of current happiness research to the valuation of non-market goods is still in its infancy. Some of the findings so far are nevertheless worth reporting here. The effects of air pollution, water pollution, noise pollution, and climate were investigated, and environmental conditions were found to have significant effects on life satisfaction in all cases. Lüchinger (2009) examined the effect of air quality on life satisfaction. Using a clever research design, he combined data on sulfur dioxide emissions of power plants and information on wind directions to identify the exposure to sulfur dioxide emissions at the county level. He found that air quality had a significant effect on individual well-being, and the monetary equivalent of the well-being loss determined by this method was much larger than that obtained by alternative methods. Welsch (2006, 2007) discovered, surprisingly that particulate pollution did *not* have any influence on life satisfaction, in contrast to the very clear effect of lead and nitrogen dioxide pollution. Since emissions of lead and nitrogen dioxide have declined significantly, this means a gain in quality of life corresponding to an annual income gain of $750 for nitrogen dioxide and $1,400 for lead. By contrast, the noise pollution at Schiphol Airport in Amsterdam is comparatively cheap. Van Praag and Baarsma (2005) conclude, in any case, that an income rise of only 0.8 percent or 2.2 percent (depending on whether noise abatement measures are implemented) would be necessary to compensate for an increase in aircraft noise of 50 percent. MacKerron (2012) gathered unique well-being data by having people report their current emotional state through a smartphone app that they had to install on their own phones. Responses were geo-located and could thus be combined with information about the quality of the environment in which the respondents were located. The study showed that people's emotional experiences were much more positive in natural environments than in congested urban areas.

The findings on climate change available so far also make interesting reading. Rehdanz and Maddison (2005) analyzed data from 67 countries and concluded that a rise in the minimum temperature of a country leads to an increase in life satisfaction whereas a rise in the maximum temperature reduces life satisfaction. Incidentally, these climate effects result in the gains in northern countries being greater than the losses in southern countries. It is clearly possible to compensate for climate change with appropriate changes in earnings (Frijters and Van Praag 1997).

On the whole, the results of studies to date show that happiness research on the valuation of non-marketable goods has substantial potential.

Personal and political freedom
Freedom is a tremendous asset. People fight for it and go into the streets to demonstrate for it, often taking great risks. It seems obvious that achieving political and personal freedom contributes to high life satisfaction. However, testing that assumption isn't easy. Several methodological problems remain to be solved. For one thing, we need a way to measure the political freedom a person enjoys. Indices have been used to do this, but of course they are somewhat arbitrary. Nevertheless, we can use indices as an approximate estimate in order to quantify the extent of political freedom in a country. In order to say something about the effects of more or less political freedom, however, it is necessary to compare different countries, and life-satisfaction data from one country can't readily be compared with life-satisfaction data from another.

Despite these limitations, life-satisfaction research provides us with findings that indicate strongly that freedom does in fact have the expected effects. Dorn et al. (2007) analyzed data on 25,000 people in 28 countries and found a strong correlation between the level of democracy prevailing in a country and the level of life satisfaction. The level of democracy was measured on a scale from 1 to 10, capturing, for instance, whether elections were run in the form of a genuine contest between politicians and whether non-elites also had access to political office. Giving people more democracy triggers long-lasting and strong effects on life satisfaction. In order to get an idea of this, Dorn et al. calculated the monetary value of one additional point on the democracy scale and found that a country's gaining of such an additional point had the same effect as raising the annual income of an adult by 4,500 euros.

The quality of the state system and the accomplishments of the government also are important. Helliwell and Huang (2008) showed that honest and efficiently run government is of great importance to people in poorer countries. Why this is so isn't difficult to imagine. Being poor and living in a poor country isn't easy, and a corrupt and incompetent government will certainly not add to your zest for life.

Minimizing corruption is also important to the inhabitants of rich countries, as are the rule of law and the quality of the government's work. Politicians affect the happiness of their voters not only by what they do but also by how they do it. If they follow the rules of law on which the constitutional state is based and go about their business in a reasonably intelligent way, this will have positive effects. Hudson's (2006) finding that trust in political institutions leads to higher life satisfaction should give us cause for thought. For years there has been talk in many European democracies of a "disenchantment with politics," accompanied by a growing loss of confidence. The crisis in the European Union and the fears associated with the euro and with governments' escalating debts are likely causes of a huge loss of confidence in political institutions.

Switzerland is a particularly rewarding object of study when it comes to the question of how democracy affects life satisfaction. Direct democracy isn't practiced to the same extent throughout Switzerland; the cantons vary considerably in how far the citizens' rights of co-determination go. This provides a good opportunity to investigate whether different forms of direct democracy result in different levels of life satisfaction. According to Frey and Stutzer (2000), the further the rights to political participation go, the higher the life-satisfaction scores are. The variations are not small. For example, a Swiss citizen who moves from Geneva to Basel is leaving the canton with the lowest level of direct democracy and settling in the canton with the highest level. This results in an increase of 11 percentage points in the probability that this person will respond to the question about his life satisfaction with the highest score (10)!

There are basically two ways direct democracy can lead people to feel better. On the one hand, political decisions have to be more closely aligned with the needs of the citizens. This could be characterized as an enhancement of the quality of political output. On the other hand, the procedure itself may play a role, meaning it could be the case that participating in the decision process may result in higher life satisfaction regardless of the outcomes of the decision. Using a trick, Frey and Stutzer distinguish between this procedural effect and the output effect. They additionally examine the life satisfaction of foreigners who don't have the right to vote and who are therefore affected by the outcome of direct democracy without being able to participate in the process. It transpires that foreigners benefit less from direct democracy than the Swiss, who are entitled to vote. There is indeed a procedural effect: an enhancement of life satisfaction that can be achieved simply by granting people a higher degree of co-determination.

5

The Economic Determinants of Happiness

There are material and non-material determinants of happiness. Happiness research, which we presented in chapter 4, emphasizes the non-material causes of happiness and unhappiness. The Easterlin Paradox appears to justify this approach—after all, it shows that income growth doesn't play a role in happiness. But can we really assume that the material side of our existence is of no significance at all? It is certainly true that money *alone* doesn't make you happy. On the other hand, no money at all isn't the answer. It almost goes without saying that we are attached to material things and that it is by no means all the same to us what alternatives we have when we think about where we want to go to eat today. We feel worse if a soup kitchen is the only possibility than if we also have a Greek (or French, or Italian) restaurant to choose from—to say nothing of German cuisine. It would be hard to dispute all this, but it does sometimes happen. This might be due to the fact that it isn't at all simple to measure the actual value of material things correctly and to take it into adequate consideration. We nonetheless want to try to do this in this chapter, and we will turn first to the most important economic determinants of life satisfaction.

Unemployment

Generally the work that a person does decisively influences his whole life. It not only fills a large part of his waking hours and establishes his income; it also determines his social recognition and self-perception and creates a feeling of being needed. Ideally, work is an important part of a person's self-realization. In view of its importance, it should probably be clear that happiness researchers have intensively explored how losing a job affects a person's life satisfaction.

The most important finding is valid worldwide: Unemployment reduces life satisfaction dramatically. Figure 5.1 exemplifies this point for

Germany. The data analyzed cover the years 1984–2010. Unemployment reduces average life satisfaction of men by more than 22 percent (1.6 points) and that of women by about 17 percent (1.18 points). Women suffer somewhat less when unemployed than men do, but the loss of quality of life caused by unemployment is also substantial in their case.

Both of the preceding observations are valid worldwide. In a study in which Stavrova et al. (2011) compared data from 28 countries, all the data point to a huge difference in life satisfaction between the employed and the unemployed. Moreover, the finding that men are more severely affected is also supported by international data. But why is the fact that becoming unemployed lowers life satisfaction an important item of news from happiness research at all? That losing your job is no reason for clicking your heels has always been known to economists (except perhaps to those economists believing in "voluntary" unemployment); it has been clear to everyone else too. Unemployment is seen as a stroke of fate—and that is nothing new. Why unemployment is bad is also common knowledge. Losing your job means losing your income. You are then reliant on

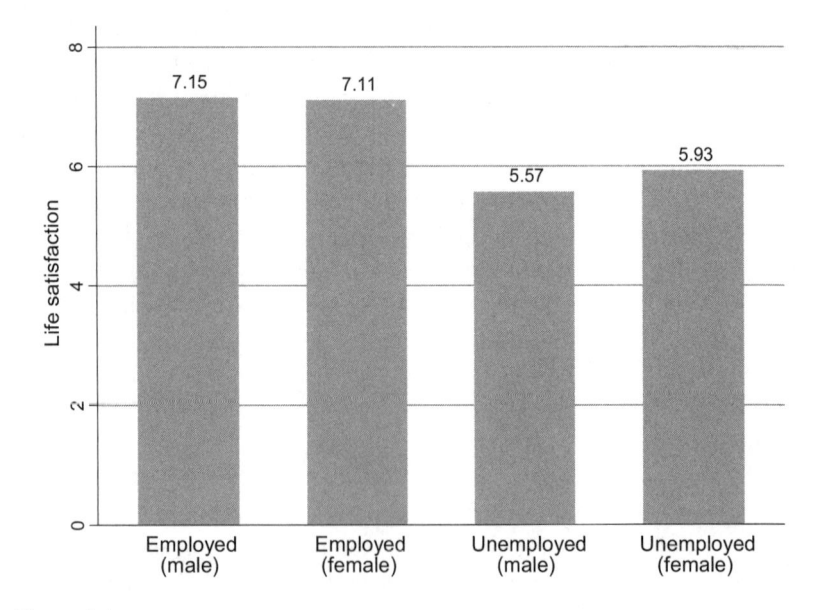

Figure 5.1

Employment status and life satisfaction in Germany. This figure shows average life satisfaction broken down into employment status and gender between 1984 and 2010 (until 1989 for the old West German states).
Source: Sozio-oekonomisches Panel, 1984–2010.

other support, and that is generally considerably less than your old salary. It is the loss of income accompanying unemployment that sees to it that life satisfaction declines. But happiness research goes one step further. It claims that reduced life satisfaction cannot be attributed entirely to loss of income. In other words, jobless people would still be less content than employed people even if income losses were completely offset by transfer payments.

Admittedly, this statistical finding needs to be put into perspective. It doesn't say that someone with a choice between working on an assembly line and not working on an assembly line, for the same pay, would always prefer to work or would have a higher life satisfaction with the assembly-line job than without it. However, if we want to explain the decline in quality of life due to loss of work only in terms of reduced income, then, purely statistically, an unexplained remainder is left over. In other words, there must be more to it than just the loss of income. Work evidently has inherent value. This is something new for economists, as they are accustomed to associating work with the disutility of labor. Perhaps they should spend some time with Luke Pittard, a 25-year-old worker from Cardiff who, despite winning £1.3 million in a lottery, decided to go back to work at McDonald's. After 18 months he realized that he missed his job and went back to flipping hamburgers—not because he had blown his winnings in record time, but because he got bored. He wanted to be with people and have something to do.

Let us look at this finding a little more closely. Figure 5.1 shows only an approximate picture of the aggregated data. The effect of unemployment becomes somewhat clearer when we take a look at how the people who lost their jobs and then were out of work for at least three years fared. The Sozio-oekonomisches Panel supplies us with German data on this too, since the same people are surveyed every year so that they can be tracked on their journey through life. Figure 5.2 shows what happens on average when unemployment becomes longer-term.

Figure 5.2 supports the finding of figure 5.1: On becoming unemployed (time t), life satisfaction declines dramatically—more for men than for women. But figure 5.2 makes one further point clear. Neither men nor women get accustomed to being unemployed! Life satisfaction is even lower after three years of being without work than after one year. This remarkable finding isn't specific to Germany. Clark (2006) obtained similar results for the British Household Panel Survey and for the European Community Household Panel, covering all countries in the European Union. As we saw in chapter 4, people normally tend to adapt to changed

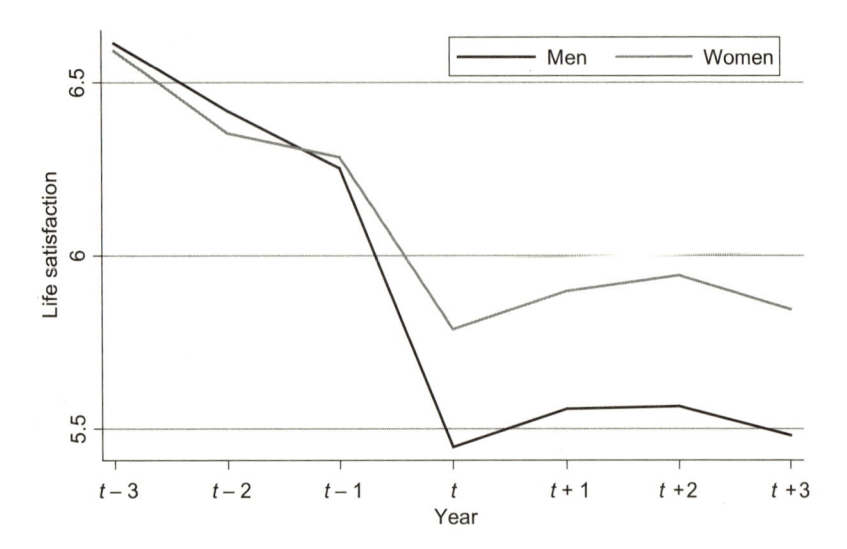

Figure 5.2

The dynamic effects of long-term unemployment on life satisfaction in Germany. This figure shows the dynamic effects of unemployment on average life satisfaction of the unemployed between 1984 and 2010 in Germany (until 1989 for the old West German states). The variable t indicates the time point of becoming unemployed; $t-3$, $t-2$, and $t-1$ represent years before becoming unemployed; $t+3$, $t+2$, and $t+1$ represent years after losing the job in year t.
Source: Sozio-oekonomisches Panel, 1984–2010.

life circumstances. We experience a shock and fall into a hole or experience good fortune and soar to the heights, but with time we approach our starting point again. This doesn't mean we always return to the long-term average. Opportunities for lasting changes in life satisfaction certainly exist, but the pattern of a rapid rise or fall followed by an adaptation phase is very common. But such is not the case with long-term unemployment. It ruins our life satisfaction unrelentingly and permanently—we don't get accustomed to it.

This naturally raises the question of what happens when unemployment is temporary. Fortunately most people only lose their jobs for a short time and then find work again. Do they regain their original level of life satisfaction? Figure 5.3 provides the answer.

The good news seems to be that unemployment doesn't leave any scars. However, that isn't completely clear. For example, studies by Winkelmann and Winkelmann (1998) and Clark, Georgellis, and Sanfey (2001) indicate that formerly unemployed people are unhappier on average than

The Economic Determinants of Happiness 61

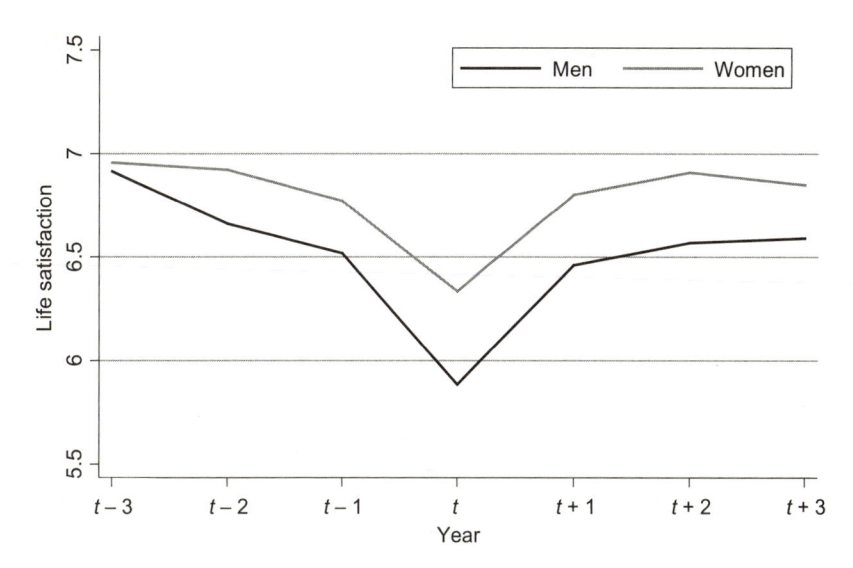

Figure 5.3

The dynamic effects of temporary unemployment on life satisfaction in Germany. This figure shows the effect of temporary unemployment in period t on average life satisfaction of the unemployed between 1984 and 2010 in Germany (until 1989 for the old West German states).
Source: Sozio-oekonomisches Panel, 1984–2010.

people who have never been unemployed. Knabe and Rätzel (2011) show that this "scarring effect" can be attributed to the observation that having suffered unemployment once can raise a person's probability of becoming unemployed again. It is the poor employment prospects that result in the sustained decline in quality of life, not the memory of past joblessness. Knabe and Rätzel's finding can be put in somewhat more dramatic terms: Unemployment has long-term negative effects not because it causes permanent psychological damage to the unemployed, but rather because it can permanently jeopardize a person's financial situation. At this point we can see how close material things are to non-material things and how easily they can be confused. Where happiness researchers see a chronic psychological problem, others identify a purely economic problem. The reason that the latter remained unnoticed for so long is that it isn't easy to separate the psychological effect from the economic effect and to make statements about their respective strengths. Knabe and Rätzel's results match the findings of Dolan and Powdthavee (2012) that employed people who reported that becoming unemployed would be an "important event" had the same level of happiness as currently unemployed people who reported that losing their jobs hadn't been an "important event."

So unemployment doesn't leave wounds, but it doesn't harden a person either. People who find a job again and then become unemployed once more suffer from the new bout of unemployment just as much as they did the first time. (See, for example, Lucas et al. 2004, Clark et al. 2008a, and Luhmann et al. 2012.) People who have been unemployed in the past therefore suffer as much as those who are experiencing unemployment for the first time. But does everyone experience the misery of being unemployed the same way? Apparently not, as we have already seen in the case of women, who face a somewhat smaller decline in happiness than men. And there is evidence of an interesting difference between people who vote for candidates of conservative parties and those who vote for candidates of left-wing parties. Alesina, Di Tella, and McCulloch (2004) found that conservative-oriented voters suffered more when unemployed. A good explanation for this difference is provided by the common assumption that supporters of conservative parties are more likely be convinced that "every man is the architect of his own fortune" whereas people of a left-wing persuasion tend to believe that chance and social factors play a much greater role than an individual's own actions. Thus, for a conservative, unemployment must seem to come as a result of his own failures, whereas a left-wing voter sees it more as a result of fate, for which chance, the system, or some other power is responsible and over which the individual has no influence.

The influence of age is less clear than that of political tendency. Pichler (2006) comes to the conclusion that unemployment is by no means as bad for people under the age of 30 as it is for those over 30. A plausible explanation for this is that younger people tend to have a better chance of finding a new job than older people, so unemployment becomes more threatening the older you get. As plausible as that may sound, Winkelmann and Winkelmann (1998) found the contrary to be the case—i.e., that people under 30 suffered the most when unemployed, and that this effect doesn't level off until after the age of 50, presumably because one's working life is gradually coming to an end anyway. But unemployment is apparently not seen as a kind of early retirement. Hetschko, Knabe, and Schöb (2013) used the Sozial-oekonomisches Panel to examine how life satisfaction changed when people who had long been unemployed retired. In contrast to the employed who go into retirement, the long-time jobless experience a dramatic increase in happiness in the year of retirement. Evidently unemployment results in suffering only in people who see themselves as members of the employable population. Only when they are officially retired do they no longer have to justify not having a job to others and to themselves.

If not having a job leads to such pronounced negative effects, does work make us happy? Having a job definitely has a positive effect on one's well-being, as we can see from the findings on unemployment. But is it work itself that brings us happiness? Do we feel better if we work more? We will deal with this question in more detail later, and we will present some rather surprising results from our own empirical studies. However, on the basis of the data sets usually used in happiness research, we come to a rather mixed conclusion.

An obvious approach is to examine whether people in part-time employment have lower life satisfaction than those in full-time employment. Such an effect was found by Schoon, Hansson, and Samela-Aro (2005) for Britain, but it was small. Blanchflower and Oswald (2005) found no difference for the United States. Luttmer (2000) even found that full-time employees under the age of 60 had lower life satisfaction.

Germans seem to have a somewhat greater preference for working than Britons or Americans. In any case, Meier and Stutzer (2008) discovered a positive correlation between working hours and life satisfaction on the basis of data from the Sozio-oekonomisches Panel, even after controlling for income. Rätzel (2012) tends to support this finding, but ultimately concludes that the relation can be best described with an inverted U: First life satisfaction rises with increased working hours, but then it reaches a point beyond which more work tends to reduce happiness rather than increase it. That seems highly plausible. Most people who want to work full-time aren't happy if able to work only a three-day week or if regularly ordered to work on a weekend.

In summary, having a job is obviously essential to people's life satisfaction. This is also the case when we control for income—that is, when the effect on life satisfaction of the loss of income arising from unemployment is eliminated, as it were. Having a job has an inherent value beyond the generation of income. This is one of the clearest and most important findings of happiness research.

Unemployment of Others: The Unemployment Rate

It is easy to understand that it is extremely important for every individual to have a job. But what is the situation with unemployment in general? Do we feel better if the unemployment rate declines even though we are not directly affected ourselves because we already have a secure job anyway? The answer to this question isn't obvious. We will let the data speak for themselves.

Why should the overall or regional unemployment rates affect life satisfaction? A direct connection to each individual's personal situation arises from the fact that the probability of employees becoming unemployed rises when overall unemployment goes up while the chances of the unemployed finding a job go down. There are indeed a large number of studies (for instance, Knabe and Rätzel 2009, Clark 2001, 2009, and De Witte 1999) showing that job security is of paramount importance for life satisfaction. Insecurity gets on a person's nerves, especially when it affects something as essential as his job. This was dramatically demonstrated by the results of Dekker and Schaufeli's (1995) study of a large publicly owned Australian transport corporation which provided train and bus services in metropolitan and rural areas. An organizational restructuring had been scheduled. Four departments were chosen as candidates to be considered for closure. Rumors about the redundancies were around and were well known to employees. Over the following two months a rigorous examination was undertaken in order to decide the closure of which departments would be most advantageous. Only then were two of the four departments selected and closed. Two-thirds of the employees found new positions in other areas of the public sector; one-third were dismissed. The crucial point is that, after the announcement of the decision as to which departments would be closed, the life satisfaction of the employees in the affected departments rose, while that of employees in the departments that were not closed remained the same. This suggests that gaining certainty about a bad outcome might be better than remaining in an uncertain situation.

The importance attached to job security suggests the existence of a negative correlation between the unemployment rate and life satisfaction, since a low unemployment rate is accompanied by a high level of job security. A multitude of studies, including one by Helliwell (2003) and one by Alesina, Di Tella, and McCulloch (2004), are, in fact, able to verify the existence of such a correlation. There are also exceptions, however. For instance, Rehdanz and Maddison (2005) analyzed data from 67 countries and found no evidence of a negative correlation.

The reason the findings aren't entirely consistent may be that unemployment also has positive effects. Those effects are, however, limited to people who are already without work. Their burden is all the greater the more strongly their joblessness is associated with the stigma of their own failure. Someone who loses his job in a prosperous region where everyone around him is employed will suffer more from his fate than someone who is in an area where unemployment is widespread. We have already noted that relative position can be highly important for life satisfaction. If the peers with whom you compare yourself have good jobs, your self-esteem will be strongly affected by your being unemployed. Social-psychological studies by Jackson and Warr (1987) and Cohn (1978) have shown this effect very clearly; Clark (2003) also verified it using life-satisfaction data. Clark showed, in particular, that the life satisfaction of an unemployed person increases if his or her spouse also becomes unemployed, whereas the spouse's unemployment reduces the happiness of an employed person. (See also Knabe, Schöb, and Weimann 2012.) In general, as Clark, Knabe, and Rätzel (2009) demonstrate, a high level of local unemployment mitigates the loss in life satisfaction of unemployed people, since their being unemployed then becomes "more normal."

A high rate of unemployment therefore has two opposing effects. On the one hand, it makes the jobs of the employed insecure, and that reduces life satisfaction. On the other hand, the losses in life satisfaction that arise from unemployment's being associated with social relegation, or with a loss of status, become less because a high rate of unemployment removes the stigma of personal failure that the individual would otherwise experience. Overall, despite the second effect, a negative correlation between the unemployment rate and life satisfaction probably exists. There are two reasons for this. First, the number of employed people who benefit from a decline in the unemployment rate is significantly greater than the number of unemployed people who suffer from larger stigmatization. Second, a declining unemployment rate has a positive effect on the unemployed too, since it promises better prospects of finding work.

The Inflation Rate

After the unemployment rate, the inflation rate is the second central macroeconomic indicator that can be expected to influence life satisfaction. In discussions on economic policy the connection between the two parameters is often reduced to the simple formula that unemployment can be fought with inflation and, conversely, monetary stability must be paid for with high unemployment. Although macroeconomic theory sees the relationship as more complex, it is possible, in the short term at least, to assume that there is a certain tradeoff between the two. This also is the case in the context of life satisfaction. Studies by Di Tella, McCulloch, and

Oswald (2001, 2003) and Alesina, Di Tella, and McCulloch (2004) indicate the existence of a negative relationship between the inflation rate and life satisfaction. Therefore, if it is indeed possible to reduce the unemployment rate by means of higher inflation, politicians can directly influence life satisfaction by allowing more (or less) inflation, thus achieving lower (or higher) unemployment.

What, then, is the relationship between the effects of inflation and the effects of the unemployment rate on life satisfaction? Does life satisfaction remain constant if inflation rises by one percentage point but, at the same time, unemployment falls by one percentage point?

Such a tradeoff at a ratio of 1:1 is suggested by the *misery index*, which is found by adding the inflation rate to the unemployment rate in order to describe the state of an economy. Chancellor Helmut Schmidt of the Federal Republic of Germany obviously had a different rate in mind when he made his famous statement that "five percent inflation is easier to bear than five percent unemployment." For Schmidt, a one-percentage-point increase in unemployment outweighed a one-percentage-point increase in inflation. But how did German citizens feel about that?

Di Tella, McCulloch, and Oswald (2001) found that fully compensating an average American for a one-percentage-point increase in inflation requires about $70 in real (i.e., inflation-adjusted) terms. Since compensation for one percent more unemployment would cost $200, an exchange ratio of 2.86:1 results. This also applies to other findings on this matter. Although the results vary from a minimum of 1.66:1 (Di Tella, McCulloch, and Oswald 2003) to a maximum of 5:1 (Wolfers 2003), what they all have in common is that they give unemployment a higher weighting than inflation. More than one percent less inflation is required to offset one percent more unemployment. That is one point against the misery index and one for the former German chancellor.

Income Equality (and Inequality)

Not only do the economic and social policies of a country affect unemployment and the inflation rate; they also change the distribution of income. Democratic societies have enormous scope when it comes to questions of distribution. Citizens of different countries evidently have greatly varying tolerances for inequality. Whereas Scandinavians are traditionally considered supporters of the highly redistributive welfare state, Americans are willing to accept a considerable degree of inequality. For this reason, it should be clear that variations in inequality probably will affect the quality of life differently in different countries, and that therefore international comparisons or studies based on cross-country data sets are problematic.

Thus, it isn't surprising that the available findings on the effects of inequality (or those of inequality-reducing redistribution) on life satisfaction don't present a uniform picture. Berg and Veenhoven (2010), using data from 119 countries for the years 2000–2006, didn't find any robust relationship between income incqualily and life satisfaction. However, Alesina, Di Tella, and McCulloch (2004) found a significant negative correlation between inequality and life satisfaction in the United States, and an even more significant negative correlation in Europe, even after controlling for individual income. The detailed findings are as one would expect: Among poor citizens and left-wing voters the aversion to inequality is exceedingly pronounced, whereas more affluent citizens and right-wing voters are more indifferent toward the issue of distribution. Any positive effects of redistribution measures could therefore only be expected from the former group.

Cross-country studies often suffer from the difficulty of distinguishing economic effects from the influence of differences in climates and in cultures. Moreover, incomes and income inequality aren't always measured in the same way in different countries. To overcome these problems, Oishi et al. (2011) conducted a study with data from the US General Social Survey for the comparatively long period 1972–2008. They found robust evidence of a negative relationship between income inequality and happiness. They also found that inequality and happiness are linked by feelings of trust and fairness. As soon as measures of these two factors are included in the analysis, one no longer finds an additional effect of inequality on happiness, so weakened trust and deteriorated fairness perceptions are the main reasons why people are less happy in times of more income inequality. Oishi et al. also found that the negative effect of inequality on happiness arose only for low-income individuals, and not for middle-income and high-income individuals. However, this effect is not attributable to the fact that low-income earners have less income when inequality is higher. Instead, it is fully explained by the fact that people with low incomes also report reduced trust and fairness perceptions.

Prosocial Spending

The possibilty that people really don't become happier when their disposable incomes increase may also be explained by the idea that people don't spend the additional money on things that would really satisfy them. Instead, they seem to spend it on things that turn out to be useless for their well-being. If this is true, then how people spend their money is at least as important as how much they have available to spend (Frank 2004).

An interesting line of research has recently begun to examine whether there are differences in the well-being effect of spending money to the benefit of others ("prosocial spending") relative to spending money on oneself ("personal spending"). In one study, Dunn et al. (2008) asked more than 600 Americans about their happiness, their income, how much they spent on themselves, and how much they gave to others as gifts or through donations to charity. They found that personal spending was entirely unrelated to individual happiness, whereas people who gave more to others also experienced higher levels of happiness. Of course, correlation is not causation. It may be that people who are generally more cheerful tend to care more about others. To shed more light on the causal effects of giving on happiness, Dunn et al. also conducted an experiment with college students. The students were randomly assigned to four groups. Students in two of the groups received $5 each; students in the other two groups received $20 each. In both the $5 group and the $20 group, one subgroup was told that it would have to spend all of the money on personal things (a bill or a gift for themselves) and one subgroup was told that it would have to spend the money on other people (for example, by buying a gift for someone or donating money to a charity). All the students had to spend all their money before the evening of that day. Participants' emotional situation was assessed before the beginning of the experiment and at the end of the day. The results of this experiment show that students who had to spend their money on others experienced a substantially larger increase in happiness than students who could spend the money on themselves. The amount that they could spend, however, did matter for their well-being. These results are quite surprising. One would typically think that it is better to spend more and to spend it on oneself. In fact, this is what a group of more than 100 other students who had been given detailed information about the experimental setup and who were interviewed separately by Dunn et al. thought. This discrepancy between what people expect and what actually happens to them suggests that people base their economic choices on false expectations. Aknin et al. (2009) have also shown that people aren't always able to predict the well-being consequences of economic events, particularly the relationship between happiness and income. They asked people to predict the well-being of other people with different levels of income. On comparing these statements against the actual well-being of people with these levels of income, they find that predicted and actual well-being are quite close to each other for high levels of income, but fall apart dramatically for lower income levels. Apparently, people tend to overestimate the well-being loss associated with becoming poorer.

One might be inclined to argue that this is a rich-world phenomenon. Only when people don't have urgent needs anymore can giving to others be better than spending money for their own purposes. The benefit of giving does seem to be quite universal, however. Aknin et al. (2013a) conducted a multi-country study similar to that of Dunn et al. First, they examined survey data from the Gallup World Poll, comprising data on more than 200,000 individuals from 136 countries. In 120 of these countries, they observed a positive cross-sectional relationship between giving to others and happiness at the individual level, and this doesn't differ between richer and poorer countries. Apparently, not only the materially well-off benefit from social spending. Again, one might worry about the direction of causality. Like Dunn et al., Aknin et al. (2013a) conducted a number of experiments to establish a causal relationship extending from giving to happiness. In one experiment, conducted in Canada and Uganda, participants were randomly divided into two groups. People in the first group were asked to recall spending money for a personal purpose. People in the second group were asked to recall spending money on someone else. After they had described the event in detail, participants were asked about their happiness. Not surprisingly (if one has seen the results of Dunn et al.), the second group turned out to be substantially happier than the first group. This corresponds well to another study by Aknin et al. (2012a), in which participants in an experiment were also asked to recall spending money on someone else. Recalling such spending made them happier, and the happier they became the more willing they were to give to someone else in the near future—which is suggestive of a positive feedback loop between prosocial spending and happiness. In fact, such feedback not only affects an individual; it might also occur between people. As Aknin et al. (2011) report, prosocial spending by one person can make that person feel better and also induce the recipients of the prosocial act to behave more prosocially.

In another experiment, Aknin et al. (2013a) randomly divided Canadian and South African students into two groups. Both groups received a small amount of money to spend in whatever way they liked. The first group was given the option to use that money to purchase a "goody bag" for themselves at a cost equal to the amount of money given to the students, but students were told that the bag was worth substantially more than that (and was filled with juice and chocolate). The second group could purchase the same bag, but was told that the bag would be delivered to a sick child in a local hospital. Almost all students in the second group bought the bag for the sick child, whereas about one third of the students in the first group opted for the money. And again, the students in the second group were substantially happier after the experiment than the students in the first group.

The finding that the "warm glow of giving" can be found in very different regions of the world raises another question: Is the happiness mechanism that rewards people for behaving prosocially a learned behavior, or is it inborn? A recent study suggests that there are good reasons to believe that at least part of this mechanism is inborn or develops in very early childhood. Aknin et al. (2012b) conducted an experiment with two-year-old children. Each child was given a pile of crackers, which were placed in a bowl in front of him. The experimenter then "introduced" the child to a monkey puppet. The child was asked to give one of his crackers to the puppet, which "ate" the cracker, making loud "yum" sounds. The experimenter also provided an extra cracker that the child was asked to give to the puppet. (Contrary to the first case, giving the extra cracker to the puppet didn't reduce the number of crackers the child could eat himself). It was observed that the children were happier when they gave a cracker to the puppet than when they initially received the crackers for themselves. (Happiness was evaluated by trained observers.) Moreover, they enjoyed giving one of their own crackers to the puppet more than giving the puppet the extra cracker that didn't belong to them (the one the experimenter had given them with the explicit request to give it to the puppet). The "warm glow" people derive from benevolent behavior thus seems to be deeply ingrained in human nature.

Even though prosocial spending generally enhances happiness, it may be the case that not all types of prosocial spending are equally beneficial for a person's subjective well-being. Prosocial activities seem to be especially beneficial if they allow people to connect with others. For example, Aknin et al. (2013b) report an experiment in which they gave Starbucks gift cards worth $10 to randomly selected students in the morning, telling the students in one group to use the card themselves and those in another group to give it to a friend. The latter group was subdivided into two further groups; members of one group were told just to give the card to a friend, whereas members of the other group were told to go to Starbucks with the friend. The students' happiness was measured at the end of the day. The happiest group was the one in which people had to give the card to a friend and accompany the friend to Starbucks. This illustrates the importance of using prosocial activities as a means to build and foster social ties. Another important factor contributing to the benefits of prosocial spending is that people see how their giving makes an immediate difference. Aknin et al. (2013c) gave students $10, which they could either keep or donate to charity. One group of students had the option to give the money to UNICEF. Another group had the option to donate to Spread the Net, a charitable organization that supports the fight against malaria by providing bed nets for children in Africa. Aknin et al. observed that students donated, on average, $5. There was no difference in charitable giving between the two organizations. Giving more to Spread the Net, however, was associated with larger increases in happiness, whereas giving to UNICEF seemed to be irrelevant to well-being. Apparently donations are more attractive when they serve a clear purpose and have a direct effect.

There is a lot of experimental and empirical evidence that the visibility of social giving is very important (Ariely et al. 2009; Harbourgh 1998a). Most donations are not made anonymously (Glazer and Konrad 1996). Thus, contributing money to a charity or in order to help others is a source of happiness not only because of the warm glow donor might feel but also because of the prestige it buys (Harbourgh 1998b; Glazer and Konrad 1996).

We can see from the overview provided in this section that prosocial spending appears to be a very beneficial way to increase subjective well-being, be it for the warm glow or to buy prestige. In either case, money does buy happiness, and it does so twice: once for the recipient and once for the donor.

Education

There is probably no other belief that is supported by such a wide consensus than that education is of overwhelming significance for a person's happiness. Unfortunately, such significance can't be deduced from the data that happiness researchers use. The reasons for this are mainly methodological. Generally, the data collected on education are purely quantitative (e.g., number of years of schooling, or diploma obtained). Apart from this very limited database, there is a methodological problem that can scarcely be solved satisfactorily, even with better data: Often education provides happiness indirectly, in that better educational attainment makes many things that increase life satisfaction possible. For example, a person's level of income, social situation, and standing in society are closely tied to his or her educational achievements. If social standing matters for a person's subjective well-being (and much points to this), it is hardly possible to isolate a direct effect of education (e.g., that a person has higher life satisfaction solely because of his education). There may be good reasons for this. For instance, educated people are in a better position to understand themselves and their environment, they potentially gain greater benefit from their sensory impressions and experiences, and they reflect on their own actions to a higher degree. All this could contribute to an enhancement of life satisfaction—but this cannot be concluded from the data.

On the other hand, one can imagine that education might have a *negative* effect on life satisfaction: Higher education leads to higher expectations in life, and it may not be possible to fulfill those higher expectations. Analysis of the effects of education suffers from the methodological difficulty that, in order to analyze the effect of educational differences, comparisons between different people are needed. Happiness researchers, however, typically don't put much trust in such comparisons, because between-person differences in happiness could also be driven by unobserved factors, such as personality differences. To circumvent this problem, they try to investigate only the effects that result when the respondents' own level of education changes over time (for example, when the respondents obtains a college degree). But this doesn't happen often, and so, on the basis of panel data, it is difficult to say anything about the effect of education.

In view of the difficulties, it isn't surprising that not many studies have been devoted explicitly to the effects of education. One important exception is a study by Oreopoulos and Salvanes (2011), who found that compulsory schooling had substantial non-pecuniary benefits, including a positive effect on life satisfaction. Studies that have looked at such effects in the context of other factors, however, have come to a variety of conclusions. Some have found an education effect; some haven't. The findings obtained from investigations of the relationship between education and health are particularly striking. Were it to turn out that more-educated people are healthier than less-educated people, then education would have a huge indirect influence on life satisfaction, since health is an important determinant of quality of life. Unfortunately, no clear statements concerning this have been made. In fact, studies provide evidence of just about every possible relationship. Sometimes the educated are healthier

(Baker et al. 2005), sometimes there is no connection between education and health (Flouri 2004), and sometimes the correlation is even negative (see, e.g., Clark 2003). It is likely that education influences life satisfaction in many ways, but only indirectly.

At this point let us briefly sum up what we have seen so far. The statistical analysis of the data gained from the question on general life satisfaction has, so far, provided the following findings: We can be certain that unemployment drastically reduces life satisfaction. Furthermore, health and a stable social environment are crucial prerequisites for a high level of life satisfaction. Social contacts, especially marriage and family, play an important role. Losing one's partner is as devastating as losing one's job. Limitations due to poor health cast a cloud over life satisfaction. Getting old doesn't necessarily mean that one's life satisfaction has to decrease—in fact, it may increase.

Admittedly, if we ignore the last point, the individual life-satisfaction findings have, until now, been relatively unspectacular. What has been spectacular and important so far is primarily the realization that the absolute level of our income allegedly doesn't play a role; instead, the role of the relative position in which we find ourselves is all the more important. The next chapter will show how far-reaching this new view is. There we are going to look at the consequences this has if it is assumed that the Easterlin Paradox as we have presented it so far really does exist.

6
What Is to Be Done If Money Doesn't Make Us Happy?

The Easterlin Paradox and the claim that it is the importance of relative position that explains it have called into question much of what economists and most other people have firmly believed until now. While presenting it, we expressed certain doubts time and again as to whether it really does behave in the manner Easterlin and some others claim. We will return to these doubts later, but for the moment we want to put them on the back burner and start with two premises:

1. Life-satisfaction measurements in the form they have been made so far provide a valid measure of people's actual life satisfaction.
2. The empirical results obtained so far using this method of measurement will not be called into question.

Both of these premises will be subjects of critical consideration later in the book, but at the moment it is necessary to present the consequences of accepting both without any restrictions.

New Goals

The consequences that will now be discussed are chiefly reactions to the central finding of happiness research, the Easterlin Paradox. That doesn't mean that other findings, which we discussed in the last chapter, shouldn't be included in the policy debate. However, it is the deep mistrust of the conventional notions of growth, prosperity, and quality of life shown by the Easterlin Paradox that stands at the center of this debate. Is it right to strive for economic prosperity? Does more money really make us happier? If we have to answer this question No—which is what the Easterlin Paradox suggests—what are the resulting implications for economic policy?

The Easterlin Paradox doesn't take this question literally, even in a milder variation. What it does is interpret it in a somewhat less radical way. The findings of happiness research are construed as suggesting that income alone—as measured by gross domestic product—doesn't suffice as an indicator of the well-being of a population. But that too leads to the question of consequences. If we no longer want to use GDP as the only indicator, which other indicators are we to use in addition? How are we then to measure people's happiness? This question has been plaguing many governments for some time. We mentioned these initiatives and efforts briefly in the first chapter. Let us now take a closer look at them.

The first step was taken by a country that draws little attention to itself and that few people know much about, apart from the fact that it exists. The Kingdom of Bhutan is the first country in the world that has decided to use Gross National Happiness (GNH) as a guide in its future policies. This index is made up of a series of sub-indicators containing both objective measures and subjective assessments. The standard of living, as measured by per capita income, is included, as are biological diversity, health, and subjective reports on the life satisfaction of the country's inhabitants. It is probably not so easy to learn from the example of Bhutan, which is located on the edge of the Himalayas, since it is a country of some extremes. One of the poorest countries in the world, it is extremely sparsely populated and largely underdeveloped. Thimphu, the capital city, has a population of only 80,000 and may well be the only capital city on the planet that doesn't have a single traffic light. The political situation bears little similarity to what we are accustomed to in Central Europe. Not until 2008 did Bhutan become a constitutional monarchy; before that no democratic structures existed. Considerable ethnic tension was caused by a controversial citizenship law, issued by the last king's predecessor, with which he consolidated his own ethnic group's hegemony. Add to this the fact that television was banned in Bhutan until 1999 and that 80 percent of the country lies more than 2,000 meters above sea level and it should be clear that Bhutan's experience with the Gross National Happiness index isn't readily transferable to the conditions of most developed economies.

However, in recent years many national governments and supranational organizations have begun to investigate what makes up quality of life and how to measure it. Both the Organisation for Economic Co-operation and Development and the European Union have been attempting to develop a system of indicators that will allow them to describe the welfare of a country better than GDP does. Since 2007 the OECD has been intensively working on developing indicators that are to measure various aspects of social, economic, and ecological conditions. Self-reported life satisfaction is used to create an indicator for "social cohesion," one of the five main "Headline Social Indicators." The EU has been intensively searching for an alternative to GDP since 2009. Under the heading "Beyond GDP," it is looking for the ultimate mix of indicators. What must not be left out, of course, are indicators that measure "sustainability." For this purpose, the EU uses no fewer than 100 individual indicators, which are then condensed into eleven "key indicators." In view of the fact that after thirty years of discussion of the concept "sustainable development" it is still not clear what "sustainable development" means, it should not come as a surprise that the EU's indicators cannot provide a uniform picture. For example, real GDP, the poverty rate, and the total energy consumption of the transport sector are included in the measurement of sustainability. Imagine that the automobile industry in your country experiences an upturn and recruits not only engineers but also many former welfare recipients. GDP rises, the poverty rate falls, but the total energy consumption of the transport sector also goes up. What happens to the sustainability?

In parallel with the efforts of the EU, in 2008 President Nicolas Sarkozy of France set up a commission whose task it was to draft recommendations to improve the quality of the statistical information on the basis of which France's economic success and its social progress were to be assessed. Four Nobel laureates in economics—Joseph Stiglitz, Amartya Sen, Daniel Kahneman, and Kenneth Arrow—were members of this commission, which became known in the literature as the Stiglitz-Sen-Fitoussi Commission. (See Stiglitz, Sen, and Fitoussi 2009.) Angus Deaton, Alan Krueger, Andrew Oswald, and Robert Putnam—four of the most renowned representatives of research into the economics of happiness—also served on the commission.

The Stiglitz-Sen-Fitoussi Commission primarily dealt with two questions that are of interest to us. First, how can the economic performance of a country, which hitherto has been measured unidimensionally with GDP, be better captured? Second, how does one get from GDP as the one-dimensional measure of welfare to a more comprehensive measurement tool? What conclusions did the commission reach?

In relation to purely economic performance, the commission points out the inadequacy of GDP in capturing quality changes. Economic growth in developed countries is generated increasingly less by more of the same goods being consumed but increasingly more by goods being replaced by new, qualitatively better goods. It is easy to find examples of this in consumer goods. But quality changes show up in sectors where they are not so obvious. They can be found not only in health care and in service industries, but also in cultural and social areas. The equipment and furnishings in museums, theaters, and opera houses have just as much a quality component as the construction of cars. Using GDP—the commission presumes—leads to an underestimation of the qualitative components of growth. This is an important point because the current critical discussion on growth suffers from the fact that growth is almost exclusively perceived as something that is purely quantitative.

In addition to the underestimation of the qualitative elements of growth, the commission criticizes above all else the way the public sector is included in GDP. The usual practice is to simply equate the inputs and the output. Police performance therefore includes the expenditures on police officers and police cars. The reason for this approach is that there are no market prices for public services, just as there are no market prices for environmental resources, the Eiffel Tower, or Cologne Cathedral. The commission, however, urges us to critically question the very simple and easy-to-use solution to this problem that has been used until now.

Without making a final, binding recommendation, the commission offers an abundance of suggestions concerning the issue of how to move from a one-dimensional GDP to a more comprehensive measurement of quality of life. Its message might be summarized as follows: Supplementing the traditional GDP with additional, complementary metrics can lead to a better database for policy decisions that aim to improve people's quality of life. Which measures would be helpful in this is not clear, however, because innumerable measurement problems remain unsolved.

Kassenboehmer and Schmidt (2011) have recently investigated how well the indicators proposed by the Stiglitz-Sen-Fitoussi Commission correlate with GDP and unemployment. The result is rather sobering for those who believe that indicators are a better measure of welfare, since it reveals that the correlation is very high and, consequently, getting the additional information with the new indicators is hardly worth the trouble. Delhey and Kroll (2012) offer a similar insight. They examine various recently developed alternative composite measures of societal well-being and conclude that most of them are not better in predicting subjective well-being than GDP is (the only exception being the OECD Better Life Index, which performs a little better than GDP alone).

It is only the *subjective* measure of life satisfaction that could, in fact, be a valuable addition. This is where happiness research comes into play. What can it really deliver? How well suited is it for improving our knowledge of our own welfare so that we can hope for better policies?

Where do the strengths of happiness research lie with regard to the question of improving our lives with better policies? Its advantages result chiefly from the disadvantages that arise from using "objective" measures. We have already discussed the disadvantages of GDP, but what is the situation with the multitude of indicators developed by the OECD, the EU, and the UN? The UN has the longest experience in this. Its Human Development Index has long been using indicators for the health system, education, or life expectancy, the intention of which is to indicate the level of development of a country. But are these indicators really objective? Even if they were, subjective assessments come into play at the latest when considering *which* indicators should be included, not to mention the issue of the weighting an indicator should have when included in the dashboard of indicators. What should have a greater weighting: more economic prosperity, or more sustainability? Do the indicators measure what we want them to measure? We can't be sure. Take internal security, for example. If a country employs a large number of police officers, is this an indicator of crime prevention, or only a consequence of the high crime rate in that country? Does the existence of many hospitals indicate that people are healthy, or that people frequently become ill?

It is clear that such indicators are anything but perfect measures. They should therefore be treated with the same degree of caution as GDP. Nevertheless, happiness research, despite being based on subjective measures, can at least help us solve some problems, for example, by delivering valuable hints as to which things are important for life satisfaction and which are not. And this occurs by relying not on the judgment of "experts," but on the judgment of those who are directly affected! No one can know better what is good for people than the people themselves.

A second, serious shortcoming of GDP and other indicators is that they can only very inadequately estimate the value of goods for which there are no market prices. This is particularly annoying because these are often goods that are of paramount importance for our life satisfaction. The secure provision of the "goods" in health care, for instance, is likely to be highly important for most of us. But the value of the health-care system that is available to us in emergencies in the interests of our health can't be read from a market price and can't be found in any catalog of indicators.

Economists use the term *public goods* for this case. Their most important feature is that no one can be excluded from their consumption. In modern welfare states, hospitals, emergency physicians, and ambulances are not permitted to exclude anyone from the guaranteed supply of medical services, and everyone benefits from this. That is, incidentally, why such goods cannot form markets. Since no one can be excluded from using them, no one is voluntarily willing to pay for using them. All forms of goods and services to which equal access has to be secured for everybody take on the character of public goods. There are many public goods, and almost all of them are important. It isn't possible to exclude anyone from consuming clean air or from living in an intact climate system. The political system, the democratic constitution, internal and external security are further examples of important public goods. It seems clear they are important, but it is hard to know what value they actually have for people.

Happiness research shows us a way to establish the value of public goods and other things that don't have market value. We have already explained how happiness research has contributed to ascertaining the value of improving the environment. Gauging life satisfaction with a one-dimensional measure has proved to be a major asset of happiness research. This makes it easier to determine rates of exchange that allow the value of goods that don't have prices to be determined. If we know, for example, how much people's life satisfaction rises if the level of fine-particulate pollution is halved, and we also know how much it rises with a 5 percent increase in income, we can get an idea of how much income growth the reduction in particulate pollution is worth. Here is another example: Let us assume that we know the size of the tax increase needed to improve internal security by 10 percent. Using the methods of happiness research, we can then determine by how much life satisfaction has fallen as a result of the tax increase and how much it has risen as a result of the better security. If the balance is positive, we should recruit more police officers.

Of course, we have to be very careful with this. The tool used to measure life satisfaction should really deliver what it promises before we base tax increases on it. Further, the measures used don't always have to be compulsory measures, such as taxes. It is possible to imagine that happiness research could provide us with some indication of how to design something like a libertarian paternalism, with government regulations that don't use direct compulsion but favor developments that lead to higher life satisfaction. The rules for donating organs have been used as an example time and again. The United States, the United Kingdom, and Germany have "opt in" clauses under which only people who have given their explicit consent are donors. For example, in Germany the organs of a person who has been proclaimed brain dead may be used only if the person has explicitly declared his consent and this declaration is documented on an organ-donor card, which a person who would genuinely like to donate his or her organs should carry. In Belgium, France, and Austria it is exactly the other way round: A person is considered a potential donor unless he or she has expressly declared that his or her organs must *not* be removed. This "dissent solution," or "opt out" clause, doesn't restrict anyone's civil liberties and is therefore just as "liberal" as the "opt in" regulation. Whereas in most "opt out" countries the proportion of organ donors in the population exceeds 90 percent, consent rates in "opt in" countries typically don't exceed 30 percent and are often much lower—e.g., only 12 percent in Germany (Johnson and Goldstein 2003). The relevance of these figures is evident if one considers that in the United States 6,000 people die per year because they don't receive a donor organ early enough (Orentlicher 2009). If it can be shown by means of happiness research that people place a high value on a secure supply of health goods, that could justify a transition to the dissent solution.

Happiness research, a new and promising tool in the valuation of public goods, has the potential to provide valuable information on how a libertarian-paternalistic state can raise the life satisfaction of its citizens. It is then all the more astounding that subjective measures of life satisfaction aren't more prominent in current efforts to improve statistical measures of progress and well-being. For example, Germany's Sachverständigenrat zur Begutachtung der gesamtwirtschaftlichen Entwicklung (Council of Economic Experts) and France's Conseil d'Analyze Économique explicitly advise against using subjective measures of well-being in a joint report that includes a comprehensive catalog of indicators based on the recommendations of the Stiglitz-Sen-Fitoussi Commission (CAE-CEE 2010). This is unfortunate. Life-satisfaction research, as a supplement to other measures of welfare, could help to solve a central problem that all the previously found "indicator dashboards" have failed to solve and all those that will be discovered in the future will fail to solve. Only if we aggregate across the different indicators will we be able to make statements that will be useful guides for political decisions. If aggregation is ignored, then we will leave the politicians alone with the contradictions and conflicting goals that each indicator system entails. It will then be political arbitrariness once again that decides, for instance, whether the poverty rate or fuel consumption is more important for sustainability. The major strength of GDP is that it is an aggregate that is able to capture many of the things that positively influence our life satisfaction. Happiness research also provides us with a highly aggregated quantity measuring something different from that measured by GDP and so offers a supplement to it.

New Taxes?

In our discussion of GDP earlier in this chapter, we interpreted the findings of happiness research as an indication that it could make sense to have a supplement to the conventional measurements of well-being. This is a very cautious interpretation. It is also possible to be much more radical.

The most prominent exponent of a radical interpretation of the Easterlin Paradox is undoubtedly Lord Richard Layard. As early as 1980, a time when happiness research was only known to a few insiders, this British economist formulated far-reaching demands on the basis of Easterlin's finding in an essay published in a prestigious international periodical, the *Economic Journal*. In 2005 Layard published a book in which he summarized the conclusions about economic policy he had drawn from happiness economics. In the end, they are all based on the necessity for the Easterlin Paradox to be considered as evidence that relative position is highly important for people.

In order to better understand Layard's argumentation, we should take another look at what is exactly meant by "important in relation to relative position." Recall that it is understood as meaning that people don't use their own absolute income as an orientation, but rather assess their income situation in relation to some reference income. One alternative is that a person measures his income against the average income of a reference group. When someone does this, the average income of the reference group is called an *external reference income*. A second alternative is that a person chooses his own income from some point in the past as a reference point and then uses the growth achieved in comparison to this internal reference income as a guide. What is so bad about using an internal or an external reference income as a guide?

Let us begin with the case in which someone uses the average income of others as a guide. If that income rises and his own income remains constant, his relative position deteriorates and he feels correspondingly worse off. On the other hand, if his own income rises and the average income of others remains unchanged, his relative position will improve and he feels better. The decisive point is that every change in income affects not only the person whose income has risen or fallen, but also the others (because their relative positions change). Economists refer to this as an *external effect*. What is problematic is that individuals don't take external effects into account when they decide how much they want to work. An example will make it clear why this is problematic.

Suppose that a group of people all work the same number of hours per week and therefore all earn the same pay. If one person in this group now decides to work an extra hour a day, he improves his relative income position and only that is of interest to him. However, he can achieve a better relative position only if the positions of the others worsen. The case of all the group's members working an hour more illustrates the inefficiency of competition clearly: Everyone has to work an hour longer, yet this doesn't change their relative positions in the slightest. No one gains an advantage, but everyone has an hour less free time every day. Such a situation cries out for state intervention. If the state caps working hours or taxes earned income, everyone works less once again and the inefficiency disappears. In the words of Layard (2005, p. 151): "The struggle for *relative* income is totally self-defeating at the level of society as a whole. If my income rises relative to yours, your income falls relative to mine by exactly the same amount. The whole process produces no net social gain, but may involve a massive sacrifice of private life and time with family and friends. It should be discouraged."

In the case of external reference income, it is because of the external effect just described that individual decisions about working hours are inefficient. With internal reference income, it is quite a different effect that drives people to work too much. The human brain possesses an inherent tendency to adapt. We adapt to the circumstances of our lives, and one part of this is getting accustomed to higher earnings. If your income increases, you feel better because you are in a better position relative to the internal reference point. Unfortunately, the reference point then changes. Your new income is now the benchmark, and as long as your situation relative to this new reference point doesn't improve you find yourself back at your old satisfaction level. Here we will again quote Layard (2005, p. 154): "Indeed, the pleasure is largely associated with the change in income rather than its level. To some extent it is like the classic forms of addiction, such as alcohol or drugs, where you have to increase the dosage all the time to get the same enjoyment."

The hypothesis behind this assessment states that people are unable to anticipate that they will become accustomed to a higher income and for this reason cannot derive a lasting gain in life satisfaction from the income increase. Since they can't predict that adaption will take place, they succumb to the temptation of becoming more satisfied with higher earnings and more consumption over and over again. They don't recognize that it is all for nothing, so they end up in a treadmill from which there appears to be no escape unless the state prevents them from working too much by taxing earned income at higher rates.

As we saw in chapter 3, there is clear empirical evidence that the internal reference income has a role to play. It is nevertheless a little odd that people, time and time again, have to go through the same experience that they gain no advantage by working more, and that they just don't understand this. Are there good reasons for this? We will return to this point later. Here it should be noted that, according to Layard's strict interpretation, the Easterlin Paradox calls upon the state to protect its citizens from the danger of working and consuming too much by taxing income—progressively, if that is possible. Layard expressly points out that this doesn't mean that income taxation as it is already implemented today has to be increased. There are no clear policy implications that can be drawn from Layard's line of reasoning. Are our income-tax rates progressive enough, are they already too progressive, or are they just right? Neither happiness research itself nor the policy consequences advocated by Layard permit such a quantification. The argument Layard develops from the Easterlin Paradox is purely qualitative. It doesn't allow a quantification of the "right" tax rate.

Nevertheless, there is some empirical support for the hypothesis that progressive taxation is positively related to subjective well-being. Oishi et al. (2012) looked at data from the 2007 Gallup World Poll and specifically examined 54 countries for which detailed information on the national tax system could be obtained. Their main finding is that people are happier in countries with more progressive taxation. The main mediator of this effect appears to be people's satisfaction with the quality of public goods and services. This, however, weakens the policy conclusion that tax progression is recommendable. The quality of public goods is more important than how they are financed, so any type of flat tax could also be compatible with high subjective well-being as long as its proceeds are used to finance good public infrastructure, education, health care, and so on. Moreover, whereas raising a certain level of tax revenues with more progressive taxes seems to be beneficial for happiness, raising more tax revenues does not. The data show that the average tax rate and the overall level of government spending are negatively related to well-being, and so give no support to the idea of "big government."

Against Layard's reasoning we could argue that far more than 90 percent of the citizens in industrial countries are not alcoholics or drug addicts, just as they are not workaholics or consumption junkies, and that they are capable of making decisions with foresight. Were heroin to be legally available in every drugstore, the number of addicts would soar, but even then the great majority of people would easily be able to resist the temptation because they can anticipate the dependency and all the negative consequences associated with it. Can we still go so far as to demand state protection against work and consumption? After all, that would mean a massive encroachment on the civil liberties of every individual.

There are economists who would go much further than to demand such protection. One of them is the renowned Australian economist Yew-Kwang Ng. Ng takes the Easterlin Paradox as a reason to seriously call conventional economics to account. He is firmly convinced that "a revolution in economic thinking and policy formulation is needed" (2008, p. 259).

Ng concludes from the existence of the Easterlin Paradox that an increase in economic prosperity doesn't have a positive effect on life satisfaction. In conjunction with the findings that economic growth puts our natural resources under stress and that the individual pursuit of higher income causes negative external effects, this stands the economic world on its head.

With respect to taxation, Ng calls for economists to stop referring to the additional burdens of taxation or generally to losses in efficiency due to taxation. This is because earning income as such is the cause of a negative external effect and therefore every kind of taxation raises efficiency: "Rather than imposing excess burdens or distortionary costs, taxes are corrective and this efficiency gain could be increased by increasing tax rates!" (ibid., p. 260) But Ng goes even further. Not only does he think that the pursuit of income is reprehensible and should be prevented with a stricter tax regime; consumption as such also seems suspect to him. Ng doesn't accept the argument that choices made by consumers are expressions of their preferences. Rather, he assumes "a consistent bias towards excessive materialism" (p. 260) and concludes that "when individual preference and welfare systematically diverge, adjustments may be necessary, even in the absence of external effects" (ibid.).

Ng also comes to conclusions about activities of the state that are completely different from those we are accustomed to hearing from the economic profession. Since government expenditure displaces private consumption, it should be seen as positive, irrespective of whatever efficiency loss might go hand in hand with it. The alternative—increased growth, higher incomes, more private consumption—is always worse.

The full extent of the far-reaching conclusions to which the Easterlin Paradox can lead becomes really clear when Ng recommends, at the conclusion of his 2008 paper, that the human feeling of happiness be made the measure of all things, and that no limits be imposed on maximizing this sense of happiness. Ng recommends helping this feeling along with "good drugs" and electrical stimulation of certain regions of the brain. Feelings of happiness that are conveyed by the peripheral nervous system are subject to deterioration or lead to adaptation. For instance, we can take in only a limited quantity of food, even though the food produces a feeling of happiness in us. Direct stimulation of the reward system in the brain, on the other hand, promises continuing happiness without a reduction in marginal happiness. Ng comes close to ideas known as the "brain in a vat" or Nozick's (1974) "experience machine." The idea is that it should be possible to isolate a brain and suspend it in a life-sustaining liquid. If the correct areas of the brain are stimulated, it may be possible to enable the owner of the brain to have a very long and extremely happy life. Honestly, would you jump at this opportunity if it were offered to you?

Ng's conclusions are certainly not shared by a majority of economists. But they show how far a consistent, logical interpretation of the Easterlin Paradox can go. If one accepts the existence of this paradox and is willing to explain it with positional preferences, one can easily arrive at conclusions similar to Ng's. One need only believe hard enough that it is the competition for relative position that drives us, that this competition is pointless and inefficient, and that only government intervention or brain manipulation can save us from this struggle. In turn, it is possible to believe this only if one considers two conditions to be fulfilled:

1. The measure used by happiness research to gauge people's life satisfaction is valid—that is, it really does measure subjective life satisfaction. Moreover, this measure is suitable for making intertemporal and international comparisons.

2. The data used to analyze the relationship between subjective life satisfaction and people's life circumstances have been collected properly and contain no serious measurement errors. The data of different countries are comparable.

Can we really assume without any doubt that both conditions are fulfilled? Or are doubts justified? We will approach this question in two steps.

In the first step, we will continue to assume that life-satisfaction research measures the correct quantity—in other words, that the first condition is fulfilled. We will then show that recent work casts serious doubts on the fulfillment of the second condition. Better data collection has shown that, in addition to relative position, absolute income also plays a significant role. The evidence suggests that radical interpretations of the Easterlin Paradox, such as Ng's, are not tenable.

In the second step, we will question whether happiness research is based on data that really do reflect people's happiness. In particular, we will ask whether statements made in relation to life satisfaction at different points in time can be compared with each other. In this context, we will also discover that the findings of life-satisfaction research as they have been reported until now should be re-examined. Then, we will see what statements we can, or cannot, make.

II
What Is Happiness Research Telling Us?

7
Are We Measuring Correctly?

How Reliable Are the Survey Data?

Collecting data is not easy. The empirical social sciences can tell us a thing or two about how difficult it is sometimes to get hold of the data needed for important scientific investigations. In many cases, data protection or something else stands in the way.

Income, working hours, health status, and moonlighting all involve objective quantities. How long a person works, or what his income is, can, without a doubt, be measured, so the data can (in principle, at least) be checked. Subjective life-satisfaction data are completely different. Only the respondents themselves really know whether what they have marked on a scale from 0 to 10 truly represents their life satisfaction. A person's life satisfaction is private information through and through, and every individual possesses an exclusive right to it. Whether or not to report life satisfaction honestly is a decision made by each individual, and it is exceedingly difficult to verify such information. To trust self-reported subjective well-being, we also have to be sure that a subject's judgments about his or her life are made in a consistent way. This implies, for instance, that, as long as nothing in life changes, people report the same level of life satisfaction when repeatedly asked about their life satisfaction. Stable answers suggest that individuals apply some consistent psychological processes when assessing their satisfaction with life (Diener et al. 2013) and thus are also able to adequately assess how income levels and changes in them affect their well-being. Stable answers enable researchers to say that the measure is reliable.

Psychological research has put an enormous amount of effort into determining the reliability of well-being measures. (For recent overviews, see Diener et al. 2009a and OECD 2013.) An influential study by Schwarz and Strack (1999) promoted a very pessimistic view of the reliability of subjective well-being measures. In the view of Schwarz and Strack (ibid., p. 61), they "do not reflect a stable inner state of well-being. Rather, they are judgments that individuals form on the spot, based on information that is chronically or temporarily accessible at that time, resulting in pronounced context effects." For instance, momentary differences in mood may explain why people, when repeatedly asked about their life satisfaction within a short period of time, don't always put their marks in the same place (Schwarz et al. 1987). We know this from our own experiences. The sun comes out from behind the clouds and our spirits rise. We meet a nice person who smiles at us or makes a friendly remark and all of a sudden our mood improves. The psychological explanation for why such moods influence people's responses to questions about life satisfaction is that making a comprehensive assessment of one's own life situation is a complex task. In order to do this, a respondent must assess different areas of life and then condense the assessments into a single measure. Respondents have to consider how happy they are in their job, how good their relationship is, how satisfied they are with their social environment, and much more, and then decide how much weight each area of life should be given. This is an extremely challenging and complex task. Psychologists assume that people tend to search for shortcuts and try to simplify things in such situations. Consequently, the mood someone happens to be in is used as an indication of his or her general satisfaction with life. Insufficient attention is given to the fact that this mood can change relatively rapidly. A famous experiment illustrates the consequences of this. Schwarz (1987) placed a dime on a photocopying machine in the hall of a library. Students who had found the dime while photocopying and pocketed it (they all had done so) were asked on their way out of the library if they were willing to participate in a short survey. They were then invited into the office of the experimenter to fill out a questionnaire that included questions on general life satisfaction. Schwarz then gave the same questionnaire to subjects who hadn't found a dime earlier. The findings were unambiguous: Subjects who had found the dime reported significantly higher life satisfaction than those who hadn't. A dime was all that was needed to put the subjects in a good mood, and they transformed this into higher life satisfaction. Mood clearly has the potential to influence a person's perception of his or her life satisfaction.

One other thing we mustn't forget while we are on the topic of what affects our mood is weather. Schwarz and Clore (1983) investigated the influence of weather in the course of a study in which subjects were interviewed by telephone. People reported being in a better mood on sunny days than on rainy days. Notably, on bad weather days a little small talk about the weather suffices to draw people's attention to the fact that it is why they are in a bad mood. This generally leads to higher life satisfaction right away, and the relationship is statistically significant. On good weather days, on the other hand, there is no statistically detectable relationship between life satisfaction and mention of the good weather in interviews.

But the weather and the mood we happen to be in at that moment aren't the only important factors in self-reported life satisfaction. Another important factor is the so-called focusing illusion. Psychologists assume that people rely on simple indicators, such as the mood they are currently in. Another way to arrive at an assessment of general life satisfaction relatively straightforwardly is to focus on one particular aspect of life that is temporarily accessible in one's mind instead of dealing with all areas of life and then laboriously weighting and aggregating them. In the context of a questionnaire survey, Strack et al. (1988) presented students with two satisfaction questions. One asked about their general life satisfaction. The other question was "How happy are you with your dating?" The answers to both questions were collected using the usual scale from 0 to 10, and the order of the questions was varied. One time the dating-satisfaction question was asked first; another time the general-satisfaction question was asked first. There was also a third arrangement in which the question about dating satisfaction was asked first, but an explicit relationship between the two questions was created additionally by informing the subjects that they would be asked about two aspects of their life satisfaction.

The focusing illusion was shown to be effective if the dating question was posed before the general life-satisfaction question without the connection between the two first being made. In this case, the focus was put on the respondent's satisfaction with dating, and it could be seen that the satisfaction with dating strongly predetermined the answers to the life-satisfaction question. Note, however, that explicitly pointing out that the questions dealt with two different aspects of life satisfaction causes this correlation to disappear. Apparently, the focusing illusion only affects the subconscious. If it is suggested to us that two different things are involved, we no longer use one as a shortcut to reach the other. Kahneman et al. (2006, p. 1909) gave a very apt description of just what this focusing illusion means: "Nothing in life is quite as important as you think it is while you are thinking about it."

These and similar studies indicate that measuring life satisfaction is connected with some inaccuracies. Andrews and Whitney (1976) confirm these inaccuracies by looking at how the answers to the life-satisfaction question differed when the question was asked twice within an hour. They find a so-called test-retest correlation in the range 0.40–0.60. If the respondents were to give the same answer in each case, ideally it would have to be 1.0! Thus, according to Schwarz and Strack (1999, p. 80), there is little to be learned from life-satisfaction data as it is "too context-dependent to provide reliable information about a population's well-being, let alone information that can guide public policy."

This pessimistic view of the reliability of the life-satisfaction measure is strongly opposed by other psychologists who argue that the measure of life satisfaction is "often not as contaminated as popular lore might suggest" (Diener and Suh 1999, p. 438). First evidence against the pessimistic view can be drawn from test-retest correlations from other studies. As times goes by, a lot happens that affects life satisfaction, and one would expect the correlation to become smaller as the time interval between the two judgments increases. But recent studies find the opposite. When the life-satisfaction question is asked after two weeks, Krueger and Schkade (2008) report a correlation coefficient of 0.59—much higher than the range reported for the retest within an hour. And for four large representative national samples such as the SOEP and the BHPS, which we used to discuss the Easterlin Paradox in preceding chapters, Lucas and Donnellan (2012) report an average reliability that exceeds 0.70. This suggests that respondents' judgments about life satisfaction are reliable. And in contrast to the illuminating examples above, where a clever manipulation of the experimental design had far-reaching consequences for where the individuals put their mark on the life-satisfaction scale, a meta-analysis by Schimmack and Oishi (2005) found some context effects due to temporarily accessible information, but only very weak ones. They also reproduced the experiment by Strack et al. (1988) where the order of the questions about dating satisfaction and life satisfaction was varied, but did not obtain the same results. In their study it simply didn't matter whether students were asked about dating satisfaction or life satisfaction first. With another experiment, Schimmack and Oishi could demonstrate that satisfaction with the family and with housing are each highly correlated with global life satisfaction, irrespective of the order in which the questions were asked. By contrast, satisfaction with weather was hardly correlated with global life satisfaction independently of the order of questions. This is evidence of the reliability of reported life satisfaction, as most of the variance in the life-satisfaction measure is determined by chronically accessible information about important life domains whereas temporarily accessible information about relatively unimportant aspects of life has only a negligible effect.

But what about the weather? Wouldn't we all judge our lives to be better on a sunny day? Another very recent study reexamined how the weather affects life-satisfaction judgments. In contrast to Schwarz and Clore (1983), who analyzed a rather small sample of only 84 participants, Lucas and Lawless (2013) made use of a sample of more than 1.9 million participants who were recruited from all fifty US states and who were each interviewed once between 2005 and 2009. These participants were asked, among other things, about their satisfaction with life. Since Lucas and Lawless knew where the individual participants were located and when they were interviewed, they could determine the local weather conditions on the day of the interview and thus analyze how the answers to the life-satisfaction question were affected by the weather conditions. Their finding was very clear cut: Most daily weather conditions had no effect on life-satisfaction judgments, and the few significant effects they found were very small in size. Since their results were derived by using exactly the type of data we used in our discussion of the Easterlin Paradox, this strongly suggests that we have indeed used a reliable measure to discuss the effect of income on subjective well-being.

Nevertheless, the reliability of happiness research depends greatly on whether the individual measurement errors lead to a systematic distortion of the results in one direction or another, or whether they are randomly distributed errors that, when aggregated, may not bias research findings. The latter is probably true in the case of mood effects, with the negative influence of the bad mood of some people being balanced out by the positive mood of others. It is, of course, debatable whether this applies to all the sources of error mentioned already. But there may be systematic distortions.

What happened on April 6, 2009? On that day the Gallup-Healthways Well-Being Index for the United States soared by an amount that, as Deaton (2012) noted, would otherwise have required doubling GDP. After April 6, the index remained at this very high level continuously. The analysis by Deaton shows that these large changes were not driven by real events but by changes in the order of questions in the survey. Gallup also uses its daily interviews to collect information about political issues and observed that changing these questions had an effect on the judgment of one's personal life. Gallup therefore randomly split the sample. Beginning January 9, 2009, half of the respondents were asked political questions as usual, whereas the other half were no longer asked any political questions but were asked about their life satisfaction right away. For the latter group, the average life satisfaction skyrocketed immediately after January 9, indicating very strong context effects. According to Deaton (2012, p. 9), "people appear to dislike politics and politicians so much that prompting them to think about them has a very large downward effect on their assessment of their lives."

These context effects can be eliminated, though. On April 6, Gallup began to ask a "transition question": "Now thinking about your personal life, are you satisfied with your personal life today?" (See Deaton 2012, p. 9.) The idea was to eliminate the context effect by refocusing a respondent's attention on his or her personal life. The effect was remarkable. The refocusing led to almost the same average life-satisfaction scores for those who were asked about politics first as for those who weren't asked about politics at all.

Deaton's analysis shows two things. First, there may be systematic context effects in survey data that may make it difficult to compare older data on life satisfaction from different sources. Second, a well-designed survey can overcome the problem of context effects. Hence, happiness researchers have at hand a potentially very reliable measure that they can use to systematically analyze the factors that affect our well-being.

Another important question is "How honestly do the respondents actually answer the life-satisfaction questions?" It would be most helpful if it were possible to directly check the truthfulness of their responses. Precisely this has been done in a series of studies. Methodologically, it is done by searching for other possibilities to determine people's life satisfaction than by means of their own subjective assessment, then examining whether the alternative measurement agrees with the result obtained subjectively. Some authors, for example, have people's life satisfaction assessed by someone who knows them well, and in this way they obtain an alternative measure. Leppert (1998) surveyed 971 senior citizens, asking them about their subjective well-being and, in addition, asking a person close to them (their partner or a close friend) to provide a corresponding evaluation. Both responses were shown to be strongly correlated with each other.

Sandvik et al. (1993) went down a similar path. In the first part of their investigation, they intensively surveyed 136 students on their life satisfaction in the course of a semester using the normal scale from 0 to 10. The "mood" of the subjects was obtained from these interviews and from a test in which the subjects had to remember positive and negative experiences within a short space of time. Conclusions on the individual feelings of happiness were drawn from the frequency of the reported positive and negative life experiences. In the second part of the study, seven "informants" for each student, at least three of whom had to be close family members and three of whom had to be close friends, were asked to judge that student's life satisfaction. Here, too, it turned out that there was a very high correlation of the assessments of the informants with the self-reported assessments of the students and the interview results. In a very recent study, Zou et al. (2013) confirm the findings that self-ratings and informant's ratings are equally valid.

Redelmeier and Kahneman (1996) took a somewhat different path to find out whether subjective assessments have a high degree of truthfulness. They asked 154 patients, after a colonoscopy, to report on how strong the pain they experienced was, using a pain scale common in medicine. The severity of the pain was also evaluated independently by a research assistant who observed the patient during the examination. Similar to the first two studies, a strong correlation was found between the patients' assessments and those of the research assistants.

The studies we have just discussed are not completely methodologically convincing, since they amount to an attempt to check the truthfulness of subjective statements with the aid of other subjective judgments. It would, of course, be better if we had an *objective* measure with which to compare the life-satisfaction responses. Obviously, there can't be an objective measure for life satisfaction itself—it is scarcely possible to find anything more subjective than one's own happiness. But one can imagine that life satisfaction has real consequences that can be objectively measured. Let us put it this way: If it is found that subjective assessments of life satisfaction are based on truth (i.e., if they really are a reliable measure of life satisfaction), that finding should have real measurable consequences.

A real consequence of very low reported life satisfaction is the probability that the individual will commit suicide. Koivumaa-Honkanen et al. (2001) investigated this for Finland and linked the life-satisfaction responses of 30,000 Finns with the data on deaths at the central registry. The finding isn't surprising: There is a strong correlation between life satisfaction and the probability of suicide. Someone in the lowest tier of life satisfaction has a 25-times-greater probability of committing suicide in the next twenty years than someone in the top tier.

There are also other cues. One is the fact that someone who reports high life satisfaction is more likely to marry or become a parent in the next few years, whereas someone with low life satisfaction is more likely to get divorced, lose a job, or relocate (Luhmann et al. 2013). Admittedly, it isn't immediately clear in which direction the causality is working. It may be that people report a higher level of happiness because they know they will be getting married soon, or perhaps it is because a person is in a happy relationship that sooner or later he or she ends up marrying. Causality in this direction can probably be ruled out if longer periods of time are considered. Harker and Keltner (2001) approached this by analyzing the photographs of women in college yearbooks and were able to demonstrate that the women whose portraits seemed to show that they were in a positive emotional state at the age of 21 had a higher probability of being married at age 27 than those who seemed to have been less cheerful and good-humored when photographed at 21. An important role was played in this by the so-called Duchenne smile, which is a smile produced by face muscles that most people cannot normally consciously control (good actors can do this after a lot of training). That's why it is possible for people to distinguish between a genuine smile and a false smile. Indeed, the probability to be married at age 27 was higher if the yearbook smiles were genuine than if they were false.

Harker and Keltner were also able to show that the moods of young women about to graduate from college were useful in predicting marital status and other circumstances of life thirty years later. An explanation that seems to suggest itself is that this correlation has something to do with attractiveness. Pretty women are sought after and are therefore good-humored, tend to marry, and are abandoned less frequently. However, controlling for attractiveness shows that it isn't the attractiveness that is important, but rather the positive emotions.

What about the correlation between subjective life satisfaction and health? We discussed the effect of health on happiness in chapter 4. Here, we want to look at the opposite direction of causality. It could be the case that happy people are also healthier and live longer on average. There are, in fact, several highly interesting studies that seem to indicate this.

Maier and Smith (1999) show that respondents' judgments of affective status (that is, of their emotional state) are good predictors of whether the respondent will die in the next three to six years. Similar studies confirm this finding, however, as was the case with weddings, it could also be that the causality is the opposite of what is suggested. It can't be ruled out that people who will later be seriously ill have already begun to notice the first signs of illness and therefore tend to become pessimistic. Snowdon (2001) and Danner et al. (2001) discovered a way to track relationships over a very long period of time and could thereby almost entirely rule out reverse causality (in which the illness determines the emotional state and not vice versa). They analyzed autobiographical essays written in the 1930s by young American nuns of a religious order known as the School Sisters of Notre Dame, then investigated whether there was a relationship between the feelings each women had in her youth and the state of her health between the ages of 80 and 90. They found a surprisingly strong correlation. The nuns who had expressed more positive emotions were significantly healthier at an advanced age than their more pessimistic sisters. On average, the nuns in the happiest quintile lived ten years longer than those in the unhappiest quintile.

In a much more arduous study, Cohen et al. (2003) sought to determine whether there was a correlation between a subject's physical condition and his or her mental condition. After surveying their subjects' levels of life satisfaction, they infected them with a cold virus. It turned out that the subjects who reported higher life satisfaction had a lower probability of becoming ill and recovered faster if they did. Kiecolt-Glaser et al. (2002) were a little rougher with their subjects: They inflicted a small wound, then observed the healing process. They found that the higher the reported life satisfaction was, the faster was the healing.

There have also been attempts to reconcile the standard economic analysis of revealed preferences with the use of subjective well-being measures by looking at where people settle. Economic theory suggests that if some region has particularly nice amenities, more people would like to move there, which in turn will drive housing prices up and wages down. The differences in housing prices for otherwise equally good houses and in wages for otherwise identical work then reflect the monetary value the regional amenities have. Known as the *hedonic pricing method*, this is a well-established instrument in cost-benefit analysis. Oswald and Wu (2010) calculated the differences in subjective well-being among the fifty US states that prevailed after controlling for other important aspects of life, such as income, age, ethnicity, education, marital status, and employment status. The differences then measured the effect of just living in one state rather than another. They then compared these with differential housing prices, rents, and wages, and found a very similar ranking for the states. Apparently, both measures—subjective well-being and the objective "compensating differentials"—provide equally important information about how people judge the amenities of the region in which they live.

What can be concluded? On the one hand, there is good reason to believe that the subjective life satisfaction expressed by people in the relevant surveys is connected to their actual emotional state. On the other hand, short-term factors (such as a person's surrounding or the mood he or she happens to be in at the moment) can have some influence on responses to life-satisfaction items, but surveys can be designed such that these effects can be minimized. It is indeed possible to learn something about people's levels of life satisfaction from their subjective statements, but we must take great care when interpreting old data (which might be subject to some of the flaws described above) and when collecting new data (because a proper design of any survey is essential for sufficiently reducing any systematic, and therefore substantial, distortions).

What Are We Actually Measuring?

Economic happiness research is, essentially, based on asking people all over the world a single question: "All in all, how satisfied are you with your life at the moment?" The responses that may be chosen are on a scale, and the scale often ranges from 0 to 10 (as, for example, in the German Sozio-oekonomisches Panel). A person can't be happier than 10 or unhappier than 0. So far, so good. But what is actually measured when respondents indicate a number between 0 and 10? Moreover, is it correct to analyze the data on life satisfaction obtained by asking this question in the customary way—that is, by investigating whether the scores obtained, just as they are, are statistically significantly correlated with other values, such as income, age, or health?

Happiness research, as we saw in part I of the book, is primarily in search of the things that determine people's life satisfaction in developed countries. Paradoxically, its greatest and most spectacular findings are that income has only a small influence on life satisfaction and that the increases in income that people in developed economies have achieved in the last few decades haven't led to an increase in average life satisfaction. Its central findings thus show what happiness *doesn't* depend on. We will see whether those findings are actually correct. First, however, let us consider more closely whether it is at all valid to assume that the choice of the methodology that led to those findings was reasonable and appropriate.

Can we really simplify things so much and reduce everything about happiness to one question and a scale with fixed lower and upper bounds? If we do this, we disregard a number of things that we would do well not to ignore, beginning with the fact that the time factor isn't taken into account at all in the interpretation of the data. We measure average life satisfaction at a particular moment in time and act as if it isn't important *how long* a person is happy. That isn't right.

Better a longer happy life than a shorter happy life
Happiness research observes average life satisfaction at a particular time. If the change in life satisfaction over time is being examined, the average life satisfactions of the consecutive years are simply strung together. Does this suffice? Aren't we forgetting a small detail? Suppose we want to know whether people in some region (let's say Lower Bavaria) have a better life today than they had in 1980. Let's suppose, further, that average life satisfaction in Lower Bavaria hasn't changed since. Life expectancy, however, has increased significantly. Today an inhabitant of Lower Bavaria lives, on average, three years longer than in 1980. People today can clearly enjoy their life satisfaction longer than in the past. Even if we correctly measure that life satisfaction hasn't risen, this still doesn't mean that we can conclude that people today don't feel better than in the past. On the contrary, if we calculate the number of days that people experience a certain quality of life, it is clear that the Lower Bavarians feel much better today.

Veenhoven and Hagerty (2006) have examined this systematically. In their opinion, a longer happy life is better than a shorter happy life, and they therefore combine life-satisfaction data with life expectancy data under the heading "Happy Life Years." This measure adds up the life satisfaction over all the years of one's life by multiplying life expectancy by subjective life satisfaction (measured on a scale from 0 to 10) (Veenhoven 1996). Someone who experiences, say, an additional year with an average life satisfaction of 7 has an increase in Happy Life Years of 0.7. Results for the United States show that from 1973 to 2004 people gained an average of 5.4 Happy Life Years, and in Western Europe the increase was even higher (6.3 years). In view of this trend, it is scarcely possible to say that in 2004 people did *not* feel better than people felt in 1974.

It should be mentioned in passing that the trend in average life expectancy has a great deal to do with economic growth. There are, of course, many reasons why we are living increasingly longer, but what they all have in common is that they are closely connected to economic success. Better diet, better hygiene, better medical care, and the enormous technological progress in medicine are the most important drivers of this development, and there are good reasons for assuming that we are far from having reached the end of it. It should be remembered that Jopie Heesters, a famous entertainer in Germany, reached the age of 108 years despite two world wars and despite having had to cope, in his youth, with conditions far worse than most people are accustomed to today. If such a long life is possible under such conditions, how will it be for those who have experienced much better conditions throughout their lives? We will not have an exact answer to this question until 2045, when the first members of the postwar generation reach the age of 100. No matter how things turn out, it is certain that the enormous economic growth that followed the Second World War has made a decisive contribution to the increase in life expectancy, and that further economic growth is a necessary prerequisite for a further increase in life expectancy. This point is notoriously disregarded by those who argue that the Easterlin Paradox shows that economic growth isn't needed. Even if increased income is good for nothing else, the mere fact that it lengthens our lives (at least statistically) makes it a magnificent thing that we shouldn't thoughtlessly put at risk.

The Weber-Fechner Law: We feel logarithmically
Any scale that is used to mark answers about subjective well-being suggests implicitly that there is a linear relationship between people's actual, "objective" well-being and the level of happiness that they feel and report when questioned in social surveys. The emphasis here is on the word "feel." Happiness, or quality of life, inevitably has something to do with feeling. We will never be able to undertake a complete cognitive appraisal of our life. Even when we unemotionally and carefully take stock because the interviewer has presented us with a scale from 0 to 10, we go about it using our gut feeling and our heart and don't let our reasoning alone decide what number we will check. This means that happiness researchers are, in the end, attempting to measure a feeling.

But what is new in that? Psychologists have been doing that for a very long time. They lean on a very old finding that forms the basis for modern psychological research. It all began with a discovery by Ernst-Heinrich Weber (1795–1878), a physiologist, that the perception of sensation could be measured. The trick behind this was to use the smallest perceptible change in a sensation as a unit of measurement. A good example is the perception of sound. Whether a person perceives a sound as loud or not so loud is naturally a matter of subjective judgment. To make an objective measurement of this subjective sensation seems problematic. Weber assumed that people could perceive a difference between two sensations only if the stimulus that triggered the sensation had undergone a certain minimum change. In general, a sound is perceived as louder only if the decibel level has risen by some minimum value. Although up until that point the sound has already become louder objectively, we are not able to perceive this. What happens if a person is presented with a sound that then slowly becomes progressively louder and is asked to press a button every time he has the feeling that the sound has become louder? Does he always press the button at the same intervals? Does our hearing follow a linear pattern? Weber found that this was not the case. Instead, our hearing responds logarithmically. The intervals necessary before we perceive something as louder become increasingly larger. This logarithmic relationship can be interpreted in such a way that the stimulus (in this case the sound) always has to increase by the same percentage for us to reach the next point at which we perceive the difference again. This means, of course, that the absolute differences between the stimuli become greater and greater.

In 1860, *Elements of Psychophysics*, a two-volume work by Gustav Theodor Fechner, was published. In it Fechner systematically developed the relationship that Weber had discovered for use in the measurement of perception. Thus was born the Weber-Fechner Law. Its extraordinary importance for psychology is easy to imagine. Until then psychological theory had to rely on assumptions about feelings that were, at best, based on introspection. Thanks to the innovation of Weber and Fechner, it became possible to replace such vague "measurements" with objective data. Since then, the fact that people perceive sensations logarithmically has been demonstrated again and again in a variety of contexts.

Those who would like to infer from the findings of happiness research that income has no real influence on people's happiness point out that the relationship between income and life satisfaction is very steep at the beginning (when the basic needs must be met) and then levels off. This is, however, an exact expression of the Weber-Fechner Law. And why should it be any different? Why shouldn't the relationship between income and life satisfaction follow the same law that has been proved reliable for so many other feelings?

When perception of noise, heat, or cold is measured, it is on an open-ended scale. There is no upper or lower limit. In happiness research, however, everything is measured on a finite scale with lower and upper bounds. This suggests that a person whose life-satisfaction score approaches the maximum needs a dramatic change in his life circumstances in order to approach the maximum even more closely. His income can go as high as he wants, but his life satisfaction stops at the maximum score. As a result, the relationship between income and life satisfaction must become increasingly flatter as earnings increase. In conjunction with the Weber-Fechner Law, this point yields a wonderful explanation for the flattening of the life-satisfaction curve at high incomes. If this explanation is correct, the claim that above a certain minimum income money doesn't make a person any happier is false. If the Weber-Fechner Law also applies to the relationship between income and life satisfaction, a logarithmic curve should be detectable. In other words, we should then be able to show that an increase in income of, say, 10 percent would have the same effect on rich people as on poor people. We will demonstrate precisely this when we deal with the question of whether the Easterlin Paradox really is so paradoxical after all.

Happiness has many faces
If we are sitting with our friends and discussing what role money, income, and other material things have in our happiness, we will find again and again that we are talking gloriously at cross purposes with each other. This is due to the fact that each person can have a very different concept of "happiness." There is certain to be one person in the circle who protests by saying something like "Income isn't important to me, because I feel real happiness when I give my children a big hug, and I don't need any money for that." It is mostly the grandchildren that make older people happy, but the principle is the same. On the other hand, what these people mean when they talk of happiness is something recognizably different from what happiness researchers try to measure with their life-satisfaction scales. These two different aspects of "feelings of happiness" are commonly referred to in the literature as "cognitive well-being" and "affective well-being." The first is what life-satisfaction research measures; the latter is what small children trigger—but not only them.

The difference between the two kinds of feelings of happiness is obvious. Affective happiness is beyond our conscious control or manipulation. It comes from our emotional system, which we don't really have under control. We experience happiness spontaneously, and we experience it only as a feeling that can be triggered by an encounter, a touching experience, or simply a memory. It affects us in exactly the same way as negative feelings. Anger, sorrow, and fear can't really be controlled either and also originate in the depths of the brain in our emotional apparatus. To keep the different faces of happiness apart, we will use the term "emotional well-being" when we mean affective well-being, which is fed entirely by our emotions.

Cognitive well-being is better captured by the life-satisfaction question. Life satisfaction has been the sole focus of our attention so far. It is the result of a process of careful consideration in which we, to an extent, take a bird's-eye view of our life. Cognitive processes play a large part in this. We compare, we judge, and we find out how we feel. Of course our feelings have a big role to play in this, but they undergo a critical examination, and that is where cognition has an important part to play.

Besides emotional well-being and life satisfaction, there is another important concept of what true happiness is. Following Aristotle, this is commonly referred to as "eudaimonia" or "eudaimonic well-being," which assumes that "true" happiness begins at the moment it comes from the fulfillment of our "true" needs.

We have already dealt with life satisfaction in detail in part I of this book. We are therefore now going to look at the other two concepts in somewhat more detail, focusing on two questions. First, what is the relationship among the three concepts. Second, what is the role of money in each of the three measures of happiness?

The title of our book claims that money does buy happiness. When is that true, and does it apply to all three of the kinds of happiness we have mentioned?

Eudaimonic well-being
The basis for eudaimonism is the philosophical notion that there are good motives and bad motives for peoples' actions. In contrast to this, a purely hedonistic definition of happiness sees the gratification of desires as the sole source of happiness, irrespective of what desire is being satisfied at the moment. Let us use an example to make this clear. If we feel like eating a bar of chocolate, our hedonistic understanding of happiness doesn't have a problem with our treating ourselves to the 600 calories in a 100-gram bar or with the considerable gain in pleasure that we experience by doing so. Admittedly, our "eudaimonic ego" might insist that eating chocolate isn't virtuous, since we would be indulging in gluttony. Wanting candy is therefore a bad motive for our actions, and consequently it can't provide us with true bliss.

According to Aristotle, well-being cannot and must not be a matter of simply following our needs and desires. Instead, it is all about leading an objectively successful life. And so before we satisfy our desires we have to decide what contributes to a successful life and what doesn't. If one manages to make this decision successfully and is able to lead a successful life, one will achieve the final definitive goal in life, since eudaimonia (literally "to have a good demon") is not the means to an end but the end in itself.

It is easy to like this concept of happiness. Being in harmony with oneself and living according to one's innermost values and moral convictions is a pleasant thought. It does, however, have two disadvantages. The first is obvious. Depending on the circumstances, it can be quite hard to lead such a life—all the more so if our feelings of pleasure are in direct conflict with our inner convictions. Someone whose ideal is an ascetic way of life will find maintaining that ideal very difficult if he always craves something sweet or can't pass a fast-food restaurant without having to deal with massive inner conflict. Will such a person be happy if he leads an ascetic life but is forced to have a fierce struggle with himself day in and day out?

The second drawback of the concept of eudaimonia becomes visible if we attempt to measure people's eudaimonic well-being. This would presuppose that it is possible to know what anyone's inner values are—something that clearly is quite difficult. In order to be able to make empirically useful statements nonetheless, psychologists have thought about an alternative that might capture at least some of the central aspects of eudaimonic well-being. Ryff and Keyes (1995) call this concept "psychological well-being" and identify six dimensions in which it can develop and can manifest itself. Self-Acceptance contributes to psychological well-being when people are prepared to accept themselves as they are, with all their strengths and weaknesses. Positive Relations with Others makes a contribution when it includes empathy and emotional commitment. Autonomy, which expresses itself in the ability to go through life self-determinedly, contributes to well-being just as much as Environmental Mastery, the discovery of a Purpose in Life, and a sense of Personal Growth (which is supplied by experience of a continuous development throughout life).

Of course, the concept of psychological well-being can be extended at will. For example, Keyes (2006) proposes also including social well-being, and specifies five further domains within which it can develop. A sense of belonging plays a role here, as does the conviction that one person is able to make a contribution to the society in which one lives. The downside is that this concept can be extended arbitrarily. To this extent, it is an open question whether psychological well-being can assist us in making the unobservable eudaimonic happiness measurable. Clark and Senik (2011) have nevertheless tried, taking a rather pragmatic path and asking six questions about aspects of eudaimonic well-being. Only those respondents who answered five out of these six questions positively were classified as "eudaimonically happy." As many as 56 percent of the subjects reported that they loved to learn new things, that they considered what they did valuable and important, that they had a positive self-assessment, that they were optimistic, and that there were people to whom they were important—and thus showed that they could be considered happy in the Aristotelian sense. Equipped with this measure for eudaimonic well-being,

Clark and Senik examined whether it made a difference whether life satisfaction, happiness, or eudaimonic well-being was investigated. Is it possible that, although people experience emotional well-being, they are still unhappy in the Aristotelian sense? The answer is interesting in two respects. First, there turns out to be no difference between these aspects of happiness. Second, all three measures depend significantly on income. In the words of Clark and Senik (2011, p. 24):

> It thus turns out that … the subjective appreciation of life satisfaction, happiness and eudaimonia are similar to each other, and are characterized by very similar socio-demographic patterns (for example, the richer and the higher-educated are both more happy, more satisfied and have higher eudaimonia scores).

Affective happiness

The fact that a great deal of attention is paid to affective happiness in happiness research is due primarily to Daniel Kahneman. In 1999, Kahneman published an article that included a highly critical assessment of the conventional method of measuring happiness. In his opinion (which he, admittedly, has since revised somewhat), subjective life satisfaction measured, for example, on a scale from 0 to 10 was the wrong measure of "objective happiness." His justification for this is based on the conviction that happiness must be understood as the sum of all the experienced utility a person has had. If we want to know how happy a person is on a particular day, we have to measure the happiness he or she feels emotionally during each activity that day, assign it an appropriate weighting based on the duration of the activity, and add the measurements up. If we take a different path and ask about global life satisfaction, we are making an error because it can be shown that people make mistakes in this kind of judgment. We have already seen some of them. (Recall the discussions of the dime effect and the dependency on context in the first section of this chapter.)

Moreover, in a 1993 paper Daniel Kahneman, Barbara Fredrickson, Charles Schreiber, and Donald Redelmeier refer to another surprising phenomenon that provides cause for concern. People are rather bad at making retrospective assessments. They neglect the duration of the event and put too large a weighting on the last impression they had at the end of the incident. Kahneman et al. demonstrated this in a simple experiment in which each subject had to hold one hand in cold water, at a temperature of 14°C (57.2°F), for one minute. After a break, the experiment was repeated; this time, though, a subject had to subsequently hold one hand in water for another 30 seconds while it was heated up to a temperature of 15°C (59°F). Although it doesn't make a big difference whether you cool your hand down to 14 or 15°C, there is a perceptible relief in going from 14 to 15°C. We know this because the subjects were asked to report their sensation of pain on a scale from 0 to 14. At the end of the short episode (only 60 seconds at 14°C), the pain level was 8.4, but at the end of the longer episode (60 seconds at 14°C plus 30 seconds at 15°C) it was only 6.5.

After the two episodes, the subjects were told that one of the two would be repeated and they could choose which one. Sixty-nine percent chose the longer option even though it entailed additional (though slighter) pain. What was decisive for the evaluation during both episodes was not the duration of the sensation of pain, but the maximum pain level and the strength of the most recently experienced pain. Clearly many people follow some simplified evaluation rule according to which only the peak sensation level and the sensation at the end are used in judging the experience. The consequence of such a *peak-end rule* is that a person's own experience is judged incorrectly. It is evident that a false evaluation is involved here, since when both experimental arrangements are verbally explained to the subjects and the subjects are asked which of the two arrangements they would like to experience once more they unfailingly select the shorter one.

The use of the peak-end rule has also been observed in experiments in which subjects are exposed to noise and also in colonoscopies. In the case of colonoscopies, people who had experienced pauses in removal of the device (which prolonged the examination but made it somewhat less unpleasant) reported a lower level of pain in general than those who hadn't experienced the pauses (Redelmeier et al. 2003).

Kahneman (1999) concludes from these findings that in order to measure objective happiness it is necessary to have methods that directly measure the emotional experience at any moment and therefore don't suffer from distortions arising from measurements of subjective well-being that are reported retrospectively. Two methods are available. In one, each respondent is given a small portable computer or smartphone that, at random times in the course of a day, asks the respondent to record his emotional state at that moment, what he was doing just before the prompt, and the duration of that activity. This method, known as the Experience Sampling Method (ESM), results in an accurate picture—not distorted by retrospection—of the participant's emotional well-being. One obvious drawback is that the method is extremely elaborate. But that isn't the only drawback. It is easy to imagine that having to lug around a device that spontaneously demands that you provide details of your current feelings over and over again must have an influence on your experience. You will have to explain to people what is going on, and this will affect your communications and your interactions. The process of observation alters the object being observed, and so ESM is not without distortion. It isn't difficult to imagine that a respondent doesn't want to be disturbed by an annoying device during an especially pleasant experience or a particularly painful experience, and will simply turn the thing off in such situations.

The Day Reconstruction Method (DRM) is considerably simpler. The respondent is asked to recall the events of the previous day, noting the duration of each activity and the emotions experienced at the time. In this way, the distortions described earlier are avoided. The DRM is, however, not entirely free of distortions. Viewing events from the perspective of the next day can, of course, also lead to the changes that have been described by Kahneman as being, at least in principle, possible with retrospective evaluations.

In a study of whether the Experience Sampling Method and the Day Reconstruction Method led to different results, Dockray et al. (2010) found that they did not. Diener and Tay (2014), on the other hand, raise concerns about the reliability and validity of the DRM. In summing up the current debate, the Panel on Measuring Subjective Well-Being in a Policy-Relevant Framework, created by the National Research Council to assess the current state of research on experienced well-being, considers the DRM to be a promising method for assessing feelings and mood but also calls for additional research to determine when the DRM is an appropriate substitute for the ESM (National Research Council 2013). We will return to this later.

In the first DRM study, Kahneman et al. (2004) surveyed 909 women in Texas. Affective happiness was measured using *net affect*. This was done as follows: Three positive feelings (enjoying myself, warm/friendly, happiness) and six negative feelings (frustrated/annoyed, depressed/blue, angry/hostile, criticized/put down, hassled/pushed around, worried/anxious) were rated on a scale of 1 to 6. The average of the negative feelings was then subtracted from the average of the positive feelings, and the result was the net affect. At the top of the chart of activities, with the highest net affect, was "intimate relations." In next-to-last position was work, followed by the morning commute. Caring for children ranked relatively low; the net affects of lunch and dinner ranked high.

The starting point for Kahneman's considerations was the hypothesis that life-satisfaction research uses wrong data because so much goes wrong in the measuring process. From this it follows, of course, that results obtained with the DRM should differ from those obtained with life-satisfaction researchers' standard question. Krueger et al. (2009) investigated this by using the DRM to assess the subjective well-being of American women and French women. American women were found to have higher life satisfaction than French women, but French women were ahead in affective well-being. Although women in France are less satisfied with their lives, they feel happier. How can that be reconciled? The decisive factor is time. Because individual net affects are weighted for time, time spent on a particular activity is only included as the fraction of the total time the person spent in this activity. For instance, although intimate relations had a high net affect in Kahneman's study, they only lasted 22 minutes on average per day, whereas work used up more than 6 hours. Of course we must take this into account appropriately if we want to say something about how happy the surveyed women were over the whole day. The French women clearly have a better understanding of how to organize their day so that activities that tend to be unpleasant take up little time and pleasant ones last longer.

In a further indication of how far apart affective happiness and cognitive happiness can lie, Kahneman et al. (2006) report that income has no part to play in affective happiness if it is measured using the DRM. Subjects confirm, however, that money is important for feeling happy when they are subsequently asked about this. A similar finding is obtained when people are asked what they believe makes other people happy or unhappy. Their answers are then compared with those provided by the other people. Participants who were asked to estimate how often people on various levels of average income would be in a bad mood predicted that people living in households with annual incomes less than $20,000 would spend 58 percent of their time in a bad mood, and that people in households with annual incomes exceeding $100,000 would spend only 26 percent of their time in a bad mood. When the members of households in both these groups were asked directly, the difference turned out to be much smaller (by 20–32 percent). Nevertheless, this study shows that people with higher earnings tend to be in a better general mood the preceding day. Although the role of income as a source of happiness is grossly overestimated, it still seems to be important for our well-being.

And so we are back to the topic of money. Can we really assume that affective happiness doesn't depend on how much a person earns? Diener et al. (2009b) analyzed the answers of 141,000 people in 132 countries to questions about life satisfaction and affective well-being. And their findings? There is a positive correlation between income and life satisfaction. There is also a positive correlation between income and affective happiness, but it is weaker than that between income and life satisfaction. Kahneman and Deaton (2010) analyzed as many as 450,000 observations of how US citizens answered the same questions. Their finding is similar to that of Diener et al., except for one important qualitative difference. Three important indicators were used to collect data on the affective status of US citizens. The first sums up the components of positive affect, i.e., the positive feelings that a person has over the course of a day. The second captures the times when a person isn't sad, angry, depressed, or, as Americans say, blue. The third component is the degree of stress a person faces, measured as the proportion of stress-free time a person has. A measure of life satisfaction (on a scale of 0 to 10) was also used in addition to these affective measures.

It turned out that life satisfaction depended heavily on income. The higher the income, the more satisfied people were. What was astounding was that this positive correlation could be shown for annual incomes higher than $120,000. There is no satiation point; additional income leads to more satisfaction at all levels. Things looked quite different for the affective measures: A positive relationship was present, but only up to an income of about $75,000. Beyond that threshold, a person doesn't become more stress-free with more income and can't purchase more positive or less negative feelings. Below that threshold, income also has a very important role to play as far as emotions are concerned. It turns out that such negative life circumstances as illness, divorce, and loneliness lead to greater suffering among the poor than among the rich.

Kahneman and Deaton conclude from their investigation that in happiness research close attention must be paid to what aspect or form of feelings of happiness is being investigated at any given time, adding that it makes an enormous difference whether it is affective happiness or cognitive happiness that is being examined. There is little doubt that this conclusion, which has also been drawn by others, is correct. These findings do show, however, that for Americans with annual incomes of up to $75,000 money plays an important role in emotional well-being. According to Kahneman and Deaton, about two-thirds of American households are below the $75,000 threshold. This means that only an unfortunate minority of the population wouldn't feel better by receiving additional income. To conclude from this that money doesn't improve our emotional well-being would be rather bold.

8

How Much Truth Is There in the Easterlin Paradox?

The Easterlin Paradox is the central finding of the research into the economics of happiness, which began in the 1970s. Until a few years ago it was relatively undisputed, and research concentrated on finding an explanation for why income was arguably so unimportant. Recently, however, research has taken a different direction. New data and improved analytical methods have raised the question of whether the Easterlin Paradox really exists. Today quite a few people tend toward a significantly more moderate interpretation of the data. They point out that although older happiness research showed that people's relative position also plays an important role, it isn't nearly as dominant as Easterlin and his successors believed. In this chapter will go over the considerations that led to this assessment and augment them with our own findings. But first a point on which there is very broad consensus among happiness researchers should be clarified.

We Are Talking About a Luxury Problem

Imagine that you are living in Zimbabwe or the Democratic Republic of the Congo—that is, in one of the world's poorest countries. You have an extremely low income, and it is very insecure because it depends on such things as whether there is enough rainfall to ensure a harvest and whether you are lucky enough not to be robbed by someone. You have scarcely enough to feed you and your family. Your life is a constant struggle for your very existence. You are alone in this struggle, for there is no social security system, there is no welfare state, and there are no charities. Now suppose that you are, instead, a relatively rich American or Western European. How important is your income to you in each situation? Is it the same? Or does it make a difference whether your basic needs are sure to be met or not? Of course it makes a difference. Money's importance in a situation in which you have to use it to ensure your own survival and that of your family is completely different from its importance in a situation in which survival is guaranteed and spending money calls for creativity and imagination.

If you are poor and your survival depends on your material resources, material income *is bound to be* extremely important to your life satisfaction. It is therefore necessary to assess very poor societies and richer ones differently. Happiness research is, therefore, dealing with a "luxury problem" when it examines the effects of higher income in rich countries. The idea that the psychological importance of income depends on the level of income is also implied by "need theory." (See, for instance, Howell and Howell 2008.) Basically, "need theory" says that income plays an extremely important role in life satisfaction as long as it involves meeting basic needs. As soon as one has sufficient income to have enough food, to have shelter, and perhaps to be able to provide for the family, income rapidly loses its importance. Income tends to be of less significance for people who are "rich" in the sense that they no longer have to worry about covering their basic needs. This view of the world seems to be confirmed by data from happiness research. In particular, international comparisons of life-satisfaction data seem to show that people in rich countries are not significantly more satisfied than people in middle-income-range countries, but feel considerably better than those in very poor countries. On the basis of data sets used by Easterlin and other researchers, it turns out that when average annual income (i.e., GDP per capita) exceeds the equivalent of 20,000 US dollars, people living in countries with higher average incomes don't have higher average life satisfaction than people in somewhat poorer countries (Layard 2005). The Easterlin Paradox's claim that increases in income don't result in higher levels of life satisfaction over time also points in the same direction.

Although the findings of Kahneman and Deaton (2010) that we noted in the preceding chapter tell us something different, we need to say more on the question of whether money still makes us happy when we can be certain that our fundamental needs are met. Before we answer this question, we should note that there is broad agreement that there is a very close relationship between income and life satisfaction for poor countries (and for poor people). The disagreement is about what is happening at the higher income levels. Seen in this light, the Easterlin Paradox is describing a "luxury problem."

New Data, New Analyses, New Insights

The data Easterlin and others use to make their far-reaching statements originate from such sources as the World Values Survey (WVS). If we take a closer look at the data for different countries in this data collection, some odd things become apparent. What particularly stands out is the phenomenal performance of Colombia. According to the 2006 World Values Survey data, Colombia had the second-highest average life satisfaction of all countries. Only the inhabitants of Denmark were more satisfied. This is truly amazing. Colombia has a per capita income of less than the equivalent of 10,000 US dollars a year, the country is terrorized by drug cartels, the crime rate is extremely high, and the living conditions of the rural population are dreadful. The excellent results of Ghana in 1996 are similarly mysterious. Ghana is one of the poorest countries in the world, but obviously no one there had heard of "need theory." Despite the bitter poverty, average life satisfaction was nearly as high in Ghana as in Colombia. In both cases, there can only be one really plausible explanation for the survey results. Presumably it was mainly rich people and members of the educated upper class (the oligarchy) who were surveyed.

In 2008, two scientific papers pointing out the shortcomings of the World Values Survey and presenting alternatives were published. Deaton (2008) and Stevenson and Wolfers (2008) arrive at radically different results than the happiness researchers who claim that income plays only a minor role in happiness. As it turns out, not only are Colombia and Ghana outliers; in addition, the data sets have fundamental shortcomings. Another very critical analysis of the "old" findings was published by Diener et al. (2010). The three aforementioned publications have radically changed the picture of economic happiness research.

Deaton (2008) names three main causes of the distortions in the data sets. First, the number of poorer countries was relatively small, and richer countries were over-represented. Second, all the states of the former Soviet Union and Eastern Europe were included. Although they don't necessarily rank among the poorest of countries, they are certainly among the most dissatisfied, owing to the fact that both their economic and their political situations have been extremely unstable for a long time. Third, it was predominantly educated people in major cities who were surveyed in the poorer countries. Deaton (ibid., p. 60) concludes that as a consequence of these three peculiarities the data sets overrepresented dissatisfied Eastern Europeans and unusually satisfied inhabitants of a few very poor countries.

As a remedy, Deaton suggests using the Gallup World Poll (GWP), which is more comprehensive than the WVS and which avoids the shortcomings of the WVS that we mentioned above. And the GWP data also differ from the WVS data in another important respect. The question used to assess subjective well-being is somewhat different from the question we have been accustomed to. It asks:

Please imagine a ladder with steps numbered from zero at the bottom to 10 at the top. The top of the ladder represents the best possible life for you and the bottom of the ladder represents the worst possible life for you. On which step of the ladder would you say you personally feel you stand at this time?

Although this question is very similar to the usual question on life satisfaction, it forces the respondents to consider their assessments of their lives even more. This is particularly the case because the question expressly asks the respondents to first imagine what both extremes look like. By doing so, the respondents are called on to choose two "anchor points" relative to which they can then rank their own satisfaction. The ladder-of-life question (also called Cantril's Ladder, in honor of the American public-opinion researcher Hadley Cantril) strengthens the cognitive aspects of the assessment of life satisfaction relative to the standard question.

To prepare figure 8.1 we used the Gallup World Poll data from 2011 and the data from the 2006 World Values Survey to plot subjective well-being against GDP per capita for more than 80 countries. The two lines, which very roughly represent the relationship between income and life satisfaction, show very clearly that the relationship is considerably stronger when the Gallup World Poll data are used. When the GWP data are used, the statement that higher income doesn't lead to a further increase in life satisfaction for incomes exceeding $20,000 doesn't hold.

Covering more than 140 countries, the Gallup data set is substantially more extensive than that used for the WVS. Above all, the number of poorer countries for which data are available is much greater than in the WVS. If we analyze the relationship between subjective well-being (measured using the ladder-of-life question) and income of all the countries reported by Gallup, taking into account that the effect of additional income on well-being might be different between those countries that have an annual income of less than the equivalent of 20,000 US dollars and those that lie above this threshold, it turns out that the increase in subjective well-being due to an increase in income is less in the richer countries than in the poorer ones. This once again confirms "need theory," but it also doesn't alter the fact that when countries become richer additional income can still raise life satisfaction. A $10,000 increase in GDP per

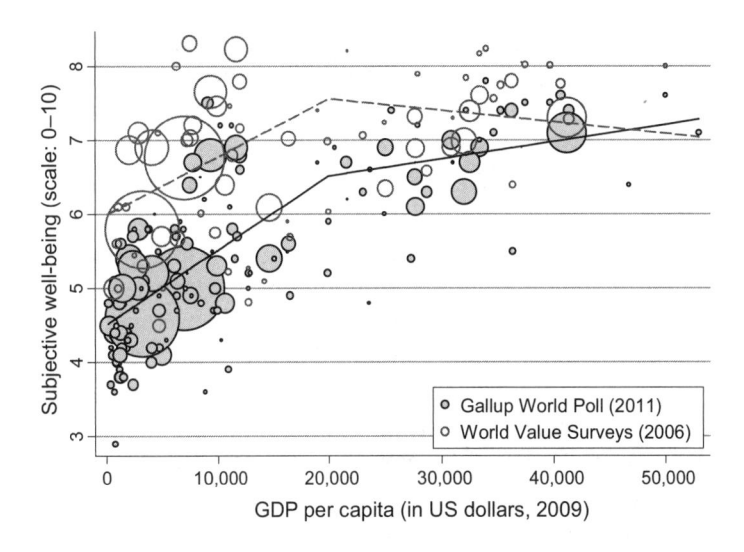

Figure 8.1

Subjective well-being and GDP per capita. The sizes of the circles represent the sizes of the populations of the countries analyzed. The lines are regression lines approximately representing the relationship between per capita income and satisfaction. Subjective well-being represents life satisfaction in the World Value Surveys and the ladder-of-life question in the Gallup World Poll.
Sources: Gallup World Poll 2011; World Values Survey 2006.

capita results in 1.0 additional ladder-of-life points in poor countries and 0.2 points in rich countries, according to the GWP. This compares with 0.8 life-satisfaction points for poor countries, but –0.16 points for rich countries (which wasn't statistically significant, though) obtained with the WVS. The transition to the Gallup data thus shows that more income will even raise people's satisfaction when they are already "rich." This also applies if the effect of an *absolute* change in income is considered—that is, if we investigate what effect an additional dollar of income has in one country or another. But does it make any sense to use this absolute change?

An alternative would be to consider relative income growth by asking (for instance) how an increase in income of 10 percent affects the life satisfaction of poor people and rich people (or countries). This would have two advantages. The first is that life satisfaction is measured on a scale that stops at 10. It should be clear that this inevitably means that the closer we get to 10 the more difficult it is to produce a further measurable increase in life satisfaction by increasing income, whereas at the other end of the scale, in the vicinity of 0, that is (for obvious reasons) very easy to do. It is therefore not particularly plausible that one more dollar in income can have the same effect at every point on the scale. The diminishing effect of absolute income changes can be taken into account by considering relative changes. The second reason for taking relative changes into consideration is the Weber-Fechner Law mentioned earlier. If human perception follows a logarithmic law, then it is rather obvious that the perception of leading a satisfying life also follows this law. Presumably most readers are no longer familiar with the exact meaning of the logarithm of a number. That doesn't matter. It is enough to know that using the logarithm of income instead of income itself implies that it isn't the absolute change in income that is being examined, but the percentage change in income. There is much to suggest that it is this change that is important to us. It is important for the Weber-Fechner Law anyway, and trade unions assume that it is important to their members. Collectively bargained wage raises are, in any case, typically formulated as a percentage pay increase.

Deaton uses the percentage change in income (by using the logarithm of income), and his findings are quite remarkable. It turns out that a certain percentage increase in income at higher incomes has a greater effect on life satisfaction than the same percentage increase has at lower incomes. Though the difference isn't large, this finding still stands in stark contrast to the view that income doesn't provide more life satisfaction at all—at least above the magic threshold of the equivalent of 20,000 US dollars a year. Similar results were found in a recent study in which Stevenson and Wolfers (2013) analyzed different international data sets and US data from a Gallup poll, which has a larger coverage of very rich individuals than other data sets.

In a second publication that is very important for present-day happiness research, Stevenson and Wolfers (2008) take the same line as Deaton and criticize the data that early happiness researchers used to derive the Easterlin Paradox. Stevenson and Wolfers also urge the use of logarithmic data, because it is the change in percentage income position that is actually important. Their most important achievement is their outstanding contribution to improving the quality of international comparisons of happiness data.

It is clear that there can be serious problems with the data if we attempt to make international comparisons or want to consider longer periods of time. A first reason for this is that we can't be sure that people all over the world use the response scale in the same way. However, there may be ways to overcome this problem, as has been proposed by King et al. (2004). They suggest using anchoring vignettes. People shouldn't be asked only about their own life satisfaction; they should also be asked about the potential life satisfaction of some hypothetical persons. If the respondents in different countries rate the life satisfaction of these hypothetical persons differently even though they are supposed to have exactly the same life circumstances, they are likely to also rank their own life satisfactions differently on the response scale. To make country-specific results comparable, it would therefore be necessary to correct for these differences in interpreting the response scale. So far, however, there has been only one attempt to do so—with very interesting results. Kapteyn et al. (2013) find that, whereas the original survey data show that Americans appear to be much less satisfied with their income than the Dutch, the difference disappears almost entirely when the difference between response behaviors in the two countries is taken into account. A second reason why comparisons over time and across countries are problematic is that we can't assume that the data were collected in the same way in different countries or at different times. The great advantage of the Gallup data is that a standardized format was used to collect them in more than 150 countries around the world—something that certainly helps to make the data from various countries more readily comparable. That certainly cannot be said for many of the data that were used to establish the Easterlin Paradox. Stevenson and Wolfers point that out and endeavor to "repair" the structural faults in the data sets.

The structural faults in the data sets may result from different causes. For example, individual countries may use differently formulated questions when measuring life satisfaction. And occasionally the way questions are asked changes over time within a country. In order to deal with such problems, Stevenson and Wolfers either resort to the Gallup World Poll data or conduct their own analysis of an individual country while keeping the respective problem in mind.

A particularly serious example of a statistical artifact is provided by Japan. For a long time Japan was considered to be the perfect example of a country where rapid economic growth wasn't able to make people happier. At the end of the Second World War, Japan and its social structures were in ruins. Economically, however, things improved considerably, with double-digit growth from the 1950s until the mid 1970s and somewhat slower but still respectable growth thereafter. But life satisfaction didn't improve. Stevenson and Wolfers show that the reason for this was that the questions had changed. As a result of that change, a Japanese person who was just as happy in 1980 as he or she had been in 1965 would have marked a lower score on the scale from 0 to 10 in 1980. Because of the change in the technique used to collect data, an increase in life satisfaction could not be discerned. That, of course, could be rectified by assessing the relationship between life satisfaction and income in the time period *before* the change in the questioning technique and the corresponding relationship in the time period *after* the change separately. That is precisely what Stevenson and Wolfers did, and it turned out that in both periods it could be shown that there was a stable positive relationship that disappeared again when the data were aggregated and the structural fault was ignored. The Easterlin Paradox vanished into thin air, at least for Japan.

Stevenson and Wolfers show that when the Gallup data are used or the structural faults are also taken into account, and when a logarithmic analysis of the data is performed, it can be demonstrated for other countries, as well as for Japan, that there is a positive relationship between income growth and life satisfaction. It can be seen once again that the positive effect of a percentage increase in income in the countries that are already richer anyway is greater than that found in countries that tend to be poorer. The exceptions Stevenson and Wolfers identify are interesting. It is particularly interesting that no positive relationship between income and life satisfaction can be found for Belgium or for the United States.

Belgium is the only European country in which life satisfaction has not increased. Indeed, despite rising earnings, life satisfaction has tended to decline. At the point we can only speculate as to what is responsible for this. Perhaps it is the long and still unresolved ethnic and linguistic conflict between the Flemings and the Walloons.

A different explanation comes to mind for the United States, where the increase in income is distributed extremely unevenly. From 1972 to 2005 the income of the lower three-fifths of the population rose by about 15–20 percent, that of the second-richest fifth by 30 percent, and that of the richest fifth by 59 percent. The size of the increase in income experienced by the upper 20 percent was thus three times that of the lower 60 percent of the population and twice as high as that of the upper middle class. This means that the relative position of the vast majority of Americans has deteriorated drastically in the last three decades. Slipping down the social ladder on account of not being able to keep up with the income growth of the upper 20 percent has been experienced by many in the middle class. If relative position plays a role—and that it does has not been disputed by Stevenson and Wolfers, Deaton, or any other happiness researchers—then we might conclude that the total negative effect seen in the United States can be attributed to the negative effect of the growing inequity outweighing the positive effect of the absolute income gains.

As we have seen, earlier studies of the Easterlin Paradox suffered from various methodological problems. Most important, the questions with which subjective well-being was measured were often not identical over the years and didn't allow a clear distinction to be made between different types of subjective well-being. Moreover, respondents in international studies were not always selected in a representative way in all countries. A recent study by Diener et al. (2013) overcomes these problems by using data from the Gallup World Poll, which uses identical questions across countries and over time and measures different types of well-being explicitly. The survey is designed to collect data from a large number of respondents in each country, representing the entire population. Moreover, it allows longitudinal analyses because it has been conducted every year since 2005. Diener et al. used data from more than 800,000 individuals from 135 countries. Their main findings are as follows: First, there are significant positive relationships between people's cognitive life evaluations and two measures of economic growth: the change in GDP per capita and the change in average household income. Second, these relationships are similarly present in wealthier and poorer countries. Third, these relationships don't attenuate over time. Diener et al. interpret these findings as supporting the claim that there may not be an Easterlin Paradox after all. They mention a number of reasons why they think that Easterlin didn't identify a positive relationship between economic growth and subjective well-being. First, they argue, Easterlin relied solely on GDP, although household income might be a more direct measure of households' actual consumption opportunities. Second, they criticize Easterlin for having "used relatively small numbers of nations or homogeneous sets of nations" (ibid., p. 274). And, finally, the Easterlin Paradox might show up only for the measure of "happiness" that is arguably more loaded with emotions than the more cognitive life-evaluation measure. Using the Gallup World Poll, Diener et al. have shown that the measure of cognitive well-being is more strongly affected by income than by emotions.

Another interesting finding presented by Diener et al. (2013) is that the relationship between income and life evaluation is as strong within countries as it is between countries. This is puzzling if one believes that relative income is more important for happiness than absolute income. A person should become happier if his income rises relative to that of his peers, but increases in proportional income for everyone within a country, leaving relative positions unaffected, should be neutral for everyone's subjective well-being. The finding by Diener et al. suggests that either it is absolute income rather than relative income that matters after all or that income comparisons take place not so much among one's closely related peers, but globally. The latter interpretation finds support in a recent study by Becchetti et al. (2013). Using data from the Eurobarometer for the years 1973–2003, they find that people not only compare themselves against other people with similar characteristics in their home country; they also compare themselves against people in neighboring countries—particular people in the richest neighboring country. Interestingly, the comparison with neighboring countries appears to be stronger for people who follow the news (either on radio and TV or in the newspapers) more intensively. Becchetti et al. interpret this as suggesting that media usage (TV, radio, newspapers) raises the visibility of neighboring countries and thus makes them more accessible as reference groups. An alternative interpretation could be that people who are more interested in international affairs compare themselves against a more global reference group and pay more attention to the news.

The studies challenging the Easterlin Paradox, most prominently the one by Stevenson and Wolfers (2008), didn't go undisputed. In a 2010 paper in which they responded to the criticism, Easterlin and four colleagues characterized some of the criticisms raised against the Easterlin Paradox as misguided. In particular, they argued, the Easterlin Paradox can't be contradicted by any studies that use cross-sectional analyses within or between countries in an attempt to show that there is no satiation point with respect to income—that is, that there isn't a certain income threshold beyond which there is no relationship between income and well-being. The simple reason for this is that the statement that people with higher incomes are happier than poorer people at any given time is part of the paradox. Without this result, it wouldn't be surprising if one didn't find a positive relation between GDP per capita and average life satisfaction over time either. We would have a paradox only if there is a positive relation between happiness and income between individuals or countries at a given time but no such relation within a country over time. Easterlin et al. (2010) conceded that the criticism based on time-series studies was more relevant. Their defense was that the time-series results of Stevenson and Wolfers (2008) had been obtained from time series that were too short. If the observed number of years is too small, changes in GDP will mainly reflect changes in the business cycle. If a survey coincidentally covers a period of a few years during which GDP grows because the economy is recovering from a recession, one might observe that people become happier, but this will not be because growth as such has been beneficial for them; it will be because the recovery reduces unemployment and thereby reduces anxiety about the future. Exactly the opposite holds true for recessionary periods. Thus, observing that GDP and happiness move in the same direction over such short periods doesn't prove that, in the long run, permanent differences in the growth rates of different countries should be associated with differences in the development of life satisfaction in these countries. In the aforementioned paper, Easterlin et al. used a sample of 37 countries for which long-run data, spanning a time interval of at least ten years, were available. They found that in that long-run perspective there was no evidence of a positive relationship between average growth rates and the change in average life satisfaction over the full length of the observed time intervals. Their defense was, thus, that the Easterlin Paradox exists if one examines sufficiently long time periods.

The defense by Easterlin et al. (2010) didn't go undisputed either. Stevenson and Wolfers, working with Daniel Sacks, accepted the challenge to examine time periods that are as long as possible. Sacks et al. (2012) compiled an extensive database by combining the six major cross-country surveys (including the World Values Survey and the Gallup World Poll), paying close attention to changes in the wording or the order of questions and to variations in the representativeness of the sample. They found clear evidence of a positive relationship between economic growth and happiness in their combined data. Even for longer time periods (12 years in the combined data set and up to 23 years in the World Values Survey), they found that the relationship between growth and income remained positive. Veenhoven and Vergunst (2013) conducted a similar analysis, using data from the World Database of Happiness (a research project, led by Ruut Veenhoven at the University of Rotterdam, that has collected more than 3,600 empirical studies of happiness and compiled the relevant information contained in them into a consistent database). The World Database of Happiness provides information on life satisfaction in 67 countries for time periods of at least 10 years, some countries having been observed for as long as 46 years. A general observation is that happiness has trended upward in two-thirds of the observed countries, and has declined in only one-third of them, with no difference between the short run and the long run. This suggests that, on average, people in the world have become happier in the past four decades. Examining the Easterlin Paradox, Veenhoven and Vergunst (2013) find that economic growth also is positively related to subjective well-being in the long run. The magnitude of this relationship is the same for periods of 10–20 years and for periods of 20–40 years. Veenhoven and Vergunst find a smaller, but still positive, association between growth and happiness for the very long run (more than 40 years). They admit that economic growth can't increase life satisfaction forever, because of the boundaries of the scale (they speculate that it will not be possible to raise average life satisfaction in a country above a level of 8.5 on a 0–10 scale); in any case, the data suggest that most countries haven't yet reached that point. Veenhoven and Vergunst conclude that the Easterlin Paradox seems to be an "Easterlin illusion."

All the new insights that we have reported so far refer to cognitive well-being. But what about the emotional side of happiness? After all, our everyday life is influenced by how we feel at a particular moment, and we rarely tend to ponder on our life at a more fundamental level or consider how satisfied we actually are. As Daniel Kahneman so beautifully put it, "Nothing in life is quite as important as you think it is while you are thinking about it." So what is the situation with the feelings we have every day? Can we be more exact in what we say about the role they play? Yes, we can.

The Two Sides of Happiness from a New Perspective

The Gallup World Poll is a very extensive data set that covers a lot more than just income and life satisfaction. In addition to the question asking which rung of the "ladder of life" you see yourself on, there is, for example, also a question asking how well you felt the previous day. In fact, a whole series of further questions are asked: Did you laugh or smile yesterday? Did you worry about anything yesterday? Were you sad yesterday? Were you stressed yesterday? Did you get annoyed yesterday? Did you feel happy yesterday? All the answers are aggregated into a measure called "daily experience." It is largely an affective measure, since it explicitly measures the feelings that a person had the previous day. The ladder-of-life question strongly appeals to our intellect, forcing us to imagine the whole ladder and to place ourselves on it. In this respect, these are two conflicting questions. One asks about the cognitive aspect of well-being; the other aims at its affective component. There is nothing new in this. As we saw in chapter 7, both affective happiness and life satisfaction changed positively in response to rising income up to an annual income of $75,000, but beyond that threshold emotional happiness displayed a weaker response to more money than life satisfaction did.

Diener et al. (2010) find a very similar relationship in the Gallup World Poll data. There is a weakly positive relationship between income and positive feelings of the previous day. So, although income has a measurable influence on people's feelings, it is rather slight. How we are doing at an emotional level depends more on other things than on income.

Happiness has many faces. When we talk about happiness we need to be aware of this, because it has become increasingly clear that the various dimensions of happiness depend on very different things. But then which dimension of happiness should we aim to maximize? If it really is the case that money makes us more satisfied, but that it doesn't necessarily provide us with more positive feelings to accompany us throughout the day, what conclusions can we draw from this? In order to find an answer to this question, it is necessary to have an idea of why income has such different effects on us and our dimensions of happiness. Why does recent research show such a strong relationship between income and life satisfaction, and why is this not found when looking at affective (that is, emotional) happiness? An important clue to how the first of these two questions can be answered is supplied by the ladder-of-life question. Recall that it forces the respondent to imagine the best and the worst possible life, meaning that the scale used to measure life satisfaction has to be adjusted by each individual respondent. Clearly, people need information to assign meaning to the endpoints of the scale and to the possible values in between. If an almost linear relationship between income and life satisfaction appears in international comparisons, respondents must have used very similar scales. And that they would have done so isn't surprising. The inhabitants of poor countries know how things look in rich countries. They certainly have an idea of what a prosperous and secure life looks like—after all, they see it on television every day. Conversely, the inhabitants of the developed world also have a pretty good idea of how the poor of this world are doing, since TV shows this too. Thus, it is highly probable that people all over the world have a rather similar idea of how a good life and a bad life look.

Delhey and Kohler (2006) show that, indeed, in Europe, cross-border references influence the life satisfaction of those who do have an idea of how people in other countries live. This is likely to be true not only for Europe. The uppermost and the lowest steps of the ladder of life are perceived in a similar way in both Ghana and Norway. Otherwise it can't be explained why the inhabitants of this planet rank themselves according to income to such a great extent on the ladder of life. This does, however, have very serious implications. If the scale used to measure life satisfaction depends on how well the rich and the poor are doing at any given moment, then this scale will change if overall economic growth spreads around the world. This is exactly what happens. The highest step moves up; the lowest step changes too. What consequence does this have? Measuring life satisfaction on a scale with lower and upper bounds makes sense if we are comparing people within a country or across countries at a particular time. It makes precious little sense if we try to compare different points in time, since it is highly likely that the scales we are using to do this are not the same. Imagine people in 100 years changing the definition of a meter to 120 centimeters. They will then find that people are exactly the same height as people today, although they are in fact taller than we are. This could be exactly the same in the case of life satisfaction, so that people seem be satisfied to the same extent irrespective of how much their income has risen in the passage of time. The Easterlin Paradox disappears when it is taken into account that the scale on which it is measured shifts with time. Because his findings are in line with this interpretation, Deaton (2008, p. 69) concludes that life-satisfaction data aren't suitable for intertemporal comparisons.

The universal measure, which is used internationally, explains the close relationship between income and life satisfaction. But why is this relationship so weak in the case of emotional happiness? There is a lot of evidence to suggest that people are true masters of adaptation. The human brain has been trained to adapt to all possible life circumstances. Humans are creatures of habit, it is said, but they are also creatures of *habituation*. This is as it should be—otherwise how would we be able to survive in an ever-changing world? If we just have a look at the diversity with which human life is lived on this planet and how different the living conditions can be, it becomes clear that our species tolerates this only because it possesses the ability to manage under the most diverse of circumstances. Emotional stability has to be a part of this too. It must also be possible for us as humans to have positive feelings if we are unfortunate enough to live in a mud-brick hut and have to spend four hours every day fetching a little water.

There is a downside to this special aspect of our survival ability. Our ability to adapt and suffer allows us to be preyed on and exploited. It isn't uncommon for rulers to secure their position by making it clear to those they govern that their subjection, their poverty, and their lack of freedom are immutable and determined by their destiny. These rulers can get away with this because a person can also get accustomed to living in poverty and subjection without freedom and still display the necessary emotional stability. How else could we imagine a state like North Korea being able to exist!

Against this background, it cannot come as a surprise that a strong relationship between income and emotional happiness can't be detected. But to conclude from this that money isn't important for our happiness would be to do just what rulers have done for hundreds of years. It would imply placing little importance on the material side of life. People can also be happy when they are poor—why should they be made richer? Not only would this be a cynical stance; it would also neglect an important aspect. Regardless of their adaptability, we should concede to people that they can, in the end, decide through their own choice what a happy life looks like for them. And this decision goes beyond the emotion felt at any one instant. An example from Hollywood may help to clarify this point.

The film *Cast Away*, with Tom Hanks in the lead role, tells the story of a FedEx employee whose plane crashes during a flight across the Pacific. He manages to reach the safety of a desert island, where he spends several years before he is rescued. At the beginning of his Robinson Crusoe life, he tries to settle in and make life comfortable. First, he tries to make a fire. There is plenty of firewood, but how do you light it if you don't have a lighter or matches? Our hero attempts this in every imaginable way, without success. He has almost reached the point of despair and is virtually ready to give up when he manages to light a fire with a stick, a piece of wood, and brushwood. The effect is tremendous. He starts a bonfire on the beach and lets the flames blaze high into the sky while dancing around the fire, beside himself with joy and happiness. But—and this is what counts—there is only one reason for his emotional high spirits. The fire provides him with the hope of being seen and the prospect of escaping from the situation in which he has just experienced what may be the happiest feeling of his life.

Should we really use emotional happiness as a guide when determining how we want to live, how much growth we would like to allow, or how much income we should have?

Let us take stock of what we have established up to this point. Recent findings in happiness research suggest that we should distinguish between two very different forms of happiness and that it is important how we measure each of these dimensions of happiness. A measure that leads people to calibrate the scale they use themselves leads to different results than a measure that avoids such a calibration. Affective happiness is to be assessed entirely differently than life satisfaction, assessment of which is based on both emotional well-being and self-reflection. Income has a positive effect on both aspects of happiness. Money makes you happy, but the strength of its effect varies.

As has been noted, the Gallup World Poll is a very extensive data set that permits a much more detailed analysis than has previously been possible—provided that one has access to the data. Diener et al. (2010) are among those who have full access to the data, and they have used the data for a very detailed analysis of the income-happiness relationship. At first, they replicate the results of Kahneman and Deaton (2010): that life satisfaction depends strongly on income whereas emotional happiness depends on income only weakly. They then go on to extend this analysis and find that the respondents' relative position (that is, the position of the respondents in the income hierarchy of their country) doesn't play a particularly important role. Although life satisfaction depends significantly on relative income, the influence of the amount of absolute income is considerably greater. Diener et al. also attribute this finding to the fact that relative position is not defined nationally but rather globally. A relatively wealthy Ghanaian is still rather poor on a global scale, and it is this that dominates his life evaluation—not the fact that he is better off than most of his fellow Ghanaians. However, it is still true that relative position and, in particular, any changes in it play an important role in a person's happiness. If a Ghanaian who was previously poor climbs up the hierarchy because he has found a better job, his life satisfaction will presumably experience a huge increase. Relative position plays a part, but (and this is the new and important message) absolute income position on the global ladder of life is more important.

Diener et al. go on to investigate the determinants of the emotional and the cognitive dimensions of happiness in more detail by analyzing how the possession of luxury conveniences, national income, and the fulfillment of psychological needs affect these two components. The psychological needs in the data set are assessed by a series of questions that collect information on things that psychologists know have a positive effect on our feelings. For example, we feel better if we do something that we are particularly good at, if we can organize our own time as we see fit, if we have friends we can rely on, and if we learn something new.

It turns out that national income, quite independently of personal income, has a strong effect on life satisfaction. This finding is of considerable significance for the question whether economic growth is good or bad. The results of Diener et al. show that it really does matter to a person's happiness in life whether he or she lives in a rich community or in a poor one. We have already pointed out that "more money" doesn't simply mean more cash in someone's pocket. It means that there are more possibilities open to people in a very broad sense. More money generally means more taxation and, with it, better provision of infrastructure, education, health facilities, and much more. It means more beautiful parks, a cleaner environment, more comfortable football stadiums, and safer streets. It would be highly unlikely if all these amenities had *no* influence on our life satisfaction. With the new data from the Gallup World Poll it is possible to empirically support this intuition, at least when comparing countries. The social context in which we live is important, and it is substantially determined by how prosperous a society is. It is simply easier to have and enjoy art, culture, and amusing events when you are rich and live in a safe environment.

Thus, economic growth has two extremely important functions that go far beyond the increase in earnings that an individual experiences. By virtue of improvements in general living conditions and developments in health care, it makes a tremendous contribution to longevity. The "amount of happiness" that one can amass becomes considerably greater because of this. This aspect alone justifies the pursuit of economic growth. The second important function of society's increasing income is that it provides us with goods that are obviously important to us and that can be made available only through collective action. We need the state to provide us with public goods. Only the state can ensure their secure supply, and the provision of infrastructure in its broadest sense often requires government action. Economic growth enables countries to provide more and better public goods. In this way, economic growth also leads to higher life satisfaction.

As we have already mentioned, Diener et al. find that emotional happiness depends positively on income, but the relationship is not as strong as that between income and life satisfaction. However, there is a strong relationship between emotional happiness and the extent to which psychological needs are met. It is plausible and logical that we will go through the day feeling better if we have the feeling that we have achieved something, that we have good friends, or that we are able to decide for ourselves what we want. And it is clear that such experiences arise even if we have less money and our society is poorer than others. This is in line with the interpretation set forth above. Emotional happiness can also be experienced by people in adverse conditions. But does that imply that it doesn't matter what our circumstances are? Hardly.

Two conclusions can be drawn. The first is that it doesn't make sense to use emotional happiness as a yardstick when we want to make decisions that will have long-lasting impacts on our lives. As we said, it is possible to be happy even under adverse conditions, but most people wouldn't choose adverse living conditions. The second conclusion also has immediate significance for policy. Suppose there are two societies with exactly equal per capita incomes and with the same conditions in all other respects. Does it follow that people in both societies necessarily have the same opportunity to have positive feelings? Obviously not. Rather, it depends on whether or not the conditions that prevail in a society are conducive to the formation of such feelings. What roles do solidarity, friendship, and a sense of community play? How well or how poorly do families function? How freely can an individual develop, and how much self-determination is allowed? These questions will be answered very differently by societies that are equally prosperous, and the answers have enormous influence on how much positive emotions people in a society can develop. A high income is helpful in developing positive feelings, but happiness research shows clearly that a person's emotional well-being depends above all on what the person *does* with this income. In what areas of life might state intervention help to create the conditions that might make people emotionally happier, and in what areas does state intervention tend to be damaging? Further investigation may be worthwhile.

Let us now summarize the last two chapters. Recent happiness research is based on better data than previous research, has a clear measuring concept, neatly separates the different dimensions of happiness, and thus has changed our views of people's happiness and of the importance of income and economic prosperity. The Easterlin Paradox is no longer tenable in its original form. The cases in which it turns out that more prosperity doesn't lead to higher life satisfaction have proved not to be the rule, but rather the exception, and it is necessary to find explanations for this. In the meantime, it can basically be considered as proven that a positive relationship exists between income and cognitive well-being. What remains from the findings of the older happiness research is the insight that relative position plays a significant role. It doesn't dominate, as Easterlin believed; however, it is important, and we still need to establish what its implications actually are. How are we to judge the importance of relative position? What are its implications for policy? We will turn to these questions in chapter 10.

First, we need deal with another question that is of considerable importance for interpreting happiness research. How do we deal with the fact that affective happiness only depends weakly on income, and what implications arise from it? So far, we have argued that it isn't a good idea to use affective happiness as a guide or signpost to the right way of life or the best blueprint for society, or to answer the question of whether economic growth is good or bad. We will provide more support for this argument in the next chapter by presenting our own research.

9
Unemployed and Happy?!

Unemployment makes you unhappy! There is probably no other result of happiness research for which there is anywhere nearly as much evidence or that is anywhere near as well founded. According to the data, unemployed people judge their lives unhappy even if the influences of income and health are removed. But it isn't only that the negative effects of unemployment can be seen in the unemployed people's responses in the relevant surveys. It is also that unemployment has destructive effects, and why that is the case is easy to understand. People define themselves by their work to a great extent. In a society based on the division of labor, people need to be employed to be integrated in society. Losing one's job means that one stops fending for oneself and becomes dependent on others. It doesn't help an unemployed person much to keep in mind that the slowdown in the economy or the structural change that swept his job away wasn't his fault. His self-esteem is still affected deeply. And so are the social contacts that arise through work. No, it really isn't surprising that the unemployed report considerably lower life satisfaction than the employed and that they don't get accustomed to being unemployed.

If we use the cognitive measure for happiness, the matter is clear. An unemployed person almost certainly will assess his life more negatively than someone who is employed. But does this mean the unemployed person spends his days feeling worse? At first glance this doesn't seem to be a particularly interesting question—if the life satisfaction of the unemployed is that much lower than that of the employed, then it should be clear that they also *feel* worse, and that they feel worse all day long. But the unemployed have something that people with jobs may well be envious of sometimes: a lot of time. Furthermore, they can use that time freely. That being employed may lead to higher life satisfaction doesn't necessarily mean that working is fun. Even a person with a difficult and unsatisfying job may have positive feelings about life, but nonetheless a person with such a job is likely to be happy when the workday is over.

Could it be that the negative effect of tiresome work and the positive effect of having free time available provides for an emotional compensation so that jobless people don't feel much worse than people with jobs? This is a question that can't be answered with the standard question of life-satisfaction research. To do this, we need a method with which affective well-being can be measured throughout the day. We have already become familiar with this in the Day Reconstruction Method (DRM), in which people write down what they did, and for how long, the preceding day, and are then asked what they felt during the individual activities. We used this method in 2008 to find out something about the affective happiness of the unemployed and the employed. (Also see Knabe et al. 2010.)

A more detailed description of how feelings people have during the course of a day can be measured, and what problems arise when doing this, may be useful. First, respondents are asked to recall the previous day and to prepare a kind of diary by making notes of all the activities that took place during their waking hours, who they were with at the time, and how long each activity lasted. They are then asked how intensely various positive and negative emotions were felt during each of the activities—for example, whether an activity was fun, or whether they felt happy during an activity, whether a meeting was pleasant, or whether the respondent was frustrated, depressed, annoyed, or sad. The intensity of each feeling was measured in a similar way to the measurement of life satisfaction: on a scale from 0 to 10, 0 meaning that the emotion wasn't felt at all and 10 meaning that it was felt very intensely.

Equipped with the measurements of each individual feeling, we can construct a measure that says something about the *experienced utility* resulting from an activity. In order to calculate the *net affect*, the difference between the average score of the positive emotions and the average score of the negative emotions is determined. That yields a number that says something about the emotional value of the activity. If we calculate the net affect for all the activities, weight the individual net affects with the fraction of the respondent's total waking time spent on that activity, and add them all up, we obtain a measure that says something about the respondent's average emotional state over the course of the day.

The net affect is a cardinal measure. Not only does it tell us whether one feeling is stronger or weaker than another; it also measures the distance between them, much as we can measure by how many centimeters one person is taller than another. This measure can then be used to make feelings directly measurable. But it has a weakness. Like every cardinal measure, it depends on the scale with which it is measured. When we measure a person's height in the metric system, we have all agreed on how long a meter is. Although all the respondents have the same eleven possibilities when they the put their marks on the scale from 0 to 10, what each individual associates with a score of, say, 5 or 7 is a personal matter. For example, Krueger et al. (2009) found that, when asked about their emotional well-being, American women tended to use the extremes of the scale more than French women did. That means that the scale used by respondents could be very different and that a direct comparison between different respondents is therefore no longer strictly possible. To avoid this weakness, an ordinal measure is needed—one that measures whether Mr. A is doing better or worse than Mr. B without having to measure how much better or worse he is doing. One such measure is the U-index, with U standing for unhappy or undesirable (Kahneman and Krueger 2006). In order to calculate the U-index, we consider only the activities in which a negative emotion received the highest score of all the emotions. The idea is that this will apply only to activities that really are experienced as very negative. It doesn't matter how much stronger the intensity reported on the scale is, or whether the answers for positive or negative emotions are mainly at the upper end of the scale or mainly the lower end. Only the ordinal comparison counts. The actual index consists of the proportion of time in a day spent on this unpleasant activity. For example, if someone was angry over a period of 2 hours (this being his strongest emotion during this episode) and he was in a good mood in the remaining 14 hours of a total of 16 waking hours, his U-index will be 1/8 or 0.125.

Of course, the U-index also has its weaknesses. One of them is that it depends on which emotions the researcher asks about. If, for instance, we ask whether the respondent felt ecstatic, rather than happy, the score for the positive emotion will be smaller and a negative emotion may receive the highest score. Mindful of this weakness, we used a third measure—one for which the necessary aggregation of positive and negative emotions isn't imposed from outside, but is carried out by the respondent himself. The respondents were asked to report how satisfied they were with each activity, and they could answer on the familiar scale from 0 to 10. This measure can be called *episode satisfaction*. As with the other two measures, the episode satisfaction of all the activities can be weighted with the respective proportion of time and then added up to yield a value that says something about the emotional satisfaction experienced during a day. We also asked the standard question of life-satisfaction research—that is, we asked the respondents for cognitive assessments of their lives. Thus, we had four measures in all: three for the emotional situation (what we have called affective happiness) and one for cognitive life satisfaction.

In addition, at the end of the survey we collected data on various demographic characteristics, including age, marital status, number of children, job satisfaction (if the respondent had a job), health status, and social contacts (how often the respondent sees relatives and friends).

In all, 1,054 people were interviewed, each interview lasting between 30 and 60 minutes. Of the respondents, 737 were either employed or unemployed without being engaged in any kind of "workfare" scheme. The rest were engaged in "workfare" measures and thus were neither unemployed nor in regular employment. In the discussion that follows, we limit ourselves to a comparison of the 366 full-time employed people with the 348 long-term unemployed people (who received "Unemployment Benefit II," the means-tested lower tier of unemployment benefits) in our sample. The unemployed were approached directly in local unemployment offices and asked whether they would be willing to participate in a survey. They received 10 euros as compensation. Employed people living in the same district were recruited by random selection from the telephone book. To our surprise, pre-tests carried out before the actual study showed that it wasn't advisable to offer 10 euros to the employed respondents, because they were then markedly less willing to participate. The employed clearly had a kind of intrinsic motivation to take part in a scientific survey which was then crowded out if they were paid to participate. Quite the reverse was true of the unemployed; they were more willing to participate if they received 10 euros. Recruiting more than 1,000 respondents was an arduous task. Only 15 percent of the unemployed who were approached agreed to participate. Of the employed people we called, 55 percent met the requirements for our target group (the other 45 percent were mainly pensioners). Of these, 20 percent were willing to be interviewed.

An initial rough comparison produces the following picture of our sample: On average, the unemployed get up an hour later than the employed. They are not as well educated as the employed. Their household income, which includes the incomes of other household members, is 890 euros a month, considerably less than the 2,974 euros a month that employed people have. Whereas the employed respondents performed 12.6 activities per day on average, the unemployed carried out 11.4.

The differences in life satisfaction between employed and unemployed respondents in our sample are in line with the standard findings of happiness economics. Those who have a job are considerably more satisfied than those who don't. On average, the employed respondents give their lives a score of 7.1 and are therefore more satisfied than dissatisfied. The unemployed respondents only reach a score of 4.6, and the difference is statistically significant.

But how do things look with affective happiness? If the individual activities are sorted according to their average episode satisfaction, we obtain almost identical rankings. At the top are leisure activities, such as entertainment or cultural activities, pursuing hobbies, playing sports, and spending time with friends. Listening to music, going for walks, and eating tend to produce pleasant feelings but are more middle ranking. Surprisingly, spending time with one's children is not one of the activities that gives a great deal of pleasure. With an average episode-satisfaction score of 7.47, spending time with one's children is ranked toward the lower end of the range of leisure activities. With a score of 8.53, it is the only activity that unemployed respondents feel more satisfied about than the employed. This may well be connected to the fact that the employed respondents report extremely low satisfaction scores for anything associated with work. Neither working itself and commuting to and from work is a source of enjoyment either. Housework receives a particularly poor assessment.

Having a job produces life satisfaction but it isn't much fun. Presumably looking after the children is less satisfying for employed people after they have spent a hard and less than joyous day at work than it is for people who are jobless.

Apart from child care, the list of rankings of activities for the employed and unemployed respondents are very similar and this still applies if the sorting takes place according to the U-index or the net affect. That raises the question of whether the three measures we have used to gauge affective happiness really lead to different results. Statistical analysis shows that episode satisfaction, the net affect, and the U-index are highly correlated with one another. Obviously all three measure the same thing and arrive at very similar, though not identical, results. Things look entirely different when we consider the relationship between these three measures and cognitive life satisfaction. It turns out here that only a relatively weak correlation exists. It is indeed the case that life satisfaction is completely different from affective happiness. This finding is in line with the findings we have reported from the literature. Quite different dimensions of happiness are being measured.

Let's return to the comparison of employed people with unemployed people. The ranking of activities is relatively similar, but that is the only thing they have in common. The two groups differ substantially in all other respects. In particular, it turns out that the unemployed respondents have considerably lower satisfaction scores than the employed for almost all the activities (apart from child care). No matter what they do, whether they read, get together with friends, or go for a walk, it is all a source of less enjoyment, less affective happiness, and less happiness than employed people experience while doing the same activities. Only watching television results in no difference, both groups feeling only moderate satisfaction (something that should give the producers of TV programs food for thought). Unemployment dampens positive emotions, producing a rather melancholic general mood that doesn't let people enjoy their lives as much. This finding is consistent with that of Krueger and Mueller (2012a,b), who also find that unemployment makes people sadder. We call this the *saddening effect* of unemployment. Krueger and Mueller (2012b) interpret the saddening effect as the emotional toll of unemployment that quickly fades away when someone finds a job.

The affective happiness that people feel throughout the day depends not only on how positively or negatively they experience each individual episode that day, but also on the duration of that episode. The most important difference between the two groups is, of course, that the employed spend an average of 6 hours and 32 minutes per workday on their work. On top of that comes the 40 minutes spent traveling to and from work. The unemployed can spend this total of more than 8 hours per workday on activities other than work. It should be clear that this will contribute to an enhancement of affective happiness, insofar as work doesn't produce any good feelings. It does indeed turn out that the unemployed fill these 8 hours with activities that have considerably better satisfaction scores than work, with one exception. Aside from one hour's more sleep (which doesn't count, since we are only investigating waking hours), they spend twice as much time on social contacts and on TV and games as the employed. Even child care, at 40 minutes, takes up twice as much time as for the working respondents, although this is relatively little relative to the 160 minutes spent in front of the TV. The one exception mentioned above is housework, which provides even less utility than paid employment. In spite of this, the unemployed spend an average of 3 hours and 12 minutes on it; the employed spend somewhat more than 2 hours on washing up, tidying up, and cleaning.

This means that, in addition to the saddening effect, which makes the unemployed unhappier, we have a *time-composition effect*, which acts in the opposite direction. The question is how much can this second effect compensate for the first. In order to get some information on this, we can isolate the time-composition effect with a small thought experiment. Imagine that someone who has a job becomes unemployed and immediately has the net affect values and the episode affect values of an unemployed person without changing his time composition (the value of his working hours will be maintained at his employed level). This will naturally lead to a decline in his affective well-being, which can be entirely attributed to the saddening effect. If we now subtract this saddening effect from the net affect of the whole day of the employed, the difference from the calculated net affect of the unemployed is the time-composition effect. This exercise can be carried out for all three affective measures. (See table 9.1.)

The results shown in the table are somewhat surprising. It really is possible for the time-composition effect to compensate for the saddening effect almost completely so that there is no statistically significant difference between the affective well-being of the employed and that of the unemployed.

The role of the time-composition effect can be demonstrated in yet another way. The interviews took place from Monday to Friday. Since the questions were about the preceding day in each case, Sunday and four of the five weekdays are included. Sunday represents a special case here—the time-composition effect doesn't play a role, since the employed can also freely decide how to use their time. If we examine the duration-weighted affective life satisfaction for this day only, it becomes apparent that the employed have significantly higher values than the unemployed. In the case of net affect this is even reversed on workdays.

Table 9.1
Saddening effect and time-composition effect.

	Life satisfaction	Net affect	U-index	Episode satisfaction
Employed	7.047	4.404	0.142	7.282
Saddening effect	—	-0.328	0.022	-0.153
Time-composition effect	—	0.496	-0.010	0.051
Unemployed	4.385	4.572	0.153	7.181
Difference	-2.689	0.168	0.011	-0.101

Source: Knabe et al. 2010

The difference between Sundays and workdays is particularly drastic in the case of the U-index for employed respondents: the U-index is 0.17 on workdays and 0.08 on Sundays. The unemployed, however, have a virtually unchanged U-index of about 0.16 on workdays and on Sundays. This result once again makes it clear how strong the negative effect of work is on affective happiness, since it is work that leads to the index that measures unhappiness being twice as high on workdays as it is on Sundays. Recently these findings were confirmed by von Scheve et al. (2013), who used recent SOEP data that also included questions about the emotional well-being.

Of course, we should take our result with a grain of salt. It may be that the DRM may lead to other results concerning the difference in the emotional well-being of the unemployed and the employed. Bylsma et al. (2011), for instance, compared the results from experience sampling with the results from the DRM for groups of depressed, mildly depressed, and nondepressed people; they found that all groups reported more negative and less positive feelings when assessed by experience sampling than with the DRM, and that these biases resulted in smaller group differences for the DRM than for experience sampling. Diener and Tay (2014) warn that the biased selection of feelings and the equal-unit time weighting we applied might affect the results. Nevertheless, our study shows very clearly that it makes an enormous difference whether we examine the cognitive dimension of happiness or its affective dimension, and it is thus fully in line with the conclusions of the Panel on Measuring Subjective Well-Being in a Policy-Relevant Framework (National Research Council 2013, p. 43). If we wanted to employ measures of happiness as a guide for making policy, the message from this finding would be rather ambivalent. On the basis of cognitive life satisfaction, there is much to suggest that considerable gains in welfare may be achieved by implementing policy measures that get people back to work. If we consider affective happiness, however, then there is no reason for such policies, since unemployed people are just as happy as employed people throughout the day.

And happiness research may have some even more drastic policy implications. If one is of the opinion that affective happiness is decisive, and concludes from this that income and growth don't play big parts in happiness, then it must be realized as a consequence of this that unemployment is only a minor problem. We don't draw this conclusion. Instead, we believe that affective happiness isn't a suitable guide for evaluating social conditions at all. People can still develop good feelings even under extremely bad conditions, but these good feelings can't be a justification for the bad conditions. That doesn't mean that we shouldn't pay any attention to affective happiness. It is quite possible that the opportunities to experience positive emotions are limited even under relatively comfortable conditions—that is, in a relatively rich society. If affective happiness is lower than it could be, there is a need for the individual, the family, or society at large to take action. On the other hand, that people are able to experience affective happiness doesn't mean that there is no need for action and that things are as they should be.

Life satisfaction depends not only on emotional well-being but also on meaning and purpose. Just summing up the pleasant moments may not lead to a satisfied life. There is therefore much to be said for using cognitive life satisfaction to evaluate living conditions and social circumstances. If we do that, what messages can we discern and how can we answer the question "How important are money, income, and economic prosperity?"

It is possible to discern two central messages. The first is that, despite the early findings of Easterlin and those who followed him, it can be regarded as certain that the absolute level of income plays an important role in people's life satisfaction. Economic growth and a general increase in the level of income have a positive effect in both poor countries and rich ones. Recent happiness research has shown that the Easterlin Paradox is largely a statistical artifact. Nevertheless, the debate centered around it has had two very beneficial effects. First, it has gained respectability for empirical life-satisfaction research. Today it is an integral part of economic discussion; it has even become part of the toolbox of economic policy advisors. None of this would have been possible without the irritation that the Easterlin Paradox caused.

The second central message that can be derived from the analysis of cognitive life satisfaction is also closely linked with the Easterlin Paradox. This message states that, in addition to the absolute income level, an individual's relative position is also of great importance for his life satisfaction. What are the policy implications of this message? Easterlin and his successors had in mind only the negative external effects that income gains must have if relative position is important. If someone increases his income, he may well improve his own relative position, but he simultaneously worsens the position of someone else. This immediately leads to the conclusion that income gains should be prevented because they don't achieve any good on balance. We no longer have to draw this radical conclusion if we recognize that an absolute income gain also confers an advantage. But what are the consequences of the importance of relative position? Is striving for a higher position in the income hierarchy really to be judged only negatively, or are there also positive aspects? Why are people so keen to aspire to relative heights?

The answers to these questions are important because, in the end, it is our aim to draw the right conclusions from happiness research. If all the efforts made to decode people's happiness are not to be in vain, we need to know exactly how to understand and interpret the findings of happiness research. As we will see in the next chapter, interpreting the finding that relative position is important isn't as straightforward as it might seem at first glance.

10
The Importance of Relative Position

It can't be denied that a person's relative position has considerable importance for his or her well-being. But why is that the case? Only when we can understand the reasons why the position people have relative to others is so important to them can we draw the right conclusions from the observations made by happiness researchers.

Let's imagine two people who are in the same situation. The first is interested only in his absolute income. He simply wants to earn as much money as possible. The second uses the income of his peer group as a guide and would like to improve his position relative to the others by earning more than they do and also more than he has earned himself in the previous year. Will these two people act differently? Probably not. Each will try very hard to achieve a higher income. From the point of view of the individual, aspiring to an absolute gain in income boils down to the same behavior as aspiring to an improvement in his own relative position. But the person striving for absolute income growth will become more satisfied as soon as his earnings rise, whereas the person pursuing a relative improvement will be satisfied only if all the others meet with less success. The difference results from the external effect that the income gain has if people care about their relative position.

We therefore have to go into quite some detail in our search for the reason for the importance of relative position. The line of argument we are going to present in this chapter will not be easy to follow, since it refers to very complex relationships. We will endeavor to explain them as simply as is possible, using mathematics only where it is necessary to do so.

The argument we are now going to present was developed in two highly respected papers by Rayo and Becker (2007a,b). The starting point for their considerations is the idea that using a reference point as a guide is not something that we learn but rather part of our genetic makeup.

Accepting this then raises the question of why evolution made sure that this gene prevailed. Is there some evolutionary advantage of being programmed to use some reference point as a guide? Does doing so enable a person to make better decisions, thereby increasing that person's likelihood of surviving and reproducing? Rayo and Becker claim precisely this.

At the beginning of their line of argument is the premise that nature doesn't really care whether we are happy or not. For nature, the pursuit of happiness is a means to an end. Nature's goal is to provide people with the tools they need to survive and pass on their genes to future generations. Here we encounter the "selfish gene." Development occurs by way of those genes that prevail against other genes surviving in the evolutionary process. The competition between rival hereditary characteristics is decided by which gene provides the best conditions for its own reproduction. Continuation of the species is the ultimate, decisive goal, and it is secured by natural selection, i.e., the survival of the fittest. The trick used by nature is to set things up in such a way that the things that make us happy are precisely those that are particularly advantageous for passing on our genes. How this works can be seen clearly in the sex drive and in the genetically determined love that parents have for their children. The first secures propagation of the genes; the latter secures parental care. But why should it follow that the process of evolution has equipped us with a genetically determined orientation to a reference point or benchmark?

We need to imagine that there is a mechanism that ensures that a feeling of happiness is assigned to each stimulus we perceive. For example, a parent who gives one of his or her small children a hug is rewarded with happiness, and that happiness increases the parent's willingness to do everything to protect the child and bring it up. According to Rayo and Becker, this can be seen as a *happiness function* in a mathematical sense. Mathematical functions assign elements of one set to elements of another set. The happiness function assigns to every stimulus a corresponding feeling of happiness. Rayo and Becker show that this happiness function must use a reference level because of two characteristics of the human nervous system. The first is that the nervous system possesses only limited sensitivity, as we have already mentioned in connection with the Weber-Fechner Law. This limited sensitivity means that we can't perceive small differences in happiness. If, for instance, your annual salary rises by 100 euros, you aren't sensitive enough to feel the rise in happiness that results. On its own, this characteristic wouldn't be problematic. Evolution could simply modify the perception of happiness by making it more sensitive. For example, it could multiply our happiness perception by a sufficiently large factor so that the resulting difference would be noticeable. Unfortunately, the second characteristic of our nervous system stands in the way of this, as Rayo and Becker point out. Our perception has an upper limit and a lower limit. The intensity of a sensation we perceive depends on the frequency of the electrical impulses our nerve cells produce. And this frequency is limited by chemical processes (that is, by the refractory period—the amount of time it takes for a cell to be ready for a second stimulus once it returns to its resting state after excitation). We can't feel happiness at any old intensity, although that in itself wouldn't be problematic either. Nature could have made sure that the intensity of feeling of every possible stimulus were divided by a sufficiently large factor so that all intensities of feeling would be in the interval that our nervous system can deal with.

Together, the two limitations of our nervous system mentioned above result in a dilemma. We can't react to environmental influences very sensitively and, at the same time, do so across an arbitrarily large bandwidth. Or, to put it mathematically, it isn't possible to secure the perceptibility of a sensation by multiplying its intensity and simultaneously to ensure that it fits in an interval that we can perceive at all by using division. This means that either we have to reduce our sensitivity so far that we can no longer distinguish between two adjacent states—and are therefore not able to determine our maximum happiness precisely—or we can assign different emotions only to a small range of all possible states. In this situation, nature makes use of a trick. Instead of trying to equip us with an emotional system that can evaluate all possible states in this world, it provides us with one that specialized in evaluating highly probable states. And this leads us to the reference point.

Let's go back for a moment to the time when our ancestors were hunters and gatherers, since a great deal of our genetic predisposition originated from that time. A hunter's ability to gauge his hunting performance correctly was of great importance for his survival, because only by gauging his performance correctly could he optimize his hunting behavior. A comparison with other hunters would help him assess whether an unsuccessful hunt was due to his having done something wrong or due to the presence of fewer animals that day. Using previous hunting successes as a guide would make similar sense, since it would allow the hunter to accurately assess his own potential and he could, in this way, gain an idea of what could be expected under normal circumstances. Remaining below his capacity would be an indication to the hunter that he should change his behavior. Employing the reference point as a guide would enable the hunter to improve his hunting behavior and secure his own survival and the survival of his offspring.

We (most of us, anyway) no longer roam through the forests in search of food. We secure our survival by earning income, and the hypothesis forming the basis of the evolutionary explanations of human behavior implies that we continue to be under the control of the genetic predisposition that was put in place when "survival of the fittest" was still to be taken very literally. We still use external and internal benchmarks to assess our own potential. However, we don't use them in relation to hunting success, but rather in relation to income (among other things).

If you ask yourself "How much will I probably earn this year?" you probably will use your income in the previous year and the earnings of others around you as guides. Our happiness function is designed in such a way that it is based on these two possible reference points. There is no point in thinking about how we would feel if we had Bernie Ecclestone's income, and we don't need to concern ourselves with what would happen if our earnings plummeted to the level of that of a poor Somali. We will become neither as rich as Bernie Ecclestone nor as poor as a Somali. By concentrating on what is *likely*, we can have a happiness function that complies with the limits of our nervous system and, at the same time, puts us in the position of being able to define our happiness maximum free of doubt and ambiguity.

Our happiness function supplies us with relative values by assessing situations relative to reference points. Rayo and Becker refer to an analogy that makes it clear that this is a reasonable procedure: Our eyes supply our brains with relative information by using the difference in brightness between the center and the edge of our field of vision in order to adjust the eyes' sensitivity to light. It is possible in this way to adapt the sensitivity optimally, since only the brightness that is relevant need be taken into account. We notice that our eyes work this way only when we go from bright surroundings into dark surroundings. At first we can't recognize much; our eyes can't register the difference in brightness in the room, because they are still adjusted to the brighter surroundings. The eyes must have adapted and must have a new reference point before the differences in the surroundings can be perceived.

The theory of Rayo and Becker provides a completely new perspective on the question why people use reference points as a guide and why they attach such importance to relative positions. People don't aspire to higher positions because they want to rise above others and because they can gain approval and happiness from this relative strength; they do so because using others as an orientation is a rational strategy for making better decisions for themselves. Reference points merely serve as a guide to finding the best path to one's own happiness. And so the observations from the early days of happiness research also take on new significance. If, for instance, a person's income rises, then, gauged against the old reference point, this is an improvement, which is then reflected in a higher score on the scale that measures life satisfaction. At the same time, this scale changes because the new, higher income is now its new reference point. Consequently, the score for life satisfaction falls back to its old value in the next survey. At first sight, this looks as if some form of adaptation has taken place and the person has become accustomed to the new income level. It could in fact be the case that the scale with which we measure happiness has merely changed. The situation in which the general income level rises—say, as a result of overall growth in the economy—is very similar. In this case, the external reference point rises along with the increase in one's own income, resulting in a direct shift in the scale. The fact that reported life-satisfaction scores don't change with an increase in income is therefore no longer a paradox, but instead a direct result of our innate method of measuring our happiness.

Rayo and Becker's line of reasoning is based on the physiological limits of our perception. We must be a little careful with this. These limits apply to directly perceived feelings and sensations. With regard to the definition of happiness that we have used so far, they apply above all to affective happiness. We may have the feeling we are bursting with happiness one moment, but we remain in one piece because the feeling at this point can't go any further. But this limit doesn't necessarily say anything about any possible limit to our cognitive assessment of well-being that shows up in the measures of life satisfaction! The analogy with our eyes helps here too. Their adaptability enables us to see well in bright and dark surroundings. But this ability doesn't mean that we can't distinguish between bright rooms and dark rooms, and still less that we prefer brighter surroundings to darker surroundings when we use our sight. Padoa-Schioppa (2009) has found that the same system of neuronal adaption that regulates the visual system in the brain is at work in the valuation system. This means that after the scale has also been adjusted—which comes very close to an adaptation—it can't be concluded that our life satisfaction both before and after the adaptation must be the same. The different levels could be of great importance.

This argument can also be formulated as follows: People judge their happiness relative to their happiness potential. They estimate the level of this potential on the basis of their past and their surroundings, i.e., by comparison with reference points. Whether someone is lucky and therefore has a reason to feel happy depends upon how well he can exploit his potential. If he is very lucky, he could with fortunate circumstances even go beyond his potential. It is therefore not surprising that in most languages there is only one word for luck and happiness. In German, for instance, the word is *Glück*. A person can have *Glück* (be in luck) because an advantageous incident occurs (in a lottery, in roulette, or at a race track), or he can find his *Glück* (find happiness) by living a satisfying life. Rayo and Becker show that luck and happiness belong together because variations from one's own potential are, in the final analysis, chance events, or shocks, whose influence is only fleeting. In the end, it all depends on the potential a person possesses, because this decides at what level he is when determining his position relative to others. In other words, it makes a difference whether I compare myself with other homeless beggars or with the members of my golf club.

If we think the theory of Rayo and Becker through, we have no choice but to call into question the measurement of happiness and its suitability as a criterion for judging alternative conditions. In the end, Rayo and Becker's explanation of relative position implies that we can't compare happiness between different people or at different points in time. Even before Rayo and Becker it was clear to happiness researchers that it is very difficult, if not impossible, to make comparisons between different people. One can't say that two people are equally satisfied or equally happy just because they mark the same score (say, a 7) on a scale of 0 to 10, since each of them defines for himself what a 7 on the scale means for him. That is why happiness research focuses on panel data, which always come from surveys of the same people. Comparing different people is no longer necessary, since it is possible to compare the life satisfaction of the same people at different times. Comparing happiness levels of the same person over time had been considered unproblematic until Rayo and Becker came along. But according to Rayo and Becker, this isn't possible either, for the following reason. In much the same way that a 7 marked by Ms. A may mean something different from a 7 marked by Mr. B, Ms. A's 7 in the year 2000 doesn't mean the same thing as her 7 in the year 2013. If the reference point has changed in the thirteen years between the surveys, the scale Ms. A uses in 2013 is entirely different from the one she used in 2000. This means that comparisons between the two years are just as inadmissible as comparisons between the two individuals.

This concern is behind one of the major criticisms of subjective well-being measures made by proponents of the capability approach.

Depending on their life circumstances, people may engage in redefining their reference level in order to sustain a minimum of life satisfaction. This is exemplified in a famous passage by Amartya Sen (1990, p. 45):

> A thoroughly deprived person, leading a very reduced life, might not appear to be badly off in terms of the mental metric of utility, if the hardship is accepted with non-grumbling resignation. In situations of longstanding deprivation, the victims do not go on weeping all the time, and very often make great efforts to take pleasure in small mercies and cut down personal desires to modest—"realistic"—proportions. The person's deprivation then, may not at all show up in the metrics of pleasure, desire fulfillment, etc., even though he or she may be quite unable to be adequately nourished, decently clothed, minimally educated and so on.

In a situation such as that described by Sen, one might redefine the lower bound of the scale. For the upper bound, a group of researchers led by the Dutch economist Bernard van Praag found a reference shift. They simply asked people what levels of income they would call good, sufficient, insufficient, or bad. It turned out that as the incomes of the people they asked rose, the borders of these categories shifted upward. As we mentioned in chapter 3, van Praag and Frijters (1999) estimate that an increase in income of one euro leads to a 60-euro-cent rise in the internal reference income. Hence, we expect to need more money in order to reach the best possible life, which in turn implies that the upper bound of the life-satisfaction scale shifts upwards. A shift in the two boundaries of the frame of reference thus provides an additional explanation for the observations that form the basis of the Easterlin Paradox. To give a simple example concerning income changes, let us again consider Ms. A. She may well earn more in 2013 than she earned in 2000; however, if everyone around her has enjoyed an even greater increase in income, her position relative to the others is worse in 2013 than it was in 2000, and she will rate her quality of life lower when she uses the scale appropriate to her situation in 2013. That doesn't mean that she would prefer her situation thirteen years earlier to her current situation. It merely means that she has adapted her frame of reference so as to be able to make decisions in her best interest in the new situation. There is no room for a paradox in this interpretation and the question arises what sense a comparison between two points in time could make at all.

Rayo and Becker's theory is based on the supposition that the way we perceive our happiness is genetically determined and that it has proved advantageous in the evolutionary process to use a reference point as an orientation. It is the individual who benefits from this process. One is more likely to survive if one sticks to the relative values, and one will also be more successful in passing on his genes to later generations if one does this. A genome type will prevail only if it possesses these characteristics.

We would like to support the theory of Rayo and Becker with another argument, which, on the one hand, further supports the thesis that relative valuations win out and, on the other hand, allows us to view this pursuit of improvements in our relative position from another perspective. In essence, the argument says that it isn't beneficial only to the *individual* to use reference points as a guide—that the *group* also can benefit.

The competition for better relative positions (that is, for "positional goods") has gained a bad reputation. It tends to enjoy greatest acceptance in sports. There is always only one winner in the 100-meter sprint, and if one of the runners moves forward into first place then the previous leader falls back into second. One person winning always means another person losing. It is typical of every positional competition that the efforts made by the individual seem to be wasted efforts from the point of view of the group. No matter how things look at the finish line of the 100-meter sprint, it could also have been reached if all the runners had run half as fast. If everyone has a gentle jog to the finish line, no one needs to make an effort.

Carrying this over to everyday life commonly leads to the conclusion that positional competition is a bad thing. We battle for more money in order to climb up the pecking order, but our gain is another person's loss. As a group, we gain nothing from this competition. In economic terms, every person who goes up the hierarchy causes a negative external effect for the other person. The existence of this effect is what led Richard Layard, Richard Easterlin, and others to deduce from happiness research that it is better to prevent people from aspiring to earn more and consume more.

Perhaps we should take a moment to ask why people don't object to positional competition in sports. On the contrary, we organize huge spectacles around such competition, and sit spellbound in front of the TV waiting to see who is the fastest in the 100 meters at the Olympic Games or what country wins the World Cup in soccer. Of course, we are particularly interested in the places on the ladder or the medal tally—in other words, how the relative order looks at the end of the competition. But often we are interested in the absolute level of performance. Bob Beamon was renowned because of his victory in the 1968 Olympic Games but even more so for his unbelievably long jump. Clearly people are delighted with such positional competition and see nothing wrong in it. Could it be the case that this is linked to positive external effects generated if such competitions cause the general level of achievements of all participants to rise?

Apart from the record holder, no one gains anything when the 100-meter world record is broken—so where is the external effect? It becomes obvious if we leave the sports analogy behind and think of other contexts in which relative positions people have are important. Human societies almost always have a hierarchical structure. Some people have leadership positions, others don't. It wouldn't have been different in the early societies in which our evolution took place. There would have been leaders, and it would have been extremely important for the survival of the clan that they be high-quality leaders. They had to be good hunters and be wise and courageous in order to be able to defend their own group against others, and much more. Imagine a group of people whose members aren't interested in rising to the top of the hierarchy and who don't care about their position relative to the others. There would be no competition for the leadership positions in such populations, and so there wouldn't be a selection process to ensure that the best and most efficient take over the leadership. Would such a population have a chance of succeeding in a fight to get leadership in a contest against a population in which there is positional competition? Probably not. The focus on one's own relative position is inevitably linked to the presence of positional competition. But this competition can also have positive effects for those who are unsuccessful and land at the bottom of the hierarchy, because it ensures that leading the clan is left to those who are competent.

It wasn't only leadership positions in prehistoric societies that were subject to positional competition. Such competition has, of course, existed through the ages, and when we look at the behavior of modern politicians it quickly becomes clear that it still takes place today every day wherever power and domination are at play. But not only there. Such competition can be encountered throughout society. The number of tenured professorial positions is limited, and the fierce competition for them is a contest for status and position. The hierarchical order in companies, in hospitals, in public authorities, in government offices, and in non-government organizations provokes positional competition at all points. Market competition has positional elements too, since the success of one must be accompanied by the lack of success of another in markets that are no longer growing.

Competition has many positive attributes. It releases energy, it provides creative challenges, and, not least, it leads competitors to keep each other's power in check. Thanks to competition, suppliers on goods markets can't exploit consumers. Those who hold power in society have to perform well to justify keeping their position; otherwise competition will drive them out. Positional competitions are often fought, the rivals having to prove themselves with their performance. The fighting rivals' actions often not only benefit themselves, but are also beneficial to others. Positional competitions that involve position and nothing else are extremely rare—most have been shifted to the sporting world. Political leaders have to make wise decisions that will benefit society, or they will lose their high position in the hierarchy. A scientist must be a successful researcher if he wants to get a professorship. An executive has to see to it that his company manufactures good products at competitive prices or else he will lose his leadership position.

Ultimately all such competitions have one thing in common: They show that positional competition changes not only our relative position but also the competitors' absolute levels. Without the immense forces that such competitions unleash, neither the scientific progress nor the economic growth of the nineteenth and twentieth centuries would have been conceivable. Both have put the vast majority of the world's people in a position of being able to live better lives. They have allowed people to live longer and protect themselves against existential risks. They provide them with leisure time they can spend with their children and friends. Economic growth and scientific progress provide people with better food, better health, better and more satisfying work, and all the ingredients people need to lead a meaningful, contented life. (See, for instance, Smith et al. 2005.)

At this point we have come full circle. We have shown in the last few chapters that the absolute income level is just as important for life satisfaction as relative position. Now it turns out that nature has managed to miraculously link the two. One is of use to the other. Aspiring to the highest possible relative position undoubtedly has negative external effects as a consequence. But as soon as this competition is decided by accomplishments that also are of use to others, a positive external effect also arises, and it can't be ruled out that this serves the purpose of survival. If this is true, then we shouldn't be surprised that we feel the urge to "rise to the top," and we shouldn't, therefore, accept criticism from anyone for this.

11
Conclusion

Forty years ago, research into the economics of happiness set out to find out what makes people happy. After so much time spent on searching and researching, one would think it would be easy to give a clear and unambiguous answer to this question. This applies all the more in light of the ever-increasing intensity with which this search has been carried out. At the end of the book the reader might, therefore, expect us to tell him quite clearly what makes people happy. Unfortunately, we can't fulfill that expectation completely. Gaps and doubts remain. And, as is right and proper for scientists, we must name the doubts and mustn't disregard them.

Can one really expect clear and simple answers to the question of what makes us happy? If there are easy answers, why are people still searching and why is the preoccupation with this question so popular? Such a high and unrealistic expectation of finding such answers can only lead to disappointment.

Despite all that, we can claim that we know a lot more and can see some things more clearly at the end of the book than at the beginning. Some doubts remain, though. First, it was apparent from the beginning of happiness research that it would never be feasible to compare the happiness of two different people. This was clear because happiness is quintessentially something personal, subjective, and private that simply doesn't lend itself to being measured by a standard. Second, we haven't progressed any further toward being able to compare happiness or life satisfaction at different points in time. Such comparisons once seemed practicable if data on the same individual were used. Even when that was done, however, it couldn't be guaranteed that the same scale was being used during measurement. But only when the same scale is used can meaningful statements be made about how someone's happiness has changed. There is much to suggest that the scale a person uses to gauge his or her life satisfaction changes over time. If it does change, however, then scoring the same number twice doesn't mean that the person who reported that number at the two different times felt exactly the same at both times.

Rayo and Becker point out that there are boundaries to our feelings. We can perceive happiness only up to a certain limit, and happily the same also applies to our unhappiness. But the physiological limitations mainly affect affective happiness, which is pure emotion. The fact that we reach a limit with this cannot serve as an argument for saying that we aren't able to go beyond a certain level of life satisfaction, either. Whether we are able to raise our life satisfaction in the course of time or in the course of continuously growing prosperity must, ultimately, remain an open question, because we can't really compare our life satisfaction today with that of twenty years ago.

Although a clear answer isn't possible, we have gathered in this book a number of indicators that allow us to put together a picture that, in all likelihood, comes close to reality. We can be pretty certain that relative positions are important for people. We can also say that it isn't a good idea to conclude that competition for relatively good positions in society should be prevented or restricted. If it really is the case that our genes predispose us to participate in positional competitions, then a great deal of force would be necessary to prevent us from striving for relative improvements—if that could be done at all. What would probably happen if status competition in one life domain (e.g. income) is reduced is that people more strongly engage in status competition in other life domains (e.g. leisure, education, beauty). Wasn't it in socialist states that the party career took the place of economic success when the latter was no longer politically desirable?

Such a shift is not a good idea, if only because it would lead to the levels of absolute income and general income increasing less than they potentially could. But absolute income is a major factor in our life satisfaction. It doesn't make much sense to deny this in light of the data available today.

Money makes us happy because it enables us to afford the things that are important for a high quality of life and high life satisfaction. A high income gives us the opportunity to live more healthily and to better educate, clothe, and feed ourselves, as well as to live more comfortably and to live well. On a social level, income provides us with financial security, not least because it allows financing more generous welfare systems. Economic growth provides the community with the capacities it needs to open the door to all the possibilities modern society can offer individuals, allowing them to participate in learning and in living a secure life with cultural diversity and a functioning health system. The existence of all these things can be shown to raise people's life satisfaction. The fact that a positive correlation between rising income and life satisfaction still seems to exist even in relatively long time series underlines this. And this isn't called into question by the observation that this relationship becomes weaker the longer these time series are. The reason for this is now clear: As we have seen, the meaning of the scale shifts if income rises over a long period of time because people are forced to confine their answers to a finite range. It is therefore not surprising that an increase in reported life satisfaction can't be detected over long periods, even with better data. It shouldn't be concluded, though, that people don't feel better off.

This consideration doesn't change the fact that we probably grossly underestimate the positive influence of rising income because of the unavoidable measuring problem described above. At this point it should again be noted that human life expectancy plays a very important role in this context. Its increase can be attributed to rising prosperity, the improved living conditions that prosperity brings, and the progress in medicine that economic growth makes possible. If this were the only positive effect of economic growth, it alone would be sufficient reason for the positive effect of such growth on people's life satisfaction and happiness. It is as clear as day that a person's happiness shouldn't be understood as a condition in a given period of time, but as a stream of life satisfaction that he experiences in the course of his life. It is, therefore, of major importance for people's happiness how long this stream flows.

Let's make it clear at this point what it would mean if we claimed that raising income wouldn't have any effect on our life satisfaction. It would imply that *how long* we live and *how* we live, both of which are determined by our income to a great extent, would be of no importance for our happiness in life. That is exceedingly difficult to believe, and the findings we have amassed show that it probably isn't the case.

What other findings can we present at the end of our journey through happiness research? One important finding is that we have to distinguish very carefully between life satisfaction and affective happiness. Our feelings are not a good indicator of how good or bad our life situation is. For this reason, we should be very cautious about policy recommendations made on the basis of measurements of affective happiness. On the other hand, we shouldn't declare happiness to be an exclusively private matter. It is highly possible that the extent to which "pleasant feelings" are experienced in a person's life also depend on how the society in which the person lives functions. We admittedly know very little about these relationships, and at this point we would warn against being too hasty in assigning the task of increasing affective well-being to the state. There is much to suggest that affective happiness is primarily our own responsibility and that it should remain that way. Our considerations have shown that asking happiness research to supply a blueprint for a society that makes people as satisfied as they could possibly be is asking too much of it. The data that are available to happiness researchers can deliver only imperfect measures of the individual aspects of human life. Basing binding policy recommendations on such data would make just as little sense as ignoring the information that happiness research provides. We obtain some further important pieces of the happiness puzzle when we conduct research on the determinants of both life satisfaction and affective happiness. But so far we have only a vague ideas where to fit these pieces into the overall picture.

Right from the beginning of happiness research, and increasingly as the Easterlin Paradox has become more popular, there has been an expectation that very strong recommendations for shaping policy could be inferred from such research. Some saw happiness research as opening up a new way of justifying actions of the state by seeming to provide evidence that we—the people living in our societies—don't know what to do with freedom: We use it to enter into pointless competitions for positional goods, and end up on a treadmill from which we can be rescued only if well-meaning planners force us to get off.

If recent happiness research can provide us with a clear message, it is that this view can't be sustained. In view of everything we know today, using happiness research as a normative concept to deduce how things should be is highly questionable. The limitations and doubts we described at the beginning of this conclusion, and more recent empirical results, indicate that happiness research is of no use as a normative concept. In the end, it fails because of the incomparability of people's feeling of happiness. This incomparability can be perceived either as problematic or as an expression of the uniqueness of every one of us. We tend toward the latter view.

Appendix

This appendix differs for the main text principally in that it is considerably more scientific. Though in the main text we dealt with a great deal of scientific literature and made use of scientific methodology based on facts and empirical findings, we attempted to describe things in a way that was easy to understand and didn't require any previous knowledge. We hope that the appendix is also written in an understandable style. However, because it addresses specific scientific issues, it is more difficult to understand.

We attempt here to place happiness research into the overall context of economics research by throwing a little light on the history of economic thought, and by showing why economists wanted to know nothing of happiness research for so long and how they integrate it into economics research today. This isn't absolutely necessary for an understanding of the findings of happiness research, but the story behind actual happiness research simply seemed too interesting and exciting for us not to write it down. Perhaps it will help some readers to gain an even deeper understanding of the science of happiness.

This appendix can be thought of as a little book within the larger book. It can be read quite independently of the main text. Conversely, it isn't necessary to read the appendix to understand the main text.

The Expulsion of Happiness: More Is Better Than Less

The first economists who dealt with happiness research in the 1970s had a tough time. The profession wasn't willing to deal with data purporting to measure such a thing as happiness or life satisfaction. For an outsider, this dismissive stance may be difficult to understand. Shouldn't it be an important goal of economic analysis to find out what human welfare actually depends on? After all, it is the goal of economic research to find ways and means to improve precisely this welfare. This skepticism toward happiness research, which is still virulent today, is only understandable if we dip into the history of economic thought and realize how far removed economics is from the idea of somehow being able to measure human happiness or the utility people derive from their consumption of goods and in this way make them accessible to empirical research.

At the beginning of the development of the science of economics was the philosophy that saw the pursuit of happiness as the ultimate goal of human activity. For Jeremy Bentham (1742–1832), the founder of classical utilitarianism, and John Stuart Mill (1806–1873), who combined utilitarianism with classical economics in the nineteenth century, this pursuit was synonymous with pursuing pleasure and avoiding pain. Combining this notion with methodological individualism, which requires that all scientific explanations be derived from intentional states of individual actors, and with the utilitarian notion that the prosperity of a nation can be attributed alone to the utility of an individual member of society results in an economic program that equates the maximization of social welfare with the happiness of all individuals. Jeremy Bentham's famous statement that "it is the greatest happiness of the greatest number that is the measure of right or wrong" expresses this succinctly. Utility maximization is then identical to "happiness maximization." In order for this to become an operational program, it must all be combined with the notion of measuring utility with an objective scale and comparing it intersubjectively. If we redistribute income, for example, then we take a little from one person, thereby reducing his happiness, and give it to another, whose happiness we raise. We only attain our greatest happiness if it is known how much happiness income can generate and this, in turn, presupposes the existence of an objective scale of happiness. This methodological consequence is what has given the classical program of happiness maximization a bad name, for how should such a scale be found and what reasons could be used to back it up?

Utility is just like happiness in that it is an intensely subjective and individual matter. What makes one person happy can leave another cold, and the extent of happiness that someone feels is hard to measure, even for the individual—at least if it is to occur in a consistent way so as to provide values of happiness that can also be compared over time. How can we succeed in comparing the feeling of happiness of two people and make an objectively (i.e., intersubjectively) verifiable decision about how far apart they are from each other in terms of units of happiness? The danger is obvious: Since this isn't possible, every attempt to make an "objective" measurement must contain a more or less sizable amount of arbitrariness. Arbitrariness in measurements of utility is only a precursor to arbitrary decisions of every kind. Once we allow statements about the social preferability of allocation and distribution issues to be made on the basis of arbitrary assessments, then the floodgates are opened to the same arbitrariness in decisions concerning resource allocation and income distribution.

At the end of the nineteenth century and at the beginning of the twentieth, economics was struggling for recognition as a serious and separate academic discipline, with setting itself apart from philosophy and psychology being the main aim. This involved the young discipline finding a subject area to which it could exclusively lay claim while establishing a methodology that would help it to keep pace with the aspiring modern scientific and technical disciplines. A methodological basis fostering arbitrariness couldn't possibly be in the interests of the profession.

The transition to the twentieth century marked the historical end of classical economics and the beginning of the neoclassical age. Classical economists didn't consider utility and its measurability in much detail, since it was of little importance to them. They didn't try to derive the value that things had from the utility that these things generated, but from the things themselves. Supporters of the theory of objective value helped themselves to the labor theory of value or natural law philosophy to obtain a value of goods independent of their utility. With the advent of neoclassicism, the objective-value theory was superseded by the subjective-value theory, which was based on the premise that the value of a good depends solely on the utility it generates and on its scarcity. The theory of subjective value established itself quickly because it could easily explain many phenomena that were in total contradiction to the postulates of the theory of objective value. The classic example of this is the renowned *paradox of value* that arises in a comparison of water and diamonds. Water is a good that has a high objective value for people (because all people need this good to be able to exist), but which can in normal circumstances be purchased at a low price. A diamond, in contrast, fetches an extremely high price although everyone is able to enjoy life without diamonds. Objective value theory attempted to explain the difference between the utility of goods and their price with the objective aspects of producing the goods, such as the quantity of labor necessary to manufacture a good. The water-diamond example shows, however, that this succeeds only up to a point, since although more labor has to be invested to produce the diamond than the water, the extreme difference in price can't be explained by this alone. In addition, it doesn't seem particularly plausible that the price of a good should be completely independent of the utility it generates.

The subjective theory of value can relatively easily explain the prices for water and diamonds since they needn't only be deduced from the objective characteristics of a good (how many resources are needed to produce the good), but also from the subjective valuation of diamonds and their extreme scarcity, as well as from the virtually unlimited availability of water. Wherever water is scarce, its price rises, and beyond a certain level of water scarcity every diamond owner would be willing to exchange his stone for some water. It is precisely this connection that is captured by marginal considerations, the central element of the subjective theory of value.

With the arrival of the subjective theory of value, utility became a central idea of economics. Some of the first exponents of this new economics (neoclassical), including Francis Ysidro Edgeworth (1845–1926) and William Stanley Jevons (1835–1882), stood methodologically very close to psychology, as Bruni and Sugden (2007) show. The break between classical economics and neoclassical economics didn't, therefore, consist of a turning away from psychology, but was in fact connected with a certain convergence of the two disciplines. The starting point of the economic analysis of Edgeworth and Jevons was the assumption that an individual's action ultimately serves solely to satisfy his own interests. Self-interest is the most prominent characteristic of the economic human. In Edgeworth's own words (as quoted on page 150 of Bruni and Sugden 2007): "The first principle of economics is that every agent is actuated only by self-interest."

If human behavior involves only the satisfaction of one's own wants, the first question that comes to mind is "What is the nature of these wants?" The recourse to methods of psychology was therefore, from the point of view of the early neoclassical economists, only logical. Introspection was generally accepted as a scientific method for gaining psychological knowledge and was considered a legitimate instrument with which to obtain information on the sources of pleasure and pain. And the early neoclassical economists were convinced that it was precisely this that had to be involved, since human want consists of the pursuit of pleasure and the avoidance of pain, and thus, in the end, consists of the pursuit of happiness.

An important implication of the dependence on psychology was that there was a generic relationship between the consumption of goods or, more generally, supplying stimuli and feeling happiness. The more often a stimulus is perceived, or the more often a commodity is consumed, the weaker is the sensation produced by the stimulus. To put it simply, as the consumption of any commodity increases, the utility resulting from each further, or marginal, unit of consumption of that commodity diminishes. The real discoverer of this relationship was a German, Hermann Heinrich Gossen (1810–1858), and the relationship has come to be called Gossen's First Law. It is no exaggeration to call Gossen one of the most important forerunners of neoclassical economics, although in his lifetime he remained almost completely unnoticed. Later he was discovered by some neoclassical authors; however, a search for his name in modern economics textbooks would be in vain. Gossen's First Law describes a psychologically based, empirically verifiable relationship between the consumption of goods and the "happiness" a consumer feels. Statements of this kind have been banished from modern economics as far as possible. They are the object of psychological research and are more recently being intensively studied by the neurosciences once again. But the discussion of what factors are responsible for people's happiness has been removed from books on economics for more than half a century and is only slowly returning to a few selected areas with the advent of the discussion on empirical life satisfaction.

In the middle of the nineteenth century there was a development within psychology that gave the ideas of Edgeworth and Jevons a considerable boost. In 1860, Elements of Psychophysics, a two-volume work by Gustav Theodor Fechner (1801–1887), was published. To this day it is considered to be the foundation of modern psychology, since it describes a method with which it is possible to make quantitative statements on feelings and sensations for the first time. The starting point of this was the observation by the physiologist Ernst-Heinrich Weber (1795–1878) that changes in sensations are noticed only if they exceed certain sensory thresholds. The Weber-Fechner Law describes the functional relationship between the intensity of a stimulus and the resulting sensation it produces and states that the perceived intensity of a stimulus increases logarithmically with the intensity of the stimulus. And so a stimulus has to increase more and more in order to produce a constant increase in the perceived sensation.

Weber and Fechner paved the way for objective, quasi-scientific measurement of utility and happiness. Edgeworth probably was aware of this when he titled his main work *Mathematical Psychics*. That title expressed his basic attitude toward the measurement of utility and happiness. In principle, it should be possible to measure the perceived utility of every individual and compare it with that of other people. Explicitly referring to Fechner's work, Edgeworth suggests that the idea of utility as a decisive quantity guiding people's actions can be transformed into a concept in which differences in utility can be measured exactly and compared between individuals. And he went further, propagating two empirical regularities of perceived utility, for which he also cited psychological evidence. (See Bruni and Sugden 2007.) The first regularity is the diminishing marginal utility we already met in Gossen's First Law. From a present-day perspective, the second is much more interesting.

Edgeworth assumed not only that the additional utility that can be gained from a further unit of consumption diminishes with consumption, but also that this consumption results in a reduced ability to derive utility from future consumption. This idea is especially interesting from our present-day viewpoint because, although it doesn't have a particular role to play in neoclassical economics, it plays an important part in modern research into the economics of happiness. As we will see, there is some reason to believe that the happiness people experience from consumption is path dependent—that is, it depends on what was previously consumed.

Edgeworth's ideas are therefore remarkably relevant from today's point of view—even if more from neurological and psychological perspectives than from the viewpoint of economics. This is because the majority of economists today are not interested in the question of how and why perceived utility changes or why things generate utility at all. Present-day economists politely refer such questions to their colleagues in psychology and declare that this is outside their area of competence. The reason for this is the fact that Edgeworth's stance could not prevail over a line of research that is inseparably associated with Vilfredo Pareto (1848–1923).

No other neoclassical economist has left such a lasting and fundamental impression on the development of economics in the twentieth century as Pareto. His fundamental influence is still evident today, and the prominent position economic research has taken in the social sciences owes much to this influence. Put simply, Pareto's research program, written and largely brought forward by Pareto himself, effectively cut economics off from psychology and sociology and brought mathematical analysis to the fore along the lines of the role it played in the natural sciences. And so the discipline, born in the Scottish moral philosophy of Adam Smith and nurtured by psychology, was developed into a grown-up, independent science by Pareto. He enabled it to move out of its former home and taught it to seek new role models in the world of science. Like a prodigal son, economics turned its back on its foster parents and, for a long time, didn't give a thought to returning or even paying an occasional visit.

It was Pareto's goal to provide economics with its own place among the established disciplines, a place it didn't have to share with any other disciplines. Uncoupling economic thought from a psychological or sociological knowledge base was seen as mandatory, since economics couldn't hope to become independent unless it could acquire its own research questions—questions to which only economics itself could provide answers. The epistemological program Pareto created, which still influences economic research today, consists of two components. The first concerns the way economists analyze the decisions of individual actors and the second deals with the question of how to evaluate the interaction of many actors, or rather the result this interplay leads to. Both components of the Paretian program are based on the idea that it must be possible to liberate economics from every element of metaphysics and remove all subjective elements from economic analysis, thus creating a research discipline that can make a legitimate claim to be a match for the natural sciences in terms of value freedom and being scientific. Scientific statements should meet the criterion of intersubjective verifiability—there was no place for introspection as a scientific method in such a research program.

How can we get rid of psychology if we want to analyze people's actions and decisions? That is the question. Or perhaps, to be more precise, the point is to describe how people make a choice when they have to choose between alternative bundles of goods—or, more simply, when they consume. The consumption process can be characterized with a choice function that says what quantity of goods will be consumed at given prices and income. The thought that psychology shouldn't play a role in this may seem absurd at first glance, but psychology really isn't needed.

The trick is that Pareto's economics doesn't pay attention to the essence of things—for example, what their utility is and how can it be measured—but instead pays attention to secondary principles that can be deduced from the essence of things. In concrete terms, this means the basis of economic analysis is not the metaphysical contemplation of the nature of utility, but only objectively observable decisions that the individual infers from his subjective utility calculus—i.e., how he calculates his own subjective utility. The idea is irresistibly simple. Let us assume that every individual knows exactly how much utility will be provided by a certain level of consumption or a certain choice. Let us assume, further, that people act according to their perceived utility, which means if they have a choice between two alternatives they choose the one that provides them with greater benefit. Using this assumption, it is possible to deduce the underlying utility concept from the observation of people making a choice. But when may we assume this? When may we conclude from the observable decisions that people have made those decisions precisely because they want to maximize their utility by doing so?

Pareto used these principles of choice to develop the concept of rational actions. The central idea here is that people act as if they are constantly optimizing. They measure the benefit they gain using a utility function that allocates a value to every choice they have; the higher the value, the better the alternative is. The optimization problem consists of choosing, with given prices and a given income, precisely the combination of goods that results in the utility function with the highest possible value. The central question here is "When can we conclude from people's observed choice that this action is actually based on a utility-maximizing calculus?"

The idea is that the *utility function* isn't as abstract and incomprehensible as it first appears. In order to be able to assume the existence of such a function, we only actually need to assume that people can construct a ranking of all the alternatives, which then enables them to indicate which one of two of the available alternatives they prefer. We can't observe this ranking, and still less can we know why people have a particular order of preferences. Whether someone prefers the opera or the theater or would rather go to the football than a ballet performance is of just as little interest as why he has a preference for one thing rather than another. The only important thing is *that* a ranking of alternatives exists. The Paretian research program consists largely of the question "When may we assume that people use a preference order that can be described by means of a utility function?" This question, termed the *integrability problem*, kept some of the best economists of the twentieth century extremely busy.

This part of the Paretian program was first solved in a way that wasn't really convincing. It finally came down to simply assuming, without any empirical basis for doing so, that people possess preference orders with certain characteristics. Essentially, it had to be assumed that the order was complete (i.e., that it included all the alternatives) and that it was transitive (i.e., if an individual prefers alternative X to alternative Y, and alternative Y to alternative Z, then he must also prefer X to Z). The requirement that preferences be transitive proves to be indispensable if we want to say something about decisions in which there is a choice among more than two alternatives.

Simply assuming that orders were transitive provided a means of introducing the existence of a utility function by assumption. From a scientific point of view, the most pleasant thing about this was that the utility function describing a particular preference wasn't clearly defined. Different functions could be used, including those that possessed mathematical properties that made them relatively easy to use. The drawback was that this method didn't really comply with the program designed by Pareto, since it required assumptions that couldn't be supported by observation but could be justified only by the fact that they led to suitable results.

Pareto's vision of being able to make conclusions about utility maximization entirely on the basis of observing the choices people make in order to describe decisions as the result of rational calculus came a step closer to fruition with the theory of revealed preference, which progressed significantly because of the contribution of Paul Samuelson (1915–2009). Samuelson is quite rightly regarded as one of the most outstanding economists of the twentieth century. This reputation is based on a series of ground-breaking papers. In the paper that laid the foundation for the theory of revealed preference, Samuelson showed that fulfillment of the Weak Axiom of Revealed Preference is sufficient for the justification of the utility-maximization hypothesis. This axiom can be described in a simple way as follows. Let us assume you have been invited to a celebration and someone offers you a cake platter with ten different pieces of cake on it. You decide to take some apple cake. If you had been offered the platter with only nine pieces of cake on it, the Weak Axiom requires that you would also have chosen the apple cake, so long as the apple cake was among the nine remaining pieces of cake. In other words, as long as the alternative you prefer is available, your decision will not change if the quantity from which you are choosing gets smaller. If you act in this way, you fulfill the Weak Axiom. Samuelson showed that your decision-making behavior (that is, your choice between two alternatives) can then be described by a utility-maximization problem. Thus Pareto's dream came true: The observation of certain regularities in behavior is sufficient to create a basis for a theory of rational choice.

Admittedly, there is a snag. It isn't possible to deduce from the Weak Axiom that transitivity is secured in a decision between more than two alternatives. (See Gale 1960.) It is secured by the "Strong Axiom of Revealed Preference" (see Houthakker 1950) by introducing transitivity as an assumption. Otherwise, as it turned out, the integrability problem can't be solved. This might water down Pareto's vision somewhat, but not excessively. Transitivity of preferences has to be used as an assumption in the theory of rational decisions, but is that so bad? Why should decisions be intransitive? If someone prefers wine to mineral water and appreciates mineral water more than cold tea, why would he then prefer cold tea to wine? Economists have come to terms with this weak spot of the theory of revealed preference and have been comfortable with it for seventy years.

Pareto's program is not yet complete, however. It doesn't consist only of the removal of psychology from decision theory. In fact, it goes one important step further. With the aid of rational theory, which has a reasonably solid foundation that was created with the theory of revealed preference, the behavior of individuals can be described as the solution of mathematical optimization problems in a very elegant way. But this alone doesn't provide an epistemological program for economics. The fundamental problem of economics doesn't involve an isolated individual; it involves an entire economy. It involves the sum of the wants and needs of individuals, which in principle exceeds the quantity of resources available to satisfy these. The basic economic problem is scarcity. In simple terms, it is all about the question of how the available resources ought to be used to meet people's needs. The problem here is that satisfaction of one need places limits on the satisfaction of other needs. Resources used for the construction of kindergartens, thus meeting the needs of families with children, are no longer available for extending highways or for protecting the environment. The different interests in the use of resources stand in competition with each other, and the question is how this competition is to be decided.

At first sight, this returns us to Edgeworth's theme for how are we to decide which utilization of resources is preferable if we are not in a position to compare the utilities that arise from the different uses with each other? Don't we have to weigh the children's needs for care and playing together against the wants of drivers and environmentalists if we can't satisfy all three demands at once? It seems, at first glance, as though we can't get around evaluating needs (i.e., assessing happiness) if we turn our attention away from the individual and focus on society as a whole. "The greatest happiness of the greatest numbers," as Bentham formulated it, can be achieved only if we can measure the happiness of the individual and make the use of resources dependent on where it generates the greatest happiness. Imagine how arbitrary such an undertaking would be and how much conflict would be associated with it. This would be too much for economics to handle if it had developed into a psychology-based discipline. Measuring and comparing utility is completely ruled out on the basis of the theory of revealed preference, since the concept of utility used specifies only a ranking order—it uses only information concerning whether one alternative or another is preferred, i.e., whether A is better or worse than B. How far (in whatever units) the two alternatives are apart from each other can't be measured, and this information is completely unnecessary in the rational model anyway. Pareto's second fundamental achievement was to find a way of making this basic problem of scarcity accessible to scientific analysis nonetheless.

Pareto wasn't only an economist and a sociologist; he was also an engineer, and in that capacity he devoted himself to, among other things, the question of how to judge the quality of a design. Suppose we have a motor that can be described using different characteristics. It achieves a certain level of performance, uses a certain quantity of fuel in the process, produces a certain amount of noise, and so on. Pareto's idea behind determining the quality of a design is his requirement that the design not waste any technical possibilities. This idea is implemented by using the requirement that the motor be designed in such a way that it is no longer possible to improve one of the characteristics' values (performance, fuel consumption, noise level) without at the same time bringing about a deterioration in the value of one of the other characteristics. A motor whose performance can be improved even further while the fuel consumption and the noise level remain unchanged has obviously not been optimally designed. Since this *Pareto criterion* distinguishes a good design from a bad one, it is still used in the field of engineering today. Of course, there are any number of designs that may meet the Pareto criterion, so it doesn't provide any instructions on how to design the optimal motor. It doesn't differentiate between a high-performance motor with high fuel consumption and a motor with lesser performance and low fuel consumption.

This principle can be carried over to society as a whole. Pareto has provided economies with a universal efficiency criterion: So long as it is still possible for an individual to be better off with a changed allocation of resources (economists use the term *reallocation*) without another individual being forced to be worse off, the economy is not yet in an efficient state. Essentially, *Pareto efficiency* requires that no resources be wasted. As long as resources can make an additional contribution to satisfying needs, they should be used accordingly.

Pareto efficiency and the concept of utility based on ranking order go hand in hand. Both manage without an evaluation of consumption choices of individuals, both are free of psychological statements about the causes of happiness and utility, and both are motivated by the desire to put together an economic epistemological program that can claim to have a high degree of value freedom. The theory of revealed preference did indeed come about to create a foundation for economic research based on observation alone and free of value-based judgments. Although it has not completely managed to live up to this claim, assuming transitivity is a characteristic of individual preferences is not an overly powerful value judgment.

Requiring Pareto efficiency is, of course, a normative act. Economists demand a world in which resources are not wasted. In this respect, the Paretian program is not free of value judgments; however, it might be easy, in view of the acceptance of this assessment, to secure a broad consensus. Why should a society be content with utilizing resources in a way that violates the Pareto criterion? Pareto and the neoclassical economists after him managed to put economic science on a footing that doesn't need to go beyond an elementary minimal consensus with respect to the value judgments it makes. This is most certainly one of the most important reasons for the phenomenal success of neoclassical economic theory.

At this point there is a need for a qualification. This is a concession to scientific practice, where it is necessary time and again to make a statement about what generates utility for people. In a certain sense we have to think about the essence of things after all and, by doing so, naturally risk losing the freedom from values that the neoclassical program lays claim to. In order to avoid this danger, the assumption about what generates utility is as general as it can be while following the criterion of Pareto efficiency as closely as it can. In the final analysis, the Pareto criterion is aimed at the scarcity problem. It is an answer to the question of how we are to deal with the fact that resources are scarce in the sense that all the demands on them can't be met. Doesn't it stand to reason that resources are valuable (otherwise we wouldn't have a scarcity problem), and that availability of resources should therefore be valued positively—that is, generate utility? It does stand to reason, and it explains why neoclassical economic theory rests upon the assumption that more is better than less and a high income therefore generates more utility than a lower income. *Homo economicus*, whose behavior is exactly as described by the rational model of neoclassical economics, thus appears as a soulless egoist who is interested only in his own material welfare and who can't elicit any particular feelings of sympathy or trust in others. But we are doing *Homo economicus* an injustice, because narrowing down his behavior to being able to materially provide for himself isn't the only assumption that neoclassical economics can make concerning his behavior. Criticizing *Homo economicus* as a scoundrel therefore falls short of the mark, since the rational model leaves the question of what serves people's self-interest completely open. Although pragmatically tying this to income has proved its worth, it is by no means obligatory. Making a rational choice between alternatives, in the sense of Pareto, doesn't rule out the possibility that forgoing one's own material benefits is among the alternatives. And the rational model certainly doesn't rule out the possibility that this may be preferred to the other alternatives. Altruistic behavior in its widest sense is consistent with the rational model.

As we will soon see in more detail, it hasn't really been problematic for neoclassical economic theory that, in the wake of experimental economic research, which has gained considerable significance in the last thirty years, there has been an ever-increasing popularity associated with the idea that people are systematically interested in topics such as fairness, distributive justice, or inequity aversion, and not only in material possession. The neoclassical "repair shop" simply allowed *Homo economicus* to have social preferences, and in no time the ideas that came out of the laboratories of experimental researchers were effortlessly being integrated into the standard model of the rational decision maker. The weaknesses of the rational model don't lie in the limits, of whatever kind, placed on the alternatives available or on the preferences on which people base their decisions. If this model has any weaknesses, they lie in what we must sacrifice when we accept it. What we must do without will be explained shortly, but first we must give reasons why this sacrifice did not seem to hurt economists for so long.

The Neoclassical Program: Successes and Advantages

With the theory of revealed preference, the rational model experienced an elegant legitimization that also had the advantage of being a "homegrown" product of economics. The separation from psychology was complete, and it was radical. The rational model represented the start of a program that included nothing more and nothing less than utilization of mathematics as the universal language for formulating a no less universal behavioral model. By attributing decisions explicitly and exclusively to optimization processes, the economic behavioral model is reduced to its mathematical model and analysis. And that isn't all. Mathematical behavioral theory could be applied in an almost value-free space because the belief in the Pareto criterion and the restriction to observable decisions resulted in it being possible to reduce the value base of neoclassical economic theory to only the most necessary and easily shared value judgments. This enabled economists to avoid the disagreements and the "struggles of faith" found in other parts of the scientific community and to concentrate on their real work: the ongoing expansion of normative neoclassical economic theory.

The term *normative* is appropriate in this context, since, despite legitimization through the theory of revealed preference, neoclassical economics can't really claim to be a positive theory. Had it wanted to make such a claim, it should have put more effort into the empirical viability of the rational model. It would then, admittedly, have encountered phenomena that would have set strict limits—for example, the observation that decisions are not independent of the context in which they are made and the observation that they depend on the number of alternatives and on how a decision situation is presented.

The dominance of the Paretian or neoclassical research program is only too understandable. It offered those devoted to it a normative theory that could be applied practically without limit. The economic imperialism that is sometimes referred to can be attributed to this universal usability of the rational model. No other scientific discipline that deals with human behavior and social systems has a comparable methodological tool. The thought that a normative sociology shared by all sociologists could exist seems to us, for good reason, just as far-fetched as a normative political science or a normative social psychology. That is not to say that normative theories don't exist in those disciplines. But they are not anywhere near being able to achieve the general acceptance that neoclassical economics could effortlessly achieve with its scarcely perceptible value base.

The neoclassical research program's unprecedented success cannot be attributed entirely to its having mastered the art of producing normative theory with almost no value judgments, however. The application of mathematics allowed it to "prove" the existence of relationships and causalities. Of course this succeeds only within the boundaries of the models' assumptions, but that doesn't change the fact that in this way if-then-relationships become visible with a clarity and a transparency that other disciplines that do without mathematics can only dream of. The separation from psychology has also proved effective. By being based on a few general phenomena (which are described by the theory of revealed preference) and refraining from any form of psychological speculation, the theory arrives at statements of maximum generality. The applicability of the rational model isn't conditional on the fulfillment of particular conditions. It applies to all people in all decision situations. It describes the behavior of criminals as well as it describes what is happening on the marriage market, or any other market. It can be applied to the relationship between a customer and a salesperson just as well as to that between a doctor and a patient or that between a manager and a stockholder.

It is the connection between apparent value freedom and universal applicability that accounts for the appeal and the success of the neoclassical model. The revolution in economics, decisively influenced by Pareto, led to an incredibly large and powerful research program that very successfully protected the neoclassical economics community from inner doubts, battles of opinion, and scientific revolutions for a long time. It thus gave the community the room and the time to construct a mighty and highly differentiated body of theory that, even by today's standards, still stands stable and secure and, in many respects, far surpasses any of its neighboring disciplines. If anything, neoclassical economic theory must prepare itself for the possibility that its importance in the scientific community will diminish, since researchers are increasingly turning to the task of addressing the losses that have arisen as a result of the (understandable) focus on normative theory.

The Losses

The successes of the neoclassical research program are indisputable and justify the great importance it still possesses today. But the scientific community's intense focus on this program came at a cost. For a long time, research questions outside the ambit of the program were treated as irrelevant or unimportant, and deviations from the methodological line were punished with rejection by referees. This had consequences for the qualifications of the scientists working in this area. Today mathematicians still have a real chance of becoming accomplished economists in the foreseeable future. For a long time, that was out of the question for psychologists; even today is still quite unlikely. Nonetheless, the relationship between economists and psychologists has changed significantly in the last few years. One reason for this may be the fact that contributions from psychological research seem to be indispensable at the points where the blind spots of the rational model can be found.

The theory of revealed preference excludes certain phenomena by means of implicit assumptions. For example, it explicitly excludes the decision of an actor from depending on an alternative quantity that he could choose from. But it also implicitly assumes that the *utility* that is actually experienced is also independent of the alternative quantity. Köszegi and Rabin (2008) have impressively shown that this doesn't have to be the case at all. Two examples serve to illustrate this point. If someone has a choice between an apple and a piece of cake, it is possible that he chooses the cake because he can't resist the temptation. If he had the choice between an apple and a carrot, he would choose the apple, and it can't be ruled out that in this case he would experience a higher utility than that provided by enjoying the cake.

The problem is obviously the temptation to do something that generates utility at the moment (the cake is delicious) but in the long term leads to drawbacks that a person would like to avoid (eating cake makes you fat). People therefore often follow their own self-imposed rules to protect themselves from temptation. For instance, cake lovers who have to watch their weight make sure they have lots of fruit and vegetables at home and not much cake. In this way, temptation can be held in check. However, the breakfast buffet at the hotel where they stay on their business trip leads to the failure of this strategy.

Another example shows the relevance of the blind spot being discussed. People attending church have a choice between putting money in the collection basket and keeping the money. By putting a five-euro bill in the basket, they are not revealing that they get more utility out of donating money than they could if they spent the money on themselves. The very same people who put money in the collection basket as it is passed around during mass may pass by the poor box at the entrance of the church without putting any money in it at all. It obviously makes sense to demand the collection openly. How a situation is set up influences people's preferences. For instance, visitors to a football match in the local football league are not infrequently approached by pleasant young men or women holding a collection tin and asking for donations to support the youth work carried out by the club. Placing the collection tin in a position at the entrance where it can be clearly seen would, presumably, rapidly result in the amount of money made from donations declining to zero.

Similar phenomena are familiar in the field of experimental economic research. So-called *dictator games* are used to investigate whether subjects are willing to voluntarily give money to others. In an experiment reported by Forsythe et al. (1994), a subject was given a sum of money and told that in the room next door there was a second person who hadn't received any money. The subject could then decide whether to keep the entire sum of money or to give the other person a share of it. More than a few of the subjects decided to give half of the money away. This is an odd finding, since in reality we don't often observe people giving money to strangers. There is much to suggest that it is the particular set-up of the dictator game that leads to the money being given away. In fact, List (2007) and Bardsley (2008) showed that this behavior changes dramatically if the dictator receives ten dollars, the other person receives five dollars, and the dictator isn't only allowed to give away some of his money but can also take away some of the other person's money. In this case, it turns out that there are no longer any gifts—quite the opposite, in fact.

Neither of these examples contradicts the theory of revealed preference. If the decision maker is offered apple and cake, he will always choose the cake, and the churchgoer, if she has to choose between donating and not donating, will consistently choose the former at collection time during mass. The blind spot arises because the theory of revealed preference doesn't carry out the decisive test. The reason it doesn't ask about the utility experienced in each of the different decision situations is that, owing to its own methodological implications, it must not and cannot do so. That would be asking about the essence of things—something that the Paretian program expressly forbids. Asking about the utility experienced in each of the different decision situations would mean having to leave the Paretian program. That would explain why that question wasn't asked for so long.

The situation is similar for the finding that choices depend not only on the decision problem itself, and to some extent on its mathematical model, but also on the manner in which it is presented. The *framing* (to use the technical term) of a decision problem has turned out to be highly relevant.

The discovery of the framing effect is undoubtedly one of the most important contributions that experimental research has made so far. It leads to two important consequences. First, it becomes clear that institutions (including the choices available to subjects and the rules for accepting and organizing messages) play a central role in economies. Different institutional arrangements of a decision problem lead to different frames and are therefore of systematic importance. Second, the custom of making wholesale statements about framing effects has, at least partially, given way to attempts to interpret such effects as direct expressions of the systematic influence of institutional conditions on decision behavior. List (2007) formulated this very clearly: Not only are decisions linked to the preferences of the decision makers and the conditions to which they are subject; they also are linked to the "properties of the situation." Just as the theory of revealed preference can't ask about the essence of things by investigating perceived utility, it isn't suited to directing attention to the context dependency of decisions; if it were to do so, it would violate its own methodological dictum.

Not only does the theory of revealed preference implicitly assume a certain connection between an observed choice and its utility; it must also assume that the preferences revealed in making choices are stable over time. In order to be able to use the rational model as neoclassical economics has traditionally used it, this assumption must be made. There are two serious reasons for that. First, if preferences were to change, a convincing decision theory would have to take these changes into account—i.e., would have to make explicit why and in what way preferences could change. Not doing this would reduce its applicability considerably. Even the most trivial of statements on the relationship between the price of a good and the demand for the good rely on the implicit assumption that preferences don't change when the price changes. Without the assumption of stable preferences, a systematic statement on the relationship between price and demand could no longer be made. All kinds of relationships would be possible—which relationship appeared would depend only on the preference dynamics. Second, neoclassical economic theory uses the method of comparative statics, a method that also makes the assumption of stable preferences indispensable. Bruni and Sugden (2007, p. 164) are very clear on this point: "Economic theory relies heavily on the method of comparative statics, which compares alternative equilibrium states *while holding preferences constant*. Thus the consistency properties that are attributes to preferences must hold *across equilibria*."

Do we have reason to doubt the stability of individual preferences? That question is difficult to answer. It becomes even a little more difficult because we cannot simply equate preferences and utility. For example, if it were to turn out that the utility arising from the consumption of a commodity changed over time, it wouldn't be possible to make any conclusion about the preference ordering. It could be that utility is changed by any number of possible consumption alternatives in the same way and the preference ordering therefore stays the same. This point is important because it is a central hypothesis of happiness research that utility is not static but that it possesses directed dynamics. People adapt to changing circumstances, for better or worse. A sudden rise in income will at first produce a surge of happiness, but after one gets accustomed to the additional money one's life satisfaction declines. People's life satisfaction and thus their utility from goods and income are therefore subjected to adaptation processes.

Besides neglecting the influences that alternative choice sets and framing the decision can exert on the actors and the unsettled question of the stability of preferences, the Paretian rational model has another blind spot, and it is extremely important for happiness research. The rational model leaves it to the theory of revealed preference to provide the main justification for its own universal application. This means that the theory of revealed preference is confined to—that is, can make statements only about—choices made by individuals. For that reason, it can't say anything about two phenomena that are important for the well-being of the individual.

The utility people experience doesn't always only depend on their own autonomous choices. For instance, the quality of the environment depends only to an extremely small extent on a person's own decisions, but it is nevertheless of fundamental importance for the well-being of that person. But how do people place a value on their environment? What value does an old-age pension guaranteed by the state have for them, or the provision of an efficient health-care system, or the enhancement of a country's internal and national security? People derive utility from all these things; however, all of them are independent of choices made by individuals, and therefore the neoclassical theory of value, which is based on preferences' being revealed by way of such choices, can say nothing about their value. This is a serious problem for economists, and for that reason they therefore put in a lot of effort trying to find at least provisional solutions for it.

For example, attempts have been made to estimate the value of environmental goods by considering the value of marketable complementary goods. For example, real-estate prices provide an indication of how people value the differing environmental qualities of various local areas. People can derive utility from these goods without having to reveal their preferences truthfully because nobody can be excluded from their consumption. (Economists call these goods *public goods*.) In the end, this indirect method of establishing the value of these goods has not turned out to be particularly successful. That is why an alternative approach to assessing the value of these goods has won out. And that method doesn't conform to neoclassical economic methodology at all. In the "contingent valuation" of public goods, people are simply asked how much they are willing to pay for these goods. From a neoclassical perspective this is a hopeless undertaking, because respondents have no incentive to report their willingness to pay truthfully and so the valuations reported in the interviews are worthless. In fact, it can be shown that people often exaggerate in contingent valuations. And this method has other deficiencies.

Nevertheless, such valuations are still carried out today, because the helplessness of neoclassical economics has left researchers with no other choice.

Another phenomenon about which the neoclassical theory of value can say nothing results from the fact that people's assessments of their life situations are linked not only to their own absolute positions but also to their positions relative to other people. Thus, an individual's own choice alone is no longer decisive for the utility, happiness, or life satisfaction he or she feels; what others do also figures in the individual's assessment. In the jargon of economics: Suddenly external effects play a role!

We have gone into some detail in this book about how relative position affects happiness and life satisfaction and whether absolute level is important. It should be noted here, in the historical context, that the rational model, as it is used today by normative economic theory, is fundamentally unsuited to posing such questions, let alone answering them. It is obvious that considerations of relative matters lead to external effects, and considering those effects makes it necessary to measure the utility of all concerned and thus to define utility. We can answer the question of what role absolute and relative positions play only if we look into the essence of things, even though that may be difficult. If we don't do so, eventually it will no longer be possible to make reasonably reliable statements concerning the welfare of nations. The scientific community should be grateful to happiness research if only for this insight.

Laboratory Economics

So far we have examined happiness research against the backdrop of the neoclassical epistemological program and seen a kind of reflex to the blind spots of the rational model in it. The picture we are painting of the landscape in which economic happiness research resides is not yet complete with this. An important area of economic research is missing; an area which has close links both to happiness research and to the rational model and which can therefore be seen as a kind of connection. Economics today is also an experimental discipline helping itself to methods very similar to those of experimental psychology. But this is not all. *Experimental economic research* also exhibits other close links to psychology—which might be surprising in view of Pareto's rather successful plan to completely free economics from psychology. How is it possible that a psychology-savvy methodology could become established alongside neoclassical economic theory? How could it happen that a movement that cares less and less about the methodological taboos of neoclassical economics has been able to emerge in the last forty years?

This question is important for present purposes mainly because this experimental research deals with a series of issues that are highly relevant for happiness research. In particular, many economic experiments subject the working hypothesis of neoclassical economics that more is better than less to scrutiny, and occasionally they arrive at some astounding results. First and foremost, it turns out that the neoclassical behavioral hypothesis can't explain behavior observed in the laboratory in the situations that we characterized in the preceding section as particularly problematic blind spots. For example, in the provision of public goods people act completely differently than they should if they simply wanted to maximize their income. This close connection to the blind spots, and thus to the ideas of happiness researchers who refer to these blind spots, makes it worthwhile to look at experiments in economics in more detail.

In the meantime, articles on experimental and behavioral studies can regularly be found in all the important journals of economics, and Nobel Prizes have been awarded to researchers who are committed to experimental research.[1] In other words, laboratory experimentation is now firmly established as a methodological tool in economics. Did the Paretian project to remove psychology from economics fail after all? Or do economists, in the end, conduct experiments without consulting psychologists? To come straight to the point, this is to a great extent exactly what they do. But there is a small part of experimental research that is most definitely aware of its closeness to psychology and actively seeks cooperation with the neighboring discipline. How this could come about is in need of explanation. The role that experimental research overall plays in concert with economic methods is also in need of clarification.

In 1944 a book was published that has decisively influenced the history of economics to this day. The authors were an American mathematician born in Hungary and an Austrian business economist: John von Neumann and Oskar Morgenstern. The book was titled *Theory of Games and Economic Behavior*, and its publication signaled the birth of modern game theory. Seven Nobel Prizes have been awarded for game-theoretic work, and even this isn't adequate to demonstrate the importance of game theory in economics. (Von Neumann, who is regarded as one of the most important mathematicians of the twentieth century and who laid the foundations of game theory, was not one of the Nobel laureates.)

The game-theoretic method is, only a piece of applied mathematics, without any particular thematic definition. But its tools can be used to deal with an enormous number of questions that are of relevance to economics. Game theory is devoted to the analysis of strategic interactions—that is, situations in which the success of an individual depends not only on his own behavior but also on the behavior of others. Such situations often involve conflicts of opposing interests. If, for instance, two people are negotiating the sale of a good, the seller is naturally interested in achieving as high a price as is possible; the buyer would like the opposite—to pay as little as is possible. Whether a deal will be made and what the price will be are decided through the interaction of the two people. This interaction is strategic, since the success of each party also depends on the behavior of the other.

Game theory describes such strategic interactions as parlor games. The description of a game contains instructions on who participates (who is a player) and what possible moves (strategies) each player can make. The description is completed with information on a payoff function, which describes the payoff each player receives for every conceivable combination of strategies of the players. It is, of course, not simply enough to describe strategic interactions in this way. In order to be able to analyze them and to make a prediction as to how rational players will behave in the situation described, a solution concept is needed for the game. Von Neumann and Morgenstern provided such a concept for a particular group of games: the so-called zero-sum games, in which one player's gain is the other player's loss and so the gains and the losses always add up to zero. The solution concept for such games is provided by applying the *minimax strategy*, in which the best strategy to choose is the one that minimizes the maximum payoff the other player can receive. If each of the players chooses such a strategy, then they are in equilibrium, since no player can increase his payoff by choosing a different strategy.

Zero-sum games are not normal in strategic interactions. Game theory's restriction to zero-sum games limits its applicability. This limitation was overcome by a concept introduced by John Nash at the beginning of the 1950s. A Nash equilibrium exists when the strategies of all the players represent the best responses to the other strategies. One player's best response strategy is the one that leads to a maximization of that player's payoff for the strategy choices of the other players. Let us assume that two players are participating in a game and that each can choose among five strategies, and that player A chooses strategy 3. Player B ascertains that he can, in this case, maximize his payoff by choosing strategy 4. The combination (S3, S4) is a Nash equilibrium if player A now determines that S3 is exactly the right response to S4 because, by making this choice, A receives the largest payoff that is possible if B plays S4. Nash's ground-breaking achievement (rewarded with a Nobel Prize) was to have proved mathematically that every strategy game has at least one such equilibrium. With this, it became possible to analyze a great number of strategic interactions, because the restriction to zero-sum games had been removed; moreover, it was now always certain that a solution to the game could be worked out. This made game theory a tool that could be applied to virtually all areas of economics, since strategic interactions can be found practically everywhere in the real economic world. The contributions of Reinhard Selten and John Harsanyi (who together with John Nash were awarded the Nobel Prize in 1994) did much to pave the way for a broad and comprehensive application of game-theoretic tools to economics. At the beginning of the 1970s, game theory began its triumphal march. Game-theoretic models dominated the journals and ruled the scene. It was as if economics had found its ultimate tool.

How did proponents of the Paretian research program get along with those of game theory? At first, splendidly. Game theory assumes that the actors act strictly rationally, choosing the strategy that guarantees the highest payoff. This is eminently consistent with the rational model of neoclassical economics, which in principle is based on the same behavioral assumption. Furthermore, game theory, in spite of its commitment to strict rationality of players, is completely open concerning the players' goals and motives. It is left up to the person choosing the modeling to be used to decide what strategies will be permitted, and the "payoff" to the players must be thought of as the utility that the players experience from a certain outcome of the game, not as money. What generates utility for the players is left unanswered. Thus, motives such as altruism, fairness, and aversion to inequity can generally be used in game-theoretic models. Of course, because of this, game theory is also suited to adopting the assumptions on people's motives made by neoclassical economic models. Although the neoclassical rational model, just like game theory, is in principle open to any assumption as to what generates people's utility, 99 percent of the models that adopt assumptions concerning people's behavioral goals use the premise that people are self-interested and that for them more is better than less. As we have already noted, such a "selfish assumption" is not a necessary consequence of the Paretian research program or of the rational model, but it has been the dominating assumption in scientific practice for seventy years. One reason for this dominance is that models assuming strictly rational self-interest maximization are able to explain a large number of economic phenomena successfully. Game theory could be integrated into this world of models perfectly. In a way, game theory takes the rational model to the extreme—it ascribes so much rationality to the players that one could speak of hyperrational behavior.

It was now possible to apply the standard assumptions that neoclassical economics had always used to the analysis of strategic interactions. For example, it was now possible to analyze markets in which a few suppliers mutually influence one another's decisions. Without game theory, we are limited to ideal-typical competitive markets in which individual actors have no strategic space. Industrial economics, which analyzes markets with limited competition and which is an important and large branch of economic theory, was able to develop only because of game theory. There is practically no area within economics today that could manage without game-theoretic modeling. Strategic interactions that are described by game theory are always involved, whether they concern the effect of asymmetric information, the behavior of central banks, or relationships between managers and stockholders.

Game theory has, so far, been in perfect harmony with the Paretian research program. But it has another side—one that may eventually result in inclusion of the Paretian program in a larger research framework. Game theorists treat the description of strategic interactions as a game in order to determine the equilibria of this game mathematically. It is possible, however, to take a completely different tack. The description of the game can simply be re-interpreted as a description of an experiment, and, instead of solving the game mathematically, we can have real people play the game in a laboratory. It is possible to reproduce the situation described in the game-theoretic model exactly in the laboratory. To be precise: Game-theoretic models can be tested only in the laboratory, since the assumptions used by these models are never perfectly fulfilled in reality. Let us cite an example to demonstrate what this means.

An important focus of game theory is the analysis of *auctions*. Central to this is the question of how the particular design of an auction effects the result of the auction. A game theorist can answer this question by calculating the Nash-equilibrium bid—that is, by figuring out what bid the bidder should make if he acts strictly rationally and pursues the goal of gaining the greatest possible benefit from the auction (i.e., purchasing the good being auctioned at the lowest possible price).

A common type of auction is the *second-price auction*, in which the bidder who makes the highest bid wins but pays the price of the second-highest bid. A game-theoretic analysis of such an auction was carried out as early as in the 1960s by its inventor, William Vickrey. The outstanding characteristic of a Vickrey auction is that the best a rational bidder can do is to make a bid that truly represents the maximum amount he is prepared to pay for the good.

Vickrey auctions are easy to observe in the real world. For instance, eBay's system of bidding operates according to the principles of the Vickrey auction.[2] Even with so many eBay auctions, it isn't possible to find out whether the game-theoretic prediction is correct, since only the bids of those participating in the auction can be observed but not the maximum amount they are willing to pay. Checking this by experiment is, by contrast, relatively simple. This is done as follows: The subjects are informed that they will be able to bid for a fictitious good and that the auction will proceed according to the rules of a Vickrey auction. Before the auction, every participant receives confidential information of the value the fictitious item has for the bidder. In this way, each bidder knows that if he makes the highest bid, he will receive a payoff corresponding to this value less the second-highest bid, since it is the second-highest bid that determines the price. It is therefore clear that the maximum willingness to pay corresponds exactly to the value that the experimenter confided to each participant. When the auction is carried out, it can be observed whether the bidders act in accordance with the game-theoretic prediction and make a bid exactly matching their willingness to pay.

The experiment operates according to a simple principle in that it uses the description of the game as the basis for the experimental design. The situation the game describes can be accurately produced in the laboratory, and therefore it is possible for experimental research to test game-theoretic models under laboratory conditions. And the Vickrey auction does very well in such tests. Although inexperienced bidders tend to make bids that are too high, they learn relatively quickly that it is in fact best to bid exactly what they were told was the value of the good.

Similarly to the Vickrey auction, almost any game can be played and tested in the laboratory. Game-theoretic models are perfectly suited for laboratory testing because their description can be read directly as the instructions for an experiment. Although the relationship between the theory and the experiment is so clear, it took a while before experimental research got going. There is only anecdotal evidence of the existence of experimental economic research before 1960, and relatively few papers on experimental work were published in the 1960s and the 1970s, although since 1970 scientific journals have been full of papers on game theory. Perhaps the initial reluctance was due to an experience that occurred right at the beginning of the story of the verification of the game-theoretic model—an experience that may have led to skepticism among game theoreticians.

In 1950 Melvin Dresher and Merrill Flood invented a game that has since had a remarkable career in economics: the Prisoners' Dilemma.[3] Dresher and Flood devised this game because they wanted to subject the concept of the Nash equilibrium to a particularly hard test. (Today we would call it a stress test.) The original game is illustrated here by table A.1.

The row player and the column player can each choose between the first (S1) and the second (S2) row or column, respectively. Irrespective of what the column player does, it is always the best response for the row player to choose S2, since his payoff is higher than if he chooses S1. Therefore, S2 is the *dominant strategy* for him. The column player also has a dominant strategy. If he chooses S1, his payoff is always higher than if he chooses S2. So it is clear that the Nash equilibrium is S2 for the row player and S1 for the column player. At equilibrium each player admittedly receives a payoff that is half the payoff he could achieve by choosing S1 or S2, respectively. The equilibrium is therefore extremely inefficient. The stress-test question is whether real players, in view of the foregoing, choose the rational solution all the same and play their dominant strategy.

Dresher and Flood had students play this game as an experiment. Each participant played the game 100 times in a row. The payoff was in US pennies, so at equilibrium the column player earned 50 cents and the row player nothing. If both players acted efficiently, the row player choosing S1 and the column player S2, each received 50 cents more than at equilibrium. Dresher and Flood's experiment was the first to put a game-theoretic equilibrium concept to the test, and the concept failed. The finding of the experiment was, that the players did *not* play the Nash equilibrium. Admittedly, they were also not in a position to coordinate an efficient solution with each other. In its first experiment, experimental research had

Table A.1
Payoffs in the Prisoners' Dilemma. The first number in each pair is the row player's payoff; the second number the column player's payoff.

	Column player	
Row player	S1	S2
S1	–1, 2	½, 1
S2	0, ½	1, –1

Sources: Flood 1952; Flood 1958

proved unreliable. Instead of supporting the equilibrium concept central to game theory, it showed, on the basis of a simple example, that it was by no means certain whether people acted as the game-theoretic model predicted. John Nash took a close look at Dresher and Flood's experiment and voiced some legitimate criticism about the experimental design. (See Roth 1995.) For example, he noted that the game was repeated rather than played one time only. As reasonable as this criticism was, the central finding has been confirmed time and again. We suspect that it was this bad experience with the first Prisoners' Dilemma experiment that kept game theoreticians from using experiments to investigate their models from the very beginning, and it took almost thirty years for the experimental method in economics to get a firm foothold.

It is certainly thanks to game theory that the experimental method eventually became an accepted tool in the economist's toolbox despite that initial negative experience. The connection between model and experiment is simply too close, too striking, for it to have been possible in the long run to justify why it wasn't necessary to verify game theoretical models experimentally. Today, experimental research has long been independent and no longer spends all its time testing existing theories. It is used intensively to detect regularities in behavior that can be used to develop theories that describe this behavior and allow accurate predictions to be made. Apart from that, the inevitable has come to pass. Experiments are to a large extent being used to investigate those parts of neoclassical economic theory afflicted with blind spots. That doesn't mean that experiments are in permanent opposition to the neoclassical program. Quite the opposite—there are important areas in which experiment has fully confirmed neoclassical theory. For example, neoclassical economics has proved exceptionally successful when it comes to describing how markets function. It has been proved in many experiments that markets are indeed able to achieve the efficient allocation that neoclassical economics ascribes to them. Nevertheless, the most intensive efforts of experimental economists can be found in those areas where neoclassical economics has little to say. Dresher and Flood's experiment plays an important role in this.

Since its invention, the Prisoners' Dilemma has had a remarkable career in economics. It has proved to be an excellent instrument with which to represent a contradiction that plays a large role in many situations found in economics. This is the contradiction between individual rationality and collective rationality, which can occur in certain situations. In Dresher and Flood's game, individual rational behavior means that both players choose the strategy that maximizes their own benefit. But if they both do precisely that, and don't make any mistakes while doing so, they end up in a situation that is worse for both than the situation they would have been in if they had forgone their individual benefit. Individual rationality has led them into a collective non-rational state. It is possible to speak of a *cooperation paradox* in such situations: Precisely because the players rationally seek their benefit, they end up with an unfavorable result.

The importance of the Prisoners' Dilemma results from the fact that it emerges in so many places. We dealt with public goods earlier in this chapter and explained that neoclassical economics finds it difficult to say anything about the value of such goods. This is, among other things, because people who are faced with the task of providing public goods find themselves in a Prisoners' Dilemma. From the perspective of the individual, it isn't rational to make a contribution to producing a public good, because he can't be excluded from using it even if he shows a certain polite restraint with his contribution. As this applies to everyone, it leads to the good not being provided at all—even if everyone would be better off if they all made their contribution to the provision of the good. We have already identified happiness research as a way of solving the valuation problem for public goods. Experimental research has been working intensively on the question of how people behave in reality when faced with the conflict between individual and collective rationality described above. The neoclassical rational model can't contribute anything to this other than the prediction that no one will participate in the provision of public goods. This is because it isn't capable of coming to any other result. However, the experiments of Dresher and Flood, and hundreds of public-good experiments, have shown that this prediction is wrong. People are definitely able to cooperate and overcome the Prisoners' Dilemma—albeit imperfectly. But how do they do that, and what fosters cooperation and what hinders it? The neoclassical rational model can't answer these questions. Experimental research, however, has amassed a series of important findings on this since 1980 (Chaudhuri 2011).

Thus, we now know that communication is an important prerequisite for cooperation, that the cultural background of a society plays an important part in cooperation behavior, that many people act like "contingent cooperators" (i.e., they are willing to act in the interest of the collective if others also do so), and more.

And it isn't as if the neoclassical rational model had difficulty only with public goods. It is also rather bad at modeling the context dependency of the decisions people make. It has been known in experimental research for a long time that decision behavior depends not only on the logical structure of the problem to be decided but also on its context and how the problem is presented. We saw this in the dictator game described above, for example. The behavior of the dictator clearly depends greatly on the context in which the decision to give money away is embedded. Structuring the situation in such a way that taking something away from the other person is allowed will change the willingness to give. What we do with our money depends very much on whether we worked hard for it or whether it was given to us.

In certain situations, people are prepared to sacrifice their own advantage and consider the context they are in when making decisions—even though this context may be unimportant for the logical structure of the decision problem. And so the third area that creates problems for the neoclassical rational model concerns the role of people's relative positions. Experimental research and the attempt to put the laboratory findings into a theoretical framework have amassed quite a lot of information on this too. Most of all, people's behavior in two particular experiments has fueled the suspicion that relative positions could be very important.

The first of these experiments is the *ultimatum game*, a variant of the dictator game in which the recipient can choose whether or not to accept the share of money the allocator has proposed. If the recipient rejects the proposal, both subjects go empty handed; if he accepts, the money will be shared in accordance with the proposal of the allocator. Both the rational model and game theory have a clear prediction for this game too. From the recipient's perspective, any allocation greater than zero that he receives is better than what he receives if he rejects the allocation. Therefore, he should accept every offer made to him provided that his share is greater than zero. The allocator anticipates this and makes a proposal in which the recipient gets only a minimum share. That is the theory. The experimental findings say something completely different. The allocators generally don't make proposals involving very unequal shares. If they do, the recipients in all probability reject the offer. Although they don't get any money when they reject the offer, the allocator doesn't get anything either; that is, they are in the same position as he is.

The second experiment suggesting the importance of relative positions is the *trust game*, which involves preference for equity or aversion to inequity. Once again, there are two players, and, as always, the game is played anonymously. Both players receive an initial endowment of 10 euros each. Player A has an opportunity, in the first move, to transfer some of his money to player B. If he does this, the experimenter triples the amount player A sends. In the second move, player B can give any amount back to player A. For example, if player A gives everything away to player B, player B receives 30 euros and now has 40 euros in total. If, in his countermove, he then gives 20 euros back to player A, both players have now doubled their initial endowment. This is, admittedly, based on the prerequisite that player A can trust that player B will give him something back.

What makes the trust game interesting is that, although at first glance it seems very easy to get a double payoff, rational self-interested players can't receive such a payoff. A rational self-interested player B will not give anything back to player A. And why should he? There would be nothing in it for him. Player A will anticipate this when he assumes that player B will act as the rational model advises and will, therefore, also give nothing to the second player. If self-interest is rationally pursued, both players end up in a position worse than the one they could have been in if they hadn't acted in a self-interested manner. Trust and trustworthiness pay off. But trustworthiness also means being prepared to voluntarily forgo the money for the sake of another or on the grounds of fairness. This is exactly what *Homo economicus* can't afford under the standard assumption that more is better than less.

Subjects in laboratory studies have an easier time dealing with this. At least some of them (more than half, on average) are willing to trust the second player, and in most cases the trust isn't abused. Although it doesn't often happen that when the first player gives something away he gets back half of what player B receives, the second player at least makes sure that her benefactor doesn't end up worse off than he would have done if he had transferred no money. And so once again it is the case that the behavior observed in the laboratory can't easily be reconciled with the neoclassical rational model in its standard form.

The neoclassical rational model is flexible and not at all reliant on the assumption that people are only interested in their personal income. This flexibility provides the neoclassical "repair shop" with an opportunity to integrate even the irritating results of experimental research. For instance, in two models that were developed in parallel, Bolton and Ockenfels (2000) and Fehr and Schmidt (1999) made some changes to the assumption concerning what people's utility depends on. Mathematically these changes were slight, but their effect on economic thinking was tremendous. Instead of assuming that the absolute income position alone (i.e., purely the amount of money that someone receives) is decisive for a person's utility, their *inequity-aversion model* presumes that a person's own relative position plays a role. Such a premise is consistent with the neoclassical rational model and can be used to explain various findings of experimental research—for example, the behavior of the recipient in the ultimatum game. If someone cares only about taking home as much money as is possible, he will not reject any proposals in which he is offered more than zero. But if his own relative position is important, he may well show less interest in the money if that ensures that his relative position improves. By rejecting an unfair offer, the recipient can ensure that he is not worse off than the allocator—because then *both* receive the same payoff of zero.

In a similar way, many findings of experimental research can be reconciled with the neoclassical rational model with the aid of the inequity-aversion model. Modifying the assumptions on what generates utility leaves the model intact. The subjects simply reveal preference for their relative position. The theory of revealed preference remains valid, and we can continue to assume that people's choices can be described as a consequence of a rational optimization calculus.

Does this mean that experimental research is now in perfect harmony with neoclassical economics? Have all the doubts concerning the rational model disappeared? At first view this seems to be the case. Just a relatively small change in the assumptions about the motives behind human action is all that is needed, and everything is hunky-dory. There is, however, a price to pay. The Paretian project of removing psychology from economics consisted of keeping any considerations of the essence of things as far as it concerned people's perceived utility to an unavoidable minimum. Assuming "more is better than less" was such a minimum. Now it turns out that experimental research must go even further.

Neuroeconomics

The arrival of experimental research opened the door to economics for another science. In the last few years, a new discipline called neuroeconomics has made it into the toolbox of economics.

Two developments that took place completely independently of each other are responsible for the creation of neuroeconomics. We have already described the first: the advance of the experimental method into the economic sciences. The second took place in the natural sciences (more precisely, the technical sciences). The invention of functional magnetic resonance imaging (fMRI) provided neuroscientists with a tool that enabled them to directly observe processes in all the regions of the brain. The technology used in this process exploits the fact that the flow of blood increases, and more oxygen is transported, in those areas of the brain that are particularly active at the moment. The magnetic properties of oxidized and deoxidized blood differ, and fMRI exploits this, allowing currently active areas of the brain to be observed. This technology has practically revolutionized the neurosciences. Previously, all that could be learned from brain lesions was what area of the brain was probably responsible for what tasks. Now it is possible to carry out real-time observations of healthy brains.

Neuroscientists now are able to present test subjects with carefully designed experimental set-ups and then observe what happens in the brain when they smell or taste something or solve arithmetic problems. With these new possibilities, the development of neuroeconomics was virtually inevitable. After all, what could be more obvious than combining simple experiments in economics with the new opportunities offered by imaging techniques? It didn't take long for experimental economists to make use of these new possibilities and conduct the first neuroeconomics experiments.[4]

What has emerged from these experiments that use neuroscientific techniques, and what new findings has this young discipline produced? It is too early to make final judgments on these matters, since fMRI is in its early days and since neuroscientists' abilities to analyze and interpret brain data are increasing rapidly. It hasn't yet been definitively established that this new tool is suitable for use in economics. It is, therefore, still the case that nearly all papers on neuroeconomics are published in neuroscience journals rather than in economics journals. The bibliography of a recent survey (Fehr and Rangel 2013) lists few works not published in neuroscientific journals. Fehr and Rangel also make it clear that, despite the considerable progress in neuroeconomics in the last ten years, the findings aren't terribly exciting.

Fehr and Rangel do, however, provide a very clear outline of a model that has proved to be particularly suitable for describing the neurological processes taking place when people make decisions. This basically involves the brain computing "decision values" before each decision and using these to choose between alternatives. This reminds us of the notion that people make use of preference ordering, which can be represented with the help of utility indices. In this way, the brain doesn't just make a decision; it also checks it afterward by computing some sort of "experienced utility." The only difference to the theory of revealed preference is actually that the latter assumes this experienced utility is known from the outset, whereas our brain anticipates that we can make mistakes. Neuroeconomics analyses show that people do indeed make systematic mistakes and wrong decisions, because their experienced utility is hard to calculate.

It is, however, clear-cut when the decision maker has sufficient experience. The brain never errs when it has to choose between salt and sugar—you don't intentionally put sugar on your boiled egg and salt in your coffee. It shouldn't come as a surprise, then, that we make mistakes in situations of uncertainty.

Even the finding that decisions can be manipulated isn't new; the computation of decision values, for instance, depends on things that can be manipulated. This includes the attention paid to the decision being made as well as the information available on the item being decided on. A good example of this can be found in the article by Hare, Malmoud, and Rangel (2011), in which they show that it is possible to influence the choice between "healthy" food and "tasty" (but less healthy) food by drawing people's attention to the health aspects or the taste beforehand. The contribution to neuroscience here is that this manipulation can also be captured in neural imaging. The fact that such manipulations are possible is, however, nothing new.

Douglas Bernheim (2009) has clearly expressed the skepticism that many economists have about neuroeconomics. The brain and the processes taking place within it are a black box for economists. Bernheim poses the question of whether it really makes sense to open this black box. Isn't it enough to know what decisions people make? Do we really need to know what regions of the brain participated in the decision? According to Bernheim, the answer to this question can be found in two conditions, one of which must be fulfilled so that a finding in neuroeconomics can claim to be of significance for economics: Either looking into the brain allows us to discriminate between two competing theories or direct economic consequences can be derived from neuroscientific findings. Can findings in neuroeconomics be expected to meet one of these two demands? The results have been rather disappointing, so far at least. In most cases, neuroeconomics has delivered findings that have long been known at the behavioral level and which now can be depicted using neural imaging without this leading to any direct gain in knowledge for economics. At the same time, one can certainly think of cases in which being able to directly observe processes in the brain could be important—for instance, when the question of which motive a particular decision is based upon is important for assessing theories. When applied to the issue that is the focus of this book, this suggests that it might be useful to track down the motive for the pursuit of income with a scanner. Is it absolute income growth, or is it only an improvement in relative position, that matters in this regard? This appendix isn't the place to provide an overview of neuroscientific research, but we would like to discuss two papers in more detail. These papers may give an indication as to how neuroeconomics operates and what possibilities this discipline offers and what limits it has.

The first paper, by Camillo Padoa-Schioppa (2009), has already been mentioned in chapter 10. This paper describes an experiment with monkeys. The advantage of neuroscientific research with primates is that measurements can be taken in the brain. We don't need to take the roundabout approach using blood flow, and the scanner is also superfluous. Brain activity is measured by electrodes directly implanted in the brain. (The monkeys feel no pain and suffer no lasting harm.)

Padoa-Schioppa's experiment dealt with assigning value to objects. We know that the center for valuation lies in the orbitofrontal cortex, and therefore the neuronal signal was measured in that region. The basic question was "How does the brain cope with having to handle very different valuation tasks?" This value range is particularly large in the decisions people make. Sometimes it is a matter of choosing what bread to buy, costing only a few dollars; sometimes it is a matter of having to decide on the purchase of a house or a car, a decision involving thousands of dollars. The question is whether the brain operates fundamentally differently when a person is putting a value on things that are worth a lot or whether it adapts to the level at which valuation is taking place. Padoa-Schioppa gave his monkeys different juices and observed how the juices were rated by the monkeys. The result is unambiguous: "[T]he representation of value in the orbitofrontal cortex ... adapts to the behavioral condition of choice and, more specifically, to the range of values available in any given condition." (p. 14004) Padoa-Schioppa shows not only that is the way the valuation function is independent of the level at which the assignment of values is occurring, but also that the individual assignment of values is independent of the alternatives that are not included in the choice available at that time. Hence, the monkeys' preferences are also transitive. Does this mean there has been a gain in knowledge that can claim to be economically significant in accordance with Bernheim's demands? It depends on how you look at it. Padoa-Schioppa's results don't supply us with any new economic knowledge, but they do provide evidence that it does appear to be correct to assume that preference ordering is transitive and possesses completeness in the sense of preference theory, since this is precisely what follows from the adaptability of the valuation system—nothing really new, but a confirmation of something old.

The second paper we would like to mention has somewhat more to offer. Plassmann et al. (2008) look into the valuation of objects from the point of view of marketing. How do people evaluate goods? An economist who believes in *Homo economicus* would answer that it depends on the physical characteristics of the good and on the current condition of the consumer. The valuation of a wine, for example, should depend solely on the characteristics of the wine (the taste) and whether the consumer happens to be in the mood at the time to drink wine. The valuation made during a fine meal would turn out differently than one made immediately after a sporting activity, when the main thing is to quench one's thirst. The valuation of the good should by no means depend on the price. Marketing experts have long known that this purist standpoint of economics is wrong. It has been shown in numerous experiments that the valuation of goods also depends on things that the marketing department of a company can influence. Besides the price, there are the associations that can be created by advertising, or by a brand name that guarantees the quality and particular properties of the good. Plassmann et al. raised the question of what neural processes lie behind this. The experimental set-up they chose was very simple: The subjects were given wine to drink during fMRI scans. They were instructed that they would receive five different wines to sample, each with a different price. However, there were in fact only three wines. Two of the three were given to the subjects twice, with a different price named each time. The price of wine 1 was said to be $5 and then to be $45; the price of wine 2 was said to be $10 and then to be $90. During the tasting, the subjects reported how good and how intense the wine tasted to them.

At the behavioral level, i.e., in terms of the responses concerning taste, the results were as expected: If a wine was associated with a higher price, it tasted better. More important, however, this result could be confirmed by neural activity. The increased activation in the orbitofrontal cortex was significantly greater in the case of a higher price. To this extent, the experiment therefore reproduces a result already familiar from market research. But another finding went further: Manipulating the price showed no effect on the regions of the brain responsible for the physical processing of taste. This means that the subjects physically perceived the identical wines in exactly the same way, thus experiencing the same taste. Their ratings were nevertheless different. The explanation for this is that the brain analyzes more information when rating goods than the "naive" economist thinks. Price information, therefore, is important and isn't rejected or dismissed as irrelevant by the brain. This is because the brain has learned that more expensive wines are also better wines. This experience is processed in the orbitofrontal cortex, and it doesn't matter what the systems responsible for taste perception are doing. It is obvious that associative learning plays an important role in this—that is, that people learn to associate particular valuations with particular signals. It would be highly inefficient if the brain were to neglect such learned tools, as they assist in valuation.

The experiment by Plassmann et al. demonstrates that, with the help of neuroscientific methods, it is possible to gain knowledge that can also be of economic relevance. The literature currently available is, however, not overly helpful with regard to our thesis that money does make you happy. It still isn't possible, for instance, to obtain neural representations of such sophisticated emotions as happiness or life satisfaction. The Plassmann experiment suggests that associative learning may also play a role. The question here is "To what extent do we learn that money makes us happy or that we don't need money to be happy?" The answer to this question remains completely open.

If we summarize everything we have said thus far, what picture do we arrive at? It is still, above all else, the picture of a strong neoclassical body of theory that has successfully tackled the anomalies that experimental research has brought to light. Nevertheless, there are many signs that the days when neoclassical thinking and normative theories could lay a claim to sole representation within economics are over. The blind spots of the theory of revealed preference are becoming more and more noticeable. The experimental method, which arrived in economics riding piggyback on game theory, has provided psychology with new access to economics. Overall, the scientific landscape has become more open and more sophisticated in the last thirty years. Research in the sense of the program laid down by Pareto is no longer the only kind of research that is conceivable in economics.

The fact that in the last ten years it has been possible to reappraise findings that are already thirty years old may well be attributable primarily to this newfound openness. In parallel with this reappraisal, there has also been an increased willingness to more earnestly address the questions that Easterlin raised with his paradox in the 1970s. Those questions established a new direction in economics, and out of them there arose a further challenge for the neoclassical research project: happiness research.

And thus we have come full circle.

Notes

Chapter 3

1. See, e.g., Lane 1998, 2000; Diener and Oischi 2000; Myers 2000; Blanchflower and Oswald 2004. In the meantime, some very good surveys of the literature have come out—see, e.g., Frey and Stutzer 2002; Layard 2006. Also see Frey 2008.

2. In addition to the early works by Veblen (1899) and Duesenberry (1949), see Hirsch 1976; Pollack 1976; Layard 1980; Frank 1985; Holländer 1990, 2001.

3. The findings are not entirely unambiguous. Clark, Kristensen, and Westergård-Nielsen (2009) find, using Danish data, that people's life satisfaction rises if their colleagues' incomes increase. It is difficult to interpret such a finding, particularly since the Danish are a positive exception with regard to their satisfaction with life anyway. A potential explanation is the "tunnel effect," which states that people feel happier if good things happen to others in their aspiration group because this indicates a higher likelihood that something good will happen to them.

4. See Blanchflower and Oswald 2004, Luttmer 2005, or Graham and Felton 2006.

5. Headey, Muffels, and Wooden (2008) have shown that wealth has a positive effect on life satisfaction beyond the positive effect of current income.

Chapter 4

1. For overviews, see Sagiv and Schwartz 2000 and Georgellis et al. 2009.

2. For an exhaustive survey of the evidence of the damaging effects of materialism on the quality of life, see Kasser 2002.

3. For assessments of disabilities, see Diener and Pavot 2008, Dijkers 1997, Dijkers 1999, and Lucas 2007.

Appendix

1. In addition to Vernon Smith and Daniel Kahneman, who received the Nobel Prize in 2002, there is Elinor Ostrom, who was awarded the prize in 2009.

2. The highest bidder at eBay pays the second-highest bid plus a surcharge equivalent to the minimum bid increment, and so it sometimes seems as if he is paying his own bid. However, a modified Vickrey auction is, in fact, involved.

3. The name Prisoners' Dilemma came about later and refers to the following story, which can be told with the game: Two prisoners are accused of a crime they committed together. If only one confesses, he will go free and the other will have to serve six years. If both confess, each will receive a sentence of four years. If neither confesses, each will get a sentence of one year. In this game, it is the dominant strategy to confess, which would result in each prisoner having to serve three more years than if they both remained silent.

4. For more on the relatively short history of neuroeconomics, see Glimcher et al. 2009.

References

Afriat, Sidney N. 1967. The construction of utility functions from expenditure data. *International Economic Review* 8: 67–77.

Aknin, Lara B., Michael I. Norton, and Elizabeth W. Dunn. 2009. From wealth to well-being? Money matters, but less than people think. *Journal of Positive Psychology* 4: 523–527.

Aknin, Lara B., Gillian M. Sandstrom, Elizabeth W. Dunn, and Michael I. Norton. 2011. Investing in others: Prosocial spending for (pro)social change. In *Positive Psychology as Social Change*, ed. R. Biswas-Diener. Springer.

Aknin, Lara B., Elizabeth W. Dunn, and Michael I. Norton. 2012a. Happiness runs in a circular motion: Evidence for a positive feedback loop between prosocial spending and happiness. *Journal of Happiness Studies* 13: 347–355.

Aknin, Lara B., J. Kiley Hamlin, and Elizabeth W. Dunn. 2012b. Giving leads to happiness in young children. *PLoS ONE* 7: e39211.

Aknin, Lara B., Christopher P. Barrington-Leigh, Elizabeth W. Dunn, John F. Helliwell, Justine Burns, Robert Biswas-Diener, Imelda Kemeza, Paul Nyende, Claire E. Ashton-James, and Michael I. Norton. 2013a. Prosocial spending and well-being: Cross-cultural evidence for a psychological universal. *Journal of Personality and Social Psychology* 104: 635–652.

Aknin, Lara B., Elizabeth W. Dunn, Gillian M. Sandstrom, and Michael I. Norton. 2013b. Does social connection turn good deeds into good feelings? On the value of putting the 'social' in prosocial spending. *International Journal of Happiness and Development* 1: 155–171.

Aknin, Lara B., Elizabeth W. Dunn, Ashley V. Whillans, Adam M. Grant, and Michael I. Norton. 2013c. Making a difference matters: Impact unlocks the emotional benefits of prosocial spending. *Journal of Economic Behavior & Organization* 88: 90–95.

Alesina, Alberto, Rafael Di Tella, and Robert MacCulloch. 2004. Inequality and happiness: Are Europeans and Americans different? *Journal of Public Economics* 88: 2009–2042.

Andrews, Frank M., and Stephen B. Whitey. 1976. *Social Indicators of Well-Being: Americans' Perception of Life Quality*. Plenum.

Ariely, Dan, Anat Bracha, and Stephan Meier. 2009. Doing good or doing well? Image motivation and monetary incentives in behaving prosocially. *American Economic Review* 99: 544–555.

Baker, Lindsay A., Lawrence P. Cahalin, Kerstin Gerst, and Jeffrey A. Burr. 2005. Productive activities and subjective well-being among older adults: The influence of number of activities and time commitment. *Social Indicators Research* 73: 431–458.

Bardsley, Nicholas. 2008. Dictator game giving: Altruism or artefact? A note. *Experimental Economics* 11: 122–133.

Becchetti, Leonardo, Alessandra Pelloni, and Fiammetta Rossetti. 2008. Relational goods, sociability, and happiness. *Kyklos* 61: 343–363.

Becchetti, Leonardo, Stefano Castriota, Luisa Corrado, and Elena Giachin Ricca. 2013. Beyond the Joneses: Inter-country income comparisons and happiness. *Journal of Socio-Economics* 45: 187–195.

Becker, Gary S. 1973. A theory of marriage: Part I. *Journal of Political Economy* 81: 813–846.

Becker, Gary S. 1974. A theory of marriage: Part II. *Journal of Political Economy* 82: S11–S26.

Berg, Maarten, and Ruut Veenhoven. 2010. Income inequality and happiness in 119 nations: In search for an optimum that does not appear to exist. In *Social Policy and Happiness in Europe*, ed. Bent Greve. Elgar.

Bernheim, Douglas B. 2009. The psychology and neurobiology of judgement and decision making: What's in it for economists. In *Neuroeconomics, Decision Making and the Brain*, ed. Paul W. Glimcher, Colin F. Camerer, Ernst Fehr, and Russel A. Poldrack. Academic Press.

Blanchflower, David G., and Andrew J. Oswald. 2004. Well-being over time in Britain and the USA. *Journal of Public Economics* 88: 1359–1386.

Blanchflower, David G., and Andrew J. Oswald. 2005. Happiness and the Human Development Index: The paradox of Australia. *Australian Economic Review* 38: 307–318.

Blanchflower, David G., and Andrew J. Oswald. 2008. Is well-being U-shaped over the life cycle? *Social Science & Medicine* 66: 1733–1749.

Bolton, Gary E., and Axel Ockenfels. 2000. ERC: A theory of equity, reciprocity and competition. *American Economic Review* 90: 166–193.

Breterton, Finbarr, J. Peter Clinch, and Susana Ferreira. 2008. Happiness, geography and the environment. *Ecological Economics* 65: 386–396.

Brickman, Philip, Dan Coates, and Ronnie Janoff-Bulman. 1978. Lottery winners and accident victims: Is happiness relative? *Journal of Personality and Social Psychology* 36: 917–927.

Bruni, Luigino, and Robert Sugden. 2007. The road not taken: How psychology was removed from economics, and how it might be brought back. *Economic Journal* 117: 146–173.

Bucher, Anton. 2009. *Psychologie des Glücks: Ein Handbuch*. Beltz Psychologie Verlags Union.

Burroughs, James E., and Aric Rindfleisch. 2002. Materialism and well-being: A conflicting values perspective. *Journal of Consumer Research* 29: 348–370.

Bylsma, Lauren M., April Taylor-Clift, and Jonathan Rottenberg. 2011. Emotional reactivity to daily events in major and minor depression. *Journal of Abnormal Psychology* 120: 155–167.

CAE-CEE. 2010. *Monitoring Economic Performance, Quality of Life and Sustainability*. Conseil d'Analyse Économique and German Council of Economic Experts.

Chaudhuri, Annanish. 2011. Sustaining cooperation in laboratory public goods experiments: A selective survey of the literature. *Experimental Economics* 14 (1): 47–83.

Cherry, Todd L., Peter Fryblom, and Jason F. Shogren. 2002. Hardnose the dictator. *American Economic Review* 92: 1218–1221.

Clark, Andrew E. 2001. What really matters in a job? Hedonic measurement using quit data. *Labour Economics* 8: 223–242.

Clark, Andrew E. 2003. Unemployment as a social norm: Psychological evidence from panel data. *Journal of Labor Economics* 21: 323–351.

Clark, Andrew E. 2006. A note on unhappiness and unemployment duration. *Applied Economics Quarterly* 52: 291–308.

Clark, Andrew E. 2009. Work, jobs and well-being across the millennium. In *International Differences in Well-Being*, ed. Ed Diener, John Helliwell, and Daniel Kahneman. Oxford University Press.

Clark, Andrew E., and Andrew J. Oswald. 1996. Satisfaction and comparison income. *Journal of Public Economics* 61: 359–381.

Clark, Andrew, and Claudia Senik. 2011. Is happiness different from flourishing? Cross-country evidence from the ESS. *Revue d'Economie Politique* 121: 17–34.

Clark, Andrew E., Yannis Georgellis, and Peter Sanfey. 2001. Scarring: The psychological impact of past unemployment. *Economica* 68: 221–241.

Clark, Andrew E., Ed Diener, Yannis Georgellis, and Richard E. Lucas. 2008a. Lags and leads in life satisfaction: A test of the baseline hypothesis. *Economic Journal* 118: 222–243.

Clark, Andrew E., Paul Frijters, and Michael Shields. 2008b. Relative income, happiness and utility: An explanation for the Easterlin Paradox and other puzzles. *Journal of Economic Literature* 46: 95–144.

Clark, Andrew E., Andreas Knabe, and Steffen Rätzel. 2009. Boon or bane? Others' unemployment, well-being and job insecurity. *Labour Economics* 17: 52–61.

Clark, Andrew E., Nicolai Kristensen, and Niels Westergård-Nielsen. 2009. Economic satisfaction and income rank in small neighbourhoods. *Journal of the European Economic Association* 7: 519–527.

Cohen, Sheldon, William J. Doyle, Ronald B. Turner, Cuneyt M. Alper, and David P. Skoner. 2003. Emotional style and susceptibility to the common cold. *Psychosomatic Medicine* 65: 652–657.

Cohn, Richard M. 1978. The effect of employment status change on self-attitudes. *Social Psychology* 41: 81–93.

Coleman, James S. 1988. Social capital in the creation of human capital. *American Journal of Sociology* 94: 95–120.

Danner, Deborah D., David A. Snowdon, and Wallace V. Friesen. 2001. Positive emotions in early life and longevity: Findings from the nun study. *Journal of Personality and Social Psychology* 80: 804–813.

Deaton, Angus. 2008. Income, health, and well-being around the world: Evidence from the Gallup World Poll. *Journal of Economic Perspectives* 22: 53–72.

Deaton, Angus. 2013. The financial crisis and the well-being of Americans. *Oxford Economic Papers* 64: 1–26.

Dekker, Sidney, and Wilmar B. Schaufeli. 1995. The effects of job insecurity on psychological health and withdrawal: A longitudinal study. *Australian Psychologist* 30: 57–63.

Delhey, Jan, and Ulrich Kohler. 2006. From nationally bounded to pan-European inequalities? On the importance of foreign countries as reference groups. *European Sociological Review* 22 (2): 125–140.

Delhey, Jan, and Christian Kroll. 2013. A 'happiness test' for the new measures of national well-being: How much better than GDP are they? In *Human Happiness and the Pursuit of Maximization. Is More Always Better?* ed. Hilke Brockmann and Jan Delhey. Springer.

Diener, Ed, Ronald Inglehart, and Louis Tay. 2013. Theory and validity of life satisfaction scales. *Social Indicators Research* 112: 497–527.

Diener, Ed, and Richard E. Lucas. 1999. Personality and subjective well-being. In *Well-Being: The Foundations of Hedonic Psychology*, ed. Daniel Kahneman, Ed Diener, and Norbert Schwarz. Russell Sage Foundation.

Diener, Ed, Richard E. Lucas, Ulrich Schimmack, and John F. Helliwell. 2009a. *Well-Being for Public Policy*. Oxford University Press.

Diener, Ed, Daniel Kahneman, Raksha Arora, James Harter, and William Tov. 2009b. Income's differential influence on judgments of life versus affective well-being. In *Assessing Well-Being: The Collected Works of Ed Diener*, ed. Ed Diener. Springer Netherlands.

Diener, Ed, Weiting Ng, James Harter, and Raksha Arora. 2010. Wealth and happiness across the world: Material prosperity predicts life evaluation, whereas psychosocial prosperity predicts positive feeling. *Journal of Personality and Social Psychology* 99 (1): 52–61.

Diener, Ed, and Shigehiro Oishi. 2000. Money and happiness: Income and subjective well-being across nations. In *Culture and Subjective Well-Being*, ed. Ed Diener and Eunkook M. Suh. MIT Press.

Diener, Ed, and William Pavot. 2008. The satisfaction with life scale and the emerging construct of life satisfaction. *Journal of Positive Psychology* 3: 137–152.

Diener, Ed, and Eunkook M. Suh. 1999. National differences in subjective well-being. In *Well-Being: The Foundations of Hedonic Psychology*, ed. Daniel Kahneman, Ed Diener, and Norbert Schwarz. Russell Sage Foundation.

Diener, Ed, Louis Tay, and Shigehiro Oishi. 2013. Rising income and the subjective well-being of nations. *Journal of Personality and Social Psychology* 104: 267–276.

Diener, Ed, and Louis Tay. 2014. Review of the Day Reconstruction Method (DRM). *Social Indicators Research* 116: 255–267.

Dijkers, Marcel. 1997. Quality of life after spinal cord injury: A meta analysis of the effects of disablement components. *Nature* 35: 829–840.

Dijkers, Marcel. 1999. Correlates of life satisfaction among persons with spinal cord injury. *Archives of Physical Medicine and Rehabilitation* 80: 867–876.

Di Tella, Rafael, John P. Haisken-De New, and Robert MacCulloch. 2010. Happiness adaptation to income and to status in an individual panel. *Journal of Economic Behavior & Organization* 76 (3): 834–852.

Di Tella, Rafael, Robert J. MacCulloch, and Andrew J. Oswald. 2001. Preferences over inflation and unemployment. Evidence from surveys of happiness. *American Economic Review* 91: 335–341.

Di Tella, Rafael, Robert J. MacCulloch, and Andrew J. Oswald. 2003. The macroeconomics of happiness. *Review of Economics and Statistics* 8: 809–827.

Dockray, Samantha, Nina Grant, Arthur Stone, Daniel Kahneman, Jane Wardle, and Andrew Steptoe. 2010. A comparison of affect ratings obtained with ecological momentary assessment and the Day Reconstruction Method. *Social Indicators Research* 99 (2): 269–283.

Dolan, Paul, and Daniel Kahneman. 2008. Interpretations of utility and their implications for the valuation of health. *Economic Journal* 118: 215–234.

Dolan, Paul, Tessa Peasgood, and Mathew White. 2008. Do we really know what makes us happy? A review of the economic literature on the factors associated with subjective well-being. *Journal of Economic Psychology* 29: 94–122.

Dolan, Paul, and Nattavudh Powdthavee. 2012. Thinking about it: A note on attention and well-being losses from unemployment. *Applied Economics Letters* 19: 325–328.

Dorn, David, Justina A.V. Fischer, Gebhard Kirchgässner, and Alfonso Sousa-Poza. 2007. Is it culture or democracy? The impact of democracy and culture on happiness. *Social Indicators Research* 82: 505–526.

Duesenberry, James. 1949. *Income, Savings and the Theory of Consumer Behavior*. Harvard University Press.

Dunn, Elizabeth W., Lara B. Aknin, and Michael I. Norton. 2008. Spending money on others promotes happiness. *Science* 319 (5870): 1687–1688.

Easterlin, Richard A. 1974. Does economic growth improve the human lot? Some empirical evidence?. In *Nations and Households in Economic Growth*, ed. Paul A. David and Melvin W. Reder. Stanford University Press.

Easterlin, Richard A. 1995. Will raising the incomes of all increase the happiness of all? *Journal of Economic Behavior & Organization* 27: 35–47.

Easterlin, Richard A., Laura Angelescu McVey, Malgorzata Switek, Onnicha Sawangfa, and Jacqueline Smith Zweig. 2010. The happiness–income paradox revisited. *Proceedings of the National Academy of Sciences* 107: 22463–22468.

Fechner, Gustav Theodor. 1860. *Elemente der Psychophysik*. Breitkopf and Härtel.

Fehr, Ernst, and Klaus M. Schmidt. 1999. A theory of fairness, competition and cooperation. *Quarterly Journal of Economics* 114: 817–868.

Fehr, Ernst, and Antonio Rangel. 2011. Neuroeconomic foundations of economic choice—Recent advances. *Journal of Economic Perspectives* 25: 3–30.

Ferreira, Susana, and Mirko Moro. 2010. On the use of subjective well-being data for environmental valuation. *Environmental and Resource Economics* 46: 249–273.

Ferrer-i-Carbonell, Ada. 2005. Income and well-being: An empirical analysis of the comparison income effect. *Journal of Public Economics* 89: 997–1019.

Flood, Merrill M. 1952. Some Experimental Games. Research Memorandum RM-789, RAND Corporation.

Flood, Merrill M. 1958. Some experimental games. *Management Science* 5: 5–26.

Flouri, Eirini. 2004. Subjective well-being in midlife: The role of involvement of and closeness to parents in childhood. *Journal of Happiness Studies* 5: 335–358.

Forsythe, Robert, Joel L. Horrowitz, N. Eugene Savin, and Martin Sefton. 1994. Fairness in simple bargaining experiments. *Games and Economic Behavior* 6: 347–369.

Frank, Robert H. 1985. *Choosing the Right Pond: Human Behavior and the Quest for Status*. Oxford University Press.

Frank, Robert H. 2004. How not to buy happiness. *Daedalus* 133: 69–79.

Frey, Bruno S. 2008. *Happiness. A Revolution in Economics*. MIT Press.

Frey, Bruno S., and Alois Stutzer. 2000. Happiness, economy and institutions. *Economic Journal* 110: 918–938.

Frey, Bruno S., and Alois Stutzer. 2002. *Happiness and Economics*. Princeton University Press.

Frey, Bruno S., and Alois Stutzer. 2006. Does marriage make people happy, or do happy people get married? *Journal of Socio-Economics* 35: 326–347.

Frijters, Paul, and Tony Beatton. 2012. The mystery of the U-shaped relationship between happiness and age. *Journal of Economic Behavior & Organization* 82: 525–542.

Frijters, Paul, and Bernard M. S. Van Praag. 1998. The effects of climate on welfare and well-being in Russia. *Climatic Change* 39: 61–81.

Gale, David. 1960. *The Theory of Linear Economic Models*. McGraw-Hill.

Gardner, Jonathan, and Andrew J. Oswald. 2004. How is mortality affected by money, marriage, and stress? *Journal of Health Economics* 23: 1181–1207.

Gardner, Jonathan, and Andrew J. Oswald. 2007. Money and mental wellbeing: A longitudinal study of medium-sized lottery wins. *Journal of Health Economics* 26: 49–60.

Georgellis, Yannis, Nicholas Tsitsianis, and Ya Ping Yin. 2009. Personal values as mitigating factors in the link between income and life satisfaction: Evidence from the European Social Survey. *Social Indicators Research* 91: 329–344.

Glazer, Amihai, and Kai Konrad. 1996. A signaling explanation for private charity. *American Economic Review* 86: 1019–1028.

Glimcher, Paul W, Colin F. Camerer, Ernst Fehr, and Russel A. Poldrack. 2009. Introduction: A brief history of neuroeconomics. In *Neuroeconomics, Decision Making and the Brain*, ed. Paul W Glimcher, Colin F. Camerer, Ernst Fehr, and Russel A. Poldrack. Academic Press.

Graham, Carol, and Andrew Felton. 2006. Inequality and happiness: Insights from Latin America. *Journal of Economic Inequality* 4: 107–122.

Grund, Christian, and Dirk Sliwka. 2007. Reference-dependent preferences and the impact of wage increases on job satisfaction: Theory and evidence. *Journal of Institutional and Theoretical Economics* 163: 313–335.

Harbaugh, William. 1998a. The prestige motive for making charitable transfers. *American Economic Review* 88: 277–282.

Harbaugh, William. 1998b. What do donations buy? *Journal of Public Economics* 67: 269–284.

Hare, Todd A., Jonathan Malmoud, and Antonio Rangel. 2011. Focusing attention on the health aspects of food change value signals in vmPFC and improves dietary choice. *Journal of Neuroscience* 31: 11077–11087.

Harker, LeeAnne, and Dacher Keltner. 2001. Expressions of positive emotion in women's college yearbook pictures and their relationship to personality and life outcomes across adulthood. *Journal of Personality and Social Psychology* 80: 112–124.

Headey, Bruce W., Ruud Muffels, and Mark Wooden. 2008. Money doesn't buy happiness. or does it? A reconsideration based on the combined effects of wealth, income and consumption. *Social Indicators Research* 87: 65–82.

Helliwell, John F. 2003. How's life? Combining individual and national variables to explain subjective well-being. *Economic Modelling* 20: 331–360.

Helliwell, John F., and Haifang Huang. 2008. How's your government? International evidence linking good government and well-being. *British Journal of Political Science* 38: 595–619.

Helliwell, John F., and Robert D. Putnam. 2004. *The social context of well-being*. Philosophical Transactions of the Royal Society, Series B 359: 1435-1446.

Hetschko, Clemens, Andreas Knabe, and Ronnie Schöb. 2014. Changing identity: Retiring from unemployment. *Economic Journal* 124: 149–166.

Hirsch, Fred. 1976. *Social Limits to Growth*. Harvard University Press.

Holländer, Heinz. 1990. A social exchange approach to voluntary cooperation. *American Economic Review* 80: 1157–1167.

Holländer, Heinz. 2001. On the validity of utility statements: standard theory versus Duesenberry's. *Journal of Economic Behavior & Organization* 45: 227–249.

Houthakker, Hendrik. 1950. Revealed preferences and the utility function. *Economica* 17: 159–174.

Howell, Ryan T., and Colleen J. Howell. 2008. The relation of economic status to subjective well-being in developing countries: A meta-analysis. *Psychological Bulletin* 134: 536–560.

Hudson, John. 2006. Institutional trust and subjective well-being across the EU. *Kyklos* 59 (1): 43–62.

Jackson, Paul R., and Peter Warr. 1987. Mental health of unemployed men in different parts of England and Wales. *British Medical Journal* 295: 525.

Johnson, Eric J., and Daniel Goldstein. 2003. Do defaults save lives? *Science* 302 (5649): 1338–1339.

Kahneman, Daniel. 1999. Objective happiness. In *Well-Being: The Foundations of Hedonic Psychology*, ed. Daniel Kahneman, Ed Diener, and Norbert Schwarz. Russell Sage Foundation.

Kahneman, Daniel, and Angus Deaton. 2010. High income improves evaluation of life but not emotional well-being. *Proceedings of the National Academy of Sciences* 107: 16489–16493.

Kahneman, Daniel, and Alan B. Krueger. 2006. Developments in the measurement of subjective well-being. *Journal of Economic Perspectives* 20: 3–24.

Kahneman, Daniel, Barbara Fredrickson, Charles A. Schreiber, and Donald Redelmeier. 1993. When more pain is preferred to less: Adding a better end. *Psychological Science* 4: 401–405.

Kahneman, Daniel, Alan B. Krueger, David Schkade, Norbert Schwarz, and Arthur Stone. 2004. Toward national well-being accounts. *American Economic Review* 94: 429–434.

Kahneman, Daniel, Alan B. Krueger, David Schkade, Norbert Schwarz, and Arthur Stone. 2006. Would you be happier if you were richer? A focusing illusion. *Science* 312: 1908–1910.

Kaprio, Jaako, Markku Koskenvuo, and Heli Rita. 1987. Mortality after bereavement: A prospective study of 95,647 widowed persons. *American Journal of Public Health* 77: 283–287.

Kapteyn, Arie, James P. Smith, and Arthur Van Soest. 2013. Are Americans really less happy with their incomes? *Review of Income and Wealth* 59: 44–65.

Kassenboehmer, Sonja C., and John P. Haisken-DeNew. 2012. Heresy or enlightenment? The well-being age U-shape effect is flat. *Economics Letters* 117: 235–238.

Kassenboehmer, Sonja C., and Christoph M. Schmidt. 2011. *Beyond GDP and Back: What is the Value-Added by Additional Components of Welfare Measurement?* IZA Discussion Paper No. 5453, IZA, Bonn.

Kasser, Tim. 2002. *The High Price of Materialism*. MIT Press.

Kasser, Tim, and Aaron Ahuvia. 2002. Materialistic values and well-being in business students. *European Journal of Social Psychology* 32: 137–146.

Keyes, Corey Lee M. 2006. Mental health in adolescence: Is America's youth flourishing? *American Journal of Orthopsychiatry* 76: 395–402.

Kiecolt-Glaser, Janice K., Lynanne McGuire, Theodore F. Robles, and Ronald Glaser. 2002. Emotions, morbidity, and mortality: New perspectives from sychoneuroimmunology. *Annual Review of Psychology* 53: 83–107.

King, Gary, Christopher J. L. Murray, Joshua A. Salomon, and Ajay Tandon. 2004. Enhancing the validity and cross-cultural comparability of measurement in survey research. *American Political Science Review* 98: 567–583.

Knabe, Andreas, and Steffen Rätzel. 2011. Scarring or scaring? The psychological impact of past unemployment and future unemployment risk. *Economica* 78: 283–293.

Knabe, Andreas, Ronnie Schöb, Steffen Rätzel, and Joachim Weimann. 2010. Dissatisfied with life, but having a good day: Time-use and well-being of the unemployed. *Economic Journal* 120: 867–889.

Knabe, Andreas, Ronnie Schöb, and Joachim Weimann. 2012. Partnership, Gender Roles and the Well-Being Cost of Unemployment. CESifo Working Paper No. 3932, September.

Koivumaa-Honkanen, Heli, Risto Honkanen, Heimo Viinamäki, Kauko Heikkilä, Jaakko Kaprio, and Markku Koskenvuo. 2001. Life satisfaction and suicide: A 20-year follow-up study. *American Journal of Psychiatry* 158: 433–439.

Köszegi, Botond, and Matthew Rabin. 2008. Choices, situations, and happiness. *Journal of Public Economics* 92: 1821–1832.

Krueger, Alan B., and Andreas Mueller. 2012a. The lot of the unemployed: A time use perspective. *Journal of the European Economic Association* 10 (4): 765–794.

Krueger, Alan B., and Andreas Mueller. 2012b. Time use, emotional well-being and unemployment: Evidence from longitudinal data. *American Economic Review* 102: 594–599.

Krueger, Alan B., and David A. Schkade. 2008. The reliability of subjective well-being measures. *Journal of Public Economics* 92: 1833–1845.

Krueger, Alan, Daniel Kahneman, Claude Fischler, David Schkade, Norbert Schwarz, and Arthur Stone. 2009. Time Use and Subjective Well-Being in France and the U.S. *Social Indicators Research* 93 (1): 7–18.

Lane, Robert. 1998. The joyless market economy. In *Economics, Values, and Organization*, ed. Avner Ben-Ner and Louis Putterman. Cambridge University Press.

Lane, Robert. 2000. *The Loss of Happiness in Market Democracies*. Yale ISPS Series. Yale University Press.

Larsen, Val. M., Joseph Sirgy, and Newell N. Wright. 1999. Materialism: The constructs, measures, antecedents, and consequences. *Academy of Marketing Studies Journal* 3: 78–110.

Layard, Richard. 1980. Human satisfactions and public policy. *Economic Journal* 90: 737–750.

Layard, Richard. 2005. *Happiness: Lessons from a New Science*. Penguin.

Layard, Richard. 2006. Happiness and public policy: A challenge to the profession. *Economic Journal* 16: C24–C33.

Lee, Gary R., Alfred DeMaris, Stefoni Bavin, and Rachel Sullivan. 2001. Gender differences in the depressive effect of widowhood in later life. *Journals of Gerontology. Series B, Psychological Sciences and Social Sciences* 56B: 56–61.

Lee, Sangheon, Deirdre McCann, and Jon C. Messenger. 2007. *Working Time Around the World: Trends in Working Hours, Laws and Policies in a Global Comparative Perspective*. Routledge.

Lehman, Darrin R., Camille B. Wortman, and Allan F. Williams. 1987. Long-term effects of losing a spouse or child in a motor vehicle crash. *Journal of Personality and Social Psychology* 52: 218–231.

Lepper, Heidi S. 1998. Use of other-reports to validate subjective wellbeing measures. *Social Indicators Research* 44: 367–379.

Lévy-Garboua, Louis, and Claude Montmarquette. 2004. Reported job satisfaction: What does it mean? *Journal of Socio-Economics* 33: 135–151.

List, John A. 2007. On the interpretation of giving in dictator games. *Journal of Political Economy* 115: 482–493.

Lucas, Richard E. 2007. Long-term disability is associated with lasting changes in subjective well-being: Evidence from two nationally representative longitudinal studies. *Journal of Personality and Social Psychology* 92: 717–730.

Lucas, Richard E., and M. Brent Donnellan. 2012. Estimating the reliability of single-item life satisfaction measures: Results from four national panel studies. *Social Indicators Research* 105: 323–331.

Lucas, Richard E., and Nicole E. Lawless. 2013. Does life seem better on a sunny day? Examining the association between daily weather conditions and life satisfaction judgments. *Journal of Personality and Social Psychology* 104: 872–884.

Lucas, Richard E., Andrew E. Clark, Yannis Georgellis, and Ed Diener. 2003. Reexamining adaptation and the set point model of happiness: Reactions to changes in marital status. *Journal of Personality and Social Psychology* 84: 527–539.

Lucas, Richard E., Andrew E. Clark, Yannis Georgellis, and Ed Diener. 2004. Unemployment alters the set point for life satisfaction. *Psychological Science* 15: 8–13.

Lüchinger, Simon. 2009. Valuing air quality using the life satisfaction approach. *Economic Journal* 119: 482–515.

Luhmann, Maike, Ulrich Schimmack, and Michael Eid. 2011. Stability and variability in the relationship between subjective well-being and income. *Journal of Research in Personality* 45: 186–197.

Luhmann, Maike, Wilhelm Hofmann, Michael Eid, and Richard E. Lucas. 2012. Subjective well-being and adaptation to life events: A meta-analysis. *Journal of Personality and Social Psychology* 102 (3): 592–615.

Luhmann, Maike, Richard E. Lucas, Michael Eid, and Ed Diener. 2013. The prospective effect of life satisfaction on life events. *Social Psychological and Personality Science* 4: 39–45.

Luttmer, Erzo F. P. 2000. *Inequality and Poverty Dynamics in Transition Economics: Disentangling Real Events from Noisy Data.* Policy Research Working Paper Series 2549, World Bank.

Luttmer, Erzo F. P. 2005. Neighbors as negatives: Relative earnings and well-being. *Quarterly Journal of Economics* 120: 923–1002.

Lykken, David, and Auke Tellegen. 1996. Happiness is a stochastic phenomenon. *Psychological Science* 7: 186–189.

MacKerron, George. 2012. Happiness and Environmental Quality. PhD thesis, London School of Economics and Political Science.

Maier, Heiner, and Jacqui Smith. 1999. Psychological predictors of mortality in old age. *Journals of Gerontology, Series B* 54B: P44–P54.

Meier, Stephan, and Alois Stutzer. 2008. Is volunteering rewarding in itself? *Economica* 75: 39–59.

Morillo, Fátima Gendolla. 2005. Examen + Kind = Zufrieden? Lebenszufriedenheit von Akademikerinnen und Akademikern. Dissertation, Friedrich-Alexander-Universität Erlangen-Nürnberg.

Myers, David G. 2000. The funds, friends, and faith of happy people. *American Psychologist* 55: 56–67.

National Research Council. 2013. *Subjective Well-Being: Measuring Happiness, Suffering, and Other Dimensions of Experience.* National Academies Press.

Ng, Yew-Kwang. 2008. Happiness studies: Ways to improve comparability and some public policy implications. *Economic Record* 84: 253–266.

Nolen-Hoeksema, Susan. 1991. Responses to depression and their effects on the duration of depressive episodes. *Journal of Abnormal Psychology* 100: 569–582.

Nozick, Robert. 1974. *Anarchy, state, and utopia.* Basic Books.

OECD. 2013. *OECD Guidelines on Measuring Subjective Well-being.*

Oishi, Shigehiro, Selin Kesebir, and Ed Diener. 2011. Income inequality and happiness. *Psychological Science* 22: 1095–1100.

Oishi, Shigehiro, Ulrich Schimmack, and Ed Diener. 2012. Progressive taxation and the subjective well-being of nations. *Psychological Science* 23: 86–92.

Orentlicher, David. 2009. Presumed consent to organ donation: Its rise and fall in the United States. *Rutgers Law Review* 61: 295–331.

Oreopoulos, Philip, and Kjell G. Salvanes. 2011. Priceless: The nonpecuniary benefits of schooling. *Journal of Economic Perspectives* 25: 159–184.

Oswald, Andrew J., and Nattavudh Powdthavee. 2008. Does happiness adapt? A longitudinal study of disability with implications for economists and judges. *Journal of Public Economics* 92: 1061–1077.

Oswald, Andrew J., and Stephen Wu. 2010. Objective confirmation of subjective measures of human well-being: Evidence from the U.S.A. *Science* 327: 576–579.

Padoa-Schioppa, Camillo. 2009. Range-adapting representation of economic value in the orbitofrontal cortex. *Journal of Neuroscience* 29: 14004–14014.

Patterson, David R., John J. Everett, Charles H. Bombardier, Kent A. Questadt, Victoria K. Lee, and Janet A. Marvin. 1993. Psychological effects of severe burn injuries. *Psychological Bulletin* 113: 362–378.

Pichler, Florian. 2006. Subjective quality of life of young Europeans: Feeling happy but who knows why? *Social Indicators Research* 75: 419–444.

Plassmann, Hilke, John O'Doherty, Baba Shiv, and Antonio Ranchel. 2008. Marketing actions can modulate neural representations of experienced pleasantness. *Proceedings of the National Academy of Sciences* 105: 1050–1054.

Pollak, Robert A. 1976. Interdependent preferences. *American Economic Review* 66: 309–320.

Powdthavee, Nattavudh. 2008. Putting a price tag on friends, relatives, and neighbours: Using surveys of life satisfaction to value social relationships. *Journal of Socio-Economics* 37: 1459–1480.

Putnam, Robert D. 1995. Bowling alone: America's declining social capital. *Journal of Democracy* 6: 65–78.

Putnam, Robert D., Robert Leonardi, and Raffaella Nanetti. 1993. *Making Democracy Work*. Princeton University Press.

Quari, Salmai. 2010. Marriage, adaptation and happiness: Are there long-lasting gains to marriage? Unpublished manuscript.

Quoidbach, Jordi, Elizabeth W. Dunn, K. V. Petrides, and Moira Mikolajczak. 2010. Money giveth, money taketh away: The dual effect of wealth on happiness. *Psychological Science* 21: 759–763.

Rätzel, Steffen. 2012. Labour supply, life satisfaction, and the (dis)utility of work. *Scandinavian Journal of Economics* 114: 1160–1181.

Rayo, Luis, and Gary Becker. 2007a. Habits, peers, and happiness: An evolutionary perspective. *American Economic Review* 97: 487–491.

Rayo, Luis, and Gary Becker. 2007b. Evolutionary efficiency and happiness. *Journal of Political Economy* 115: 302–337.

Redelmeier, Donald A., and Daniel Kahneman. 1996. Patients' memories of painful medical treatments: Real-time and retrospective evaluations of two minimally invasive procedures. *Pain* 66: 3–8.

Redelmeier, Donald A., Joel Katz, and Daniel Kahneman. 2003. Memories of colonoscopy: A randomized trial. *Pain* 104: 187–194.

Rehdanz, Kathrin, and David Maddison. 2005. Climate and happiness. *Ecological Economics* 52: 111–125.

Roth, Alvin E. 1995. Bargaining experiments. In *The Handbook of Experimental Economics*, ed. John H. Kagel and Alvin E. Roth. Princeton University Press.

Ryff, Carol D., and Keyes, Corey Lee M. 1995. The structure of psychological well-being revisited. *Journal of Personality and Social Psychology* 69: 719–727.

Sacks, Daniel, Betsey Stevenson, and Justin Wolfers. 2012. Growth in income and subjective well-being over time. Paper presented at Nineteenth Annual Meeting of the Society of Labor Economists, Chicago.

Sagiv, Lilach, and Shalom H. Schwartz. 2000. Value priorities and subjective well-being: Direct relations and congruity effects. *European Journal of Social Psychology* 30: 177–198.

Sandvik, Ed, Ed Diener, and Larry Seidlitz. 1993. Subjective well-being: The convergence and stability of self-report and non-self-report measures. *Journal of Personality* 61: 317–342.

Schimmack, Ulrich, and Shigehiro Oishi. 2005. The influence of chronically and temporarily accessible information on life satisfaction judgments. *Journal of Personality and Social Psychology* 89: 395–406.

Schoon, Ingrid, Leeni Hansson, and Katariina Salmela-Aro. 2005. Combining work and family life: Life satisfaction among married and divorced men and women in Estonia, Finland and the UK. *European Psychologist* 10: 309–319.

Schulz, Richard, and Susan Decker. 1985. Long-term adjustment to physical disability: The role of social support, perceived control, and self-blame. *Journal of Personality and Social Psychology* 48: 1162–1172.

Schwartz, Shalom H. 1992. Universals in the content and structure of values: Theoretical advances and empirical tests in 20 countries. In *Advances in Experimental Social Psychology*, volume 25, ed. M. Zanna. Academic Press.

Schwarz, Norbert. 1987. *Stimmung als Information: Untersuchungen zum Einfluß von Stimmungen auf die Bewertung des eigenen Lebens*. Springer.

Schwarz, Norbert, and Gerald L. Clore. 1983. Mood, misattribution, and judgments of well-being: Informative and directive functions of affective states. *Journal of Personality and Social Psychology* 45: 513–523.

Schwarz, Norbert, and Fritz Strack. 1999. Reports of subjective well-being: Judgmental processes and their methodological implications. In *Well-Being: The Foundations of Hedonic Psychology*, ed. Daniel Kahneman, Ed Diener and Norbert Schwarz. Russell Sage Foundation.

Schwarz, Norbert, Fritz Strack, Detlev Kommer, and Dirk Wagner. 1987. Soccer, rooms, and the quality of your life: Mood effects on judgments of satisfaction. *European Journal of Social Psychology* 18: 69–79.

Sen, Amartya K. 1990. Development as capability expansion. In *Human Development and the International Development Strategy for the 1990s*, ed. Keith Griffin and John Knight. Macmillan.

Sirgy, M. Joseph. 1998. Materialism and quality of life. *Social Indicators Research* 43: 227–260.

Sirgy, M. Joseph, Eda Gurel-Atay, Dave Webb, Muris Cicic, Melika Husic-Mehmedovic, Ahmet Ekici, Andreas Herrmann, Ibrahim Hegazy, Dong-Jin Lee, and J. S. Johar. 2013. Is materialism all that bad? Effects on satisfaction with material life, life satisfaction, and economic motivation. *Social Indicators Research* 110: 349–366.

Sloane, Peter J., and H. Williams. 2000. Job satisfaction, comparison earnings, and gender. *Labour* 14: 473–502.

Smith, Dylan M., Kenneth M. Langa, Mohammed U. Kabeto, and Peter A. Ubel. 2005. Health, wealth, and happiness. *Psychological Science* 16: 663–666.

Snowdon, John. 2001. Is depression more prevalent in old age? *Australian and New Zealand Journal of Psychiatry* 35: 782–787.

Stavrova, Olga, Thomas Schlösser, and Detlef Fetchenhauer. 2011. Are the unemployed equally unhappy all around the world? The role of the social norms to work and welfare state provision in 28 OECD countries. *Journal of Economic Psychology* 32: 159–171.

Stevenson, Betsey, and Justin Wolfers. 2008. Economic growth and subjective well-being: Reassessing the Easterlin Paradox. *Brookings Papers on Economic Activity* 39: 1–102.

Stiglitz, Joseph E., Amartya Sen, and Jean-Paul Fitoussi. 2009. Report by the Commission on the Measurement of Economic Performance and Social Progress. Available at www.stiglitz-sen-fitoussi.fr.

Stone, Arthur A., Joseph E. Schwartz, Joan E. Broderick, and Angus Deaton. 2010. A snapshot of the age distribution of psychological well-being in the United States. *Proceedings of the National Academy of Sciences* 107: 9985–9990.

Strack, Fritz, Leonard L. Martin, and Norbert Schwarz. 1988. Priming and communication: Social determinants of information use in judgments of life satisfaction. *European Journal of Social Psychology* 18: 429–442.

Ubel, Peter A., Heather P. Lacey, and Dylan M. Smith. 2006. Hope I die before I get old: Mispredicting happiness across the adult lifespan. *Journal of Happiness Studies* 7: 167–182.

Van Landeghem, Bert. 2012. A test for the convexity of human well-being over the life cycle: Longitudinal evidence from a 20-year panel. *Journal of Economic Behavior & Organization* 81: 571–582.

Van Praag, Bernhard, and Barbara E. Baarsma. 2005. Using happiness surveys to value intangibles: The case of airport noise. *Economic Journal* 52: 111–125.

Van Praag, Bernard M. S., and Paul Frijters. 1999. The measurement of welfare and well-being: The Leyden approach. In *Well-Being: The Foundations of Hedonic Psychology*, ed. Daniel Kahneman, Ed Diener, and Norbert Schwarz. Rusell Sage Foundation.

Vansteenkiste, Maarten, Bart Duriez, Joke Simons, and Bart Soenens. 2006. Materialistic values and well-being among business students: Further evidence of their detrimental effect. *Journal of Applied Social Psychology* 36: 2892–2908.

Veblen, Thorstein. 1899. *The Theory of Leisure Class*. Modern Library.

Veenhoven, Ruut. 2006. *World Database of Happiness. Happiness in Nations, Rank Report 2006–1*. Erasmus University, Rotterdam.

Veenhoven, Ruut, and M. Hagerty. 2006. Rising happiness in nations 1946-2004: A reply to Easterlin. *Social Indicators Research* 79: 421–436.

Veenhoven, Ruut, and Floris Vergunst. 2013. The Easterlin Illusion. EHERO Working Paper 2013/1 Erasmus University Rotterdam.

von Neumann, John, and Oskar Morgenstern. 1944. *Theory of Games and Economic Behavior*. Princeton University Press.

von Scheve, Christian, Frederike Esche, and Jürgen Schupp 2013. The Emotional Timeline of Unemployment: Anticipation, Reaction, and Adaptation. SOEP papers on Multidisciplinary Panel Data Research No. 593–2013.

Welsch, Heinz. 2002. Preferences over prosperity and pollution: Environmental valuation based on happiness surveys. *Kyklos* 55: 473–494.

Welsch, Heinz. 2006. Environment and happiness: Valuation of air pollution using life satisfaction data. *Ecological Economics* 58: 801–813.

Welsch, Heinz. 2007. Environmental welfare analysis: A life satisfaction approach. *Ecological Economics* 62: 544–551.

Wheeler, Ladd, Harry Reis, and John B. Nezlek. 1983. Loneliness, social interaction, and sex roles. *Journal of Personality and Social Psychology* 45: 943–953.

Winkelmann, Liliane, and Rainer Winkelmann. 1998. Why are the unemployed so unhappy? Evidence from panel data. *Economica* 65: 1–15.

Wolfers, Justin. 2003. Is business cycle volatility costly? Evidence from surveys of subjective well-being. *International Finance* 6: 1–26.

Wu, Stephen. 2001. Adapting to heart conditions: A test of the hedonic treadmill. *Journal of Health Economics* 20: 495–508.

Zou, Christopher, Ulrich Schimmack, and Judith Gere. 2013. The validity of well-being measures: A multiple-indicator-multiple-rater model. *Psychological Assessment* 25: 1247–1254.

Index

Affective happiness, 104, 107–111, 124–130, 154
  and life satisfaction, 153, 154
  of unemployed, 131–140
Affect, net, 109, 110, 132, 133, 135, 137
Age, 44, 45, 62
Agreeableness, 38
Altruistic behavior, 14, 38
Aristotle, 105
Australia, 64
Austria, 81

Belgium, 40, 81, 120
Benevolent behavior, 67–71
Better Life Index, 78
Bhutan, 76
British Household Panel Survey, 6, 18, 59

Canada, 69
Cantril's Ladder, 116
Charities, donations to, 71
Child care, 135, 136, 142
Children, 48, 49, 135
Cognitive well-being, 104, 110, 111, 116, 121, 124, 130, 139
Colombia, 115
Commission sur la Mesure da la Performance Économique et du Progrès Social, 7
Consumption, 15, 32, 33, 85
Costa Rica, 5
Cuba, 5

Day Reconstruction Method, 109, 110, 132, 138
Death of spouse, adaptation to, 50, 51
Democracy, 54–56
Disability, adaptation to, 36, 42–44
Disabled people, 36, 42–44
Divorce, 49, 50, 98

Easterlin illusion, 124
Easterlin line, 28
Easterlin Paradox, 5, 8, 22, 25–27, 34, 75, 82–87, 102, 113–130, 139
Easterlin, Richard, 5, 17, 148
Eastern Europe, 115
Economic determinants of happiness, 57–73
  education, 71–73
  income inequality, 66, 67
  inflation rate, 65, 66
  prosocial spending, 67–71
  unemployment, 57–65
Economic growth, 123, 129, 15, 152, 153
  and life expectancy, 101, 102
  and positional competition, 150
  qualitative and quantitative elements of, 77, 78
Economic prosperity, 3, 4
Education
  and happiness, 71–73
  and marriage, 48
Egypt, 5
Employment, full-time and part-time, 63

Environmental goods, valuation of, 52–54
Episode satisfaction, 133, 135
Eudaimonic well-being, 105–107
European Community Household Panel, 59
European Social Survey, 35
European Union, 55, 76
European Value Study, 35
Evolutionary advantage, 142, 144, 147
Experience Sampling Method, 108, 109
Extroverts, 37

Fairness, perception of, 67
Fechner, Gustav Theodor, 103
Finland, 97
Focusing illusion, 93
France, 7, 77, 78, 81, 110, 133
Freedom, personal and political, 54–56
Friendship, 51, 52

Gallup-Healthways Well-Being Index, 95, 96
Gallup World Poll, 69, 84, 116–121, 124, 127
Gender differences, 46, 50–52, 58, 62
General Social Survey, 6, 18
Genetics, 35–37, 142, 144, 147, 148
Germany, 5, 26, 58, 59, 63, 80, 81, 101
Ghana, 115
Giving to others, 67–71
Gross National Happiness, 76

Happiness function, 142, 144
Happy Planet Index, 5
Health
  education and, 72, 73
  and happiness, 41–44, 98, 99
  of married people, 46
Health care, 26, 79
Heart disease, 36
Heesters, Jopie, 101
Housework, 135, 136
Human Development Index, 5, 79

Income
  absolute, 117, 120, 121, 128, 139, 141, 150, 152
  adaptation to change in, 30–32, 83
  and affective happiness, 111
  importance of, 113, 114
  inequality in, 66, 67, 120
  and life satisfaction, 21, 22, 100, 103, 104, 110, 111, 152, 153
  marriage and, 48
  more vs. less, 13, 14
  percentage change in, 118
  periodic, 33
  permanent, 33
  of professors, 32
  reference, 27, 30, 82–84
  taxation of, 80–87, 128
  unemployment and, 59
Inflation, 65, 66
Inheritance, 35–37
Intelligence, 37
Introverts, 37
Israel, 39

Japan, 119, 120
Job security, 64

Kahneman, Daniel, 77, 107, 124

Ladder-of-life question, 116, 117, 124, 125
Layard, Richard, 82–84, 148
Leadership positions, 149, 150
Libertarian paternalism, 80, 81
Life expectancy, 5, 46, 101, 102, 153
Lottery winners, 30, 36, 59
Loudness, measurement of, 102, 103
Luck, 146
Luxury problem, 113, 114

Markets
  for environmental goods, 52, 53
  positional competition and, 149
  as solution to scarcity problem, 10
Marriage, 45–48, 97, 98
Materialism
  end of, 3–8

and personal values, 38–41
Methodological problems, 47, 48, 71, 72, 121
Misery index, 66
Momand, Arthur R., 28
Mood, and reliability of surveys, 92, 95–98
Morocco, 5

Need theory, 114, 116
Neoclassical economic theory, 13, 18
Neoclassical labor-market theory, 14
Nervous system, 142–145
Netherlands, 119
Neuroticism, 37
Ng, Yew-Kwang, 85–87
North Korea, 126

Openness to experience, 37
Organ donation, 80, 81
Organisation for Economic Co-operation and Development, 76, 78

Panel on Measuring Subjective Well-Being in a Policy-Relevant Framework, 109, 138
Paralysis, 36, 43
Parenthood, 48, 49, 97, 142
Peak-end rule, 108
Perception, measurement of, 102–104, 118, 142–145
Personality traits, 37, 38
Personal values, 38–41
Political tendencies
  and income inequality, 67
  and unemployment, 62
Pollution, 53, 54
  of air, 53, 80
  lead, 53
  nitrogen dioxide, 53
  noise, 54
Poor countries, 113–125
  importance of income in, 113, 114, 139
  income-happiness paradox in, 25
Poor people, 67
Positional competition, 148–154

Poverty, 25
Preference ordering, 12
Psychological needs, 128, 129
Psychological research, 91–94, 102, 103
Psychological well-being, 106
Public goods
  importance of, 128, 129
  taxation and, 84
  valuation of, 79–81

Rational-choice model, 11
Recessions, 122, 123
Reference groups, 29, 82, 122
Reference points, and relative position, 141–148
Reference value, 30
Relative income position, 27–29, 120, 121, 128, 130
  importance of, 139–152
  and taxation, 82, 83, 86
Retirement, 62, 63
Retrospective assessments, 107, 108
Revealed preference, theory of, 11, 12, 25, 26
Rich countries, 113–124, 139

Samuelson, Paul, 11
Sarkozy, Nicolas, 7, 77
Savoring behavior, 30, 31
Scarcity, 9, 10
Schmidt, Helmut, 66
School Sisters of Notre Dame, 99
Schweitzer, Albert, 41
Sen, Amartya, 77, 147
Sensation, measurement of, 102–104, 142–145
Singapore, 40
Smiles, 98
Social capital, 51, 52
Social cohesion, 77
Social contacts, 51, 52
Social context, 128, 129
South Africa, 69
Sozio-oekonomisches Panel, 6, 18, 46
Spending
  personal, 68
  prosocial, 67–71

Sports, 148–150
Spread the Net, 71
Standard of living, 40, 41
Starbucks, 70, 71
Stiglitz-Sen-Fitoussi Commission, 77, 78, 81
Subjective measures, in research, 78–81
Subjective well-being, 38, 39, 91, 92, 97, 116
Suicide, 97
Sundays, 137, 138
Survey data, 91–100, 110, 115–126
Survival of fittest, 142, 144
Switzerland, 55, 56

Taxation, 80–87, 128
Trust, and income inequality, 67
Truthfulness, 96, 97

Uganda, 69
U-index, 133, 135, 138
Unemployment
  adaptation to, 59, 60
  affective happiness and, 131–140
  and daily life, 134, 135
  and free time, 131, 132, 136
  and happiness, 57–63
  and inflation, 65
  of others, 63–65
  saddening effect of, 136, 137
  scarring effect of, 61
  time-composition effect of, 136, 137
UNICEF, 71
United Kingdom, 80
United States, 5, 66, 80, 95, 96, 110, 119, 133
US General Social Survey, 67

van Praag, Bernard, 147
Vietnam, 5

Weather, and reliability of surveys, 92–95
Weber, Ernst-Heinrich, 102
Weber-Fechner Law, 102–104, 118, 142

Welfare, 26, 66, 67
Work, 14, 57, 63, 131–138
World Database of Happiness, 123
World Values Survey, 115–117, 123